W9-BUP-002

Daily
Guideposts

*The LORD will watch over
your coming and going
both now and forevermore.*
—Psalm 121:8 (NIV)

IDEALS PUBLICATIONS
NASHVILLE, TENNESSEE

ISBN 0-8249-4650-2

Published by Ideals Publications
535 Metroplex Drive, Suite 250, Nashville, Tennessee 37211
www.idealsbooks.com

Acknowledgments

All Scripture quotations, unless otherwise noted, are taken from *The King James Version of the Bible*.

Scripture quotations marked (AMP) are taken from *The Amplified Bible*, © 1965 by Zondervan Publishing House. All rights reserved.

Scripture quotations marked (JB) are taken from *The Jerusalem Bible*, © 1966, 1967 and 1968 by Darton, Longman & Todd Ltd. and Doubleday & Company, Inc. All rights reserved.

Scripture quotations marked (MSG) are taken from *The Message*. Copyright © 1993, 1994, 1995, 1996, 2000, 2001, 2002 by Eugene H. Peterson.

Scripture quotations marked (NAS) are taken from the *New American Standard Bible*, © The Lockman Foundation, 1960, 1962, 1963, 1968, 1971, 1972, 1973, 1975, 1977. Used by permission.

Scripture quotations marked (NEB) are taken from *The New English Bible*. Copyright © The Delegates of the Oxford University Press and the Syndics of the Cambridge University Press 1961, 1970.

Scripture quotations marked (NIV) are taken from *The Holy Bible*, New International Version. Copyright © 1973, 1978, 1984 International Bible Society. Used by permission of Zondervan Bible Publishers.

Scripture quotations marked (NKJV) are taken from *The Holy Bible, New King James Version*. Copyright © 1997, 1990, 1985, 1983 by Thomas Nelson, Inc.

Scripture quotations marked (NLT) are taken from the *Holy Bible*, New Living Translation. Copyright © 1996. Used by permission of Tyndale House Publishers, Inc., Wheaton, Illinois 60189. All rights reserved.

Scripture quotations marked (NRSV) are taken from the *New Revised Standard Version Bible*. Copyright © 1989 by the Division of Christian Education of the National Council of the Churches of Christ in the U.S.A. Used by permission. All rights reserved.

Scripture quotations marked (RSV) are taken from the *Revised Standard Version of the Bible*. Copyright © 1946, 1952, 1971 by Division of Christian Education of the National Council of Churches of Christ in the U.S.A. Used by permission.

Scripture quotations marked (TLB) are taken from *The Living Bible*. Copyright © 1971 by Tyndale House Publishers, Wheaton, IL 60187. All rights reserved.

"Great Is Thy Faithfulness" © 1923. Renewed 1951 Hope Publishing Co., Carol Stream, IL 60188. All rights reserved. Used by permission.

Typeset by Planet Patti, Inc.
Printed in the United States of America

FOREWORD

This edition of *Daily Guideposts* has been specially designed for you, our servicemen and servicewomen on the front lines and on the bases at home and abroad. Its small size and light weight allow it to slip easily into your uniform pocket and accompany you wherever you go.

I know that you face many challenging circumstances in the course of your service to our country. I know that the danger you face is very real and that separation from your family and friends can be difficult. It is my hope that *Daily Guideposts* will prove to be a source of inspiration to you on a daily basis. Its 365 devotionals act as faith-building reminders of God's eternal presence and faithfulness in our lives, regardless of where we are and what we are facing.

As you move through your days, reach for *Daily Guideposts* whenever you need a reminder of God's presence in your life, and find comfort in reading of the many ways, large and small, in which God reveals Himself to us.

— Gaylord T. Gunhus
Chaplain (Major General), USA, Ret.

INTRODUCTION

In 586 B.C., after a long siege, the city of Jerusalem fell to the armies of Babylon. Looking over the ruins of the city, the writer of Lamentations poured out grief for the destruction of the city and the captivity of its people. Yet amid the desolation, when many thought God's promises had been given in vain, he found a precious nugget of hope: "His compassions fail not. They are new every morning: great is thy faithfulness" (Lamentations 3:22–23). Day by day, no matter how difficult the circumstances, God's mercy, like His Word, never fails; He is always faithful to the people He has chosen.

No matter what may happen in the world around us, whether our own life's journey seems like a brisk walk on a smooth road or a difficult climb up a steep mountain, God is our faithful companion all along the way. And so our theme for this edition of *Daily Guideposts* is "Great Is Thy Faithfulness."

Spend the coming year with our sixty writers as your daily companions. They'll share the ups and downs of their own journeys along life's way and show you the many ways they've come to know and rely on God's faithfulness.

Whether you read *Daily Guideposts* as part of your morning or evening devotions, or turn to it for a spiritual pick-me-up during the day, you'll find an invitation to renewed faith, a peaceful heart and confident living. And our prayer for you is that every day you'll grow in faith, hope, love and gratitude to the One Who is always with us to strengthen, comfort and inspire. Truly, great is God's faithfulness!

—Andrew Attaway
Editor, *Daily Guideposts*

The apostles said to the Lord, "Increase our faith!"
—Luke 17:5 (NIV)

Increased faith was my prayer one New Year's Day twenty years ago. It wasn't a resolution—I knew how short-lived those were! Once I'd set out to memorize a Bible verse every day of the year; I kept at it until nearly February. Another time I resolved to start each day with a half-hour of praise. Sometimes I managed fifteen minutes.

It had been the same with efforts to muster the kind of faith I'd encountered working on people's stories for *Guideposts* magazine. People who gave away their livelihoods knowing that "God will provide." People confident of healing in the face of medical impossibility. People certain in bereavement that the loved one awaited them in heaven. How I longed for a faith like that!

Jesus' closest followers did too: "Increase our faith!"

Reading Jesus' reply to them—to me—I could almost see Him shaking His head. "You don't need great faith! Faith the size of a grain of mustard seed is enough!"

And so I stopped asking for the full-grown faith of the people I admired in *Guideposts*—maybe theirs started with little seeds too. Ever since then, I've kept a record of the everyday ways God invites me to fully trust Him. Invitations in such unlikely forms as a book of cartoons, an anonymous phone call, a crying child. Small gifts in day-sized doses, scaled to the need at hand.

And oddly enough, when I pray for seeds instead of flowers, my faith life blossoms. Maybe it's the habit of looking each day for faith-builders so small they're easy to miss, but when I look back, sturdy little plants are pushing up in my garden here and there from those minuscule beginnings.

Faithful Lord, remind me again this coming year that it is not my faith but Your great faithfulness that makes all things possible. —Elizabeth Sherrill

AND I JOHN SAW THE HOLY CITY, NEW JERUSALEM, COMING DOWN FROM GOD OUT OF HEAVEN, PREPARED AS A BRIDE ADORNED FOR HER HUSBAND. —Revelation 21:2

On my drive to work I have to pass through an area of the highway called T-REX, which stands for Transportation Expansion Project. We're two years into the five years it's supposed to take the city to build a mass transit system right through the heart of Denver. To city officials, it's an exciting answer to our congested highways. To me, it's a nuisance.

I see it for what it is today; they see it for what it will be tomorrow. They have vision. And over and over, on television and in the newspapers and with signs along the highways, they try to communicate that vision to people like me. As I sit in bumper-to-bumper traffic, I need to know that the suffering is temporary and the best is yet to come.

God is the creator of vision. He Who knows the end from the beginning promises us over and over again that what's in store for us is to be in heaven with Him.

He keeps telling us the best is yet to come. So we should be encouraged while we endure disappointment or pain—or traffic snarls. God gives us His vision of heaven to hold in our hearts.

Father, help me to see Your vision, so I can look forward to what will be. —CAROL KUYKENDALL

FOR WHERE YOUR TREASURE IS, THERE WILL YOUR HEART BE ALSO. —*Matthew 6:21*

Christmas thank-you notes are mailed and the New Year's confetti swept out of the carpet. It's January, time to store the holiday finery and put out my regular decorations. To be honest, I've missed my accumulation of paintings, pottery, photos and knick-knacks.

I set great-grandmother's satin-lined spectacle box back in the rough-oak pie safe. My grandfather treasured this ivory box before it passed to me. I rehang *Little Arrow Maker* by Jerome Tiger, print number 656 of 1,500, bought by my husband Don at an auction. The red-black-yellow throw, a birthday gift from my friend Glenda, goes back over the edge of the divan.

Since I welcome each piece like an old friend, the task takes half a day. When I place my mother's polished wooden fruit bowl on the dining room table, I have a sudden scary revelation: *I love my possessions. I love everything! My white wedding china, the Navajo pots, even the pillow that says* MY FAMILY TREE IS FULL OF NUTS. But hadn't Jesus clearly taught that all our treasures should be heavenly? I know people whose lives are centered on what they own—cars, clothes, houses. Was I becoming one of them?

I run my hand over the faded cover of great-great-grandfather's Bible. As suddenly as the oppressive fear descended, it lifts. Yes, I love my possessions. But I love them because of the memories they bring to mind. Memories of dear people, some still living, others gone on to glory, who were loved and treasured parts of my life.

Lord, thank You for the precious memories forever alive in my heart. —PENNEY SCHWAB

MY LOVER IS MINE AND I AM HIS; HE BROWSES AMONG THE LILIES. —*Song of Solomon 2:16 (NIV)*

Every winter, my husband Wayne and I drive from our home in Washington to our winter home on North Hutchinson Island in Florida. In case you're wondering, that's 3,323 miles.

Over the years, we've had a number of adventures traveling across country in the middle of winter, from blizzards to breakdowns. Wayne enjoys taking the back roads, so we've spent the night in towns where the largest structure on Main Street is the car wash.

People have often asked us why we choose to drive. It took me a long time to come up with the answer: Wayne and I are guaranteed quality time together for a week. We may go several hundred miles barely speaking a word, or we may chatter nonstop for miles on end. But each year on that long drive, we fall in love all over again.

Every married couple needs to set aside special time to communicate. For some it might be a romantic weekend, a stroll on the beach or cuddle time on a Saturday morning. But for Wayne and me, it's the 3,323 miles that bring us closer to Florida, to sunshine and to each other.

Father, thank You for my husband, for the laughter and the tears, and for these special times on the road.

—DEBBIE MACOMBER

*THE STRANGER THAT DWELLETH WITH YOU SHALL BE UNTO
YOU AS ONE BORN AMONG YOU, AND THOU SHALT LOVE HIM
AS THYSELF.* . . . —*Leviticus 19:34*

My cell phone rang for the umpteenth time that morning. "Hey,
Brock, I'm running about twenty minutes late," said the voice.
Perfect, I thought. *Now I can stop for a quick cup of coffee.* I
darted into a convenience store, and as I made my way to the
back, I noticed a man in a heavy green work suit, his boots
caked with mud, with a little boy. Standing on tiptoes, the boy
watched as the man picked out doughnuts from the doughnut
case and put them in a bag.

I got my coffee and rushed into the line, six people in front
of me. I turned back and looked at the man, thinking of my
son. Just then a busy woman turned and crashed right into
them, spilling coffee all over the man and on the floor. "Oh,
ma'am, excuse me," he said.

"Watch where you're going!" she said, shaking her head
with disdain.

I told myself it wasn't my problem, I had an appointment to
make, I needed to hurry. But as I saw the man trying to mop up
the coffee, I knelt down by the boy to help him. "What a good-
looking young man," I said. "I have a boy of my own about the
same age."

A smile broke across the father's face. "Then you know
what it's like."

"And I wouldn't trade it for anything," I said.

I paid for my coffee and got back into my car, leaning back
in the seat. All of a sudden I wasn't in such a hurry anymore.

*Father of all, where I'm needed and when I'm needed, send
me.* —BROCK KIDD

*"**Bring my sons from afar and my daughters from the end of the earth, every one who is called by my name, whom I created for my glory, whom I formed and made.**" —Isaiah 43:6-7 (RSV)*

A few Christmases ago, our friend Loretta gave three-year-old Mary a doll. "Ginny" was the name on the box, and this longhaired miniature grown-up immediately became Mary's special companion.

Then one night in January, as I was tucking Mary in, I asked her if she'd like one of her dolls. She nodded. "Which one?" I asked. "Would you like Ginny?"

"Her name's not Ginny," Mary announced. "It's Ginny Mary!"

"Okay, would you like Ginny Mary?"

"Yes, please."

I searched the darkened room for the doll. "Has anyone seen Ginny?" I asked the kids.

"Mary changed her name to Ginny Mary," Elizabeth advised me from her bunk bed.

"Thank you, Elizabeth. Mary told me. Do you know where she is?"

"We were playing with her in the living room," Elizabeth said.

I retrieved the doll, put her in Mary's arms and gave my daughter a good-night kiss.

A few weeks later at bedtime, I again asked Mary if she wanted a doll and again she nodded. "Would you like Ginny Mary?" I asked, proud of myself for remembering the doll's new name.

"Her name's not Ginny Mary, it's Mary Ginny!"

"Oh, okay. Would you like Mary Ginny?"

"Yes, please," Mary answered.

Mary Ginny it was for another week or so. Then, at bedtime, as I put the doll next to Mary and said, "Here's Mary Ginny," Mary demurred.

"She's not Mary Ginny! Now her name is Mary!"

And so it was; Ginny the doll was now Mary the doll, because Mary the little girl loved her enough to call her by her very own name.

Thank You, Lord, for dolls and daughters. And thank You for calling me by Your name and transforming me after Your likeness. —ANDREW ATTAWAW

THE GOD OF ALL COMFORT, WHO COMFORTS US IN ALL OUR TROUBLES. . . . —II Corinthians 1:3-4 (NIV)

When my husband Whitney and I moved south one gray, wet January, I was terribly homesick for the house in New York where we'd lived for eighteen years. Our new cedar house atop a small mountain in Kingston Springs, Tennessee, was beautiful. *But so different from New York,* I thought sadly as I began unpacking.

Everything I pulled out held a memory of "back home." Here was a lamp from the table in the living room next to the window overlooking our rambling stone wall. Here were knick-knacks that had sat on the big windowsill where I watched the horses in the field. Here was the tea-kettle that had poured so many steaming cups for friends.

By the time dusk was falling through the bare winter woods around our new house, I was a maudlin mess. I just wanted to go *home.* But then, in the distance, my ears picked up a sound that I'd heard many times in my childhood home in Pennsylvania: the wail of a train whistle. Through the rain-beaded windows, the long-forgotten sound came closer and closer, then faded away, leaving a warm comfort, just as it had when I was a child falling asleep to its mournful wail. Every night I could count on it like clockwork. As I could count on God.

Now, fifty years and six hundred miles away in Kingston Springs, the sound of home had followed, a timely reminder that, like clockwork, I could still count on God.

Father God, thank You for the housewarming Your presence brings. —SHARI SMYTH

*THE LORD IS IN HIS HOLY TEMPLE: LET ALL THE EARTH
KEEP SILENCE BEFORE HIM.* —*Habakkuk 2:20*

There was simply too much noise. Sunday morning I was teaching, as usual, my rambunctious class of third-, fourth- and fifth-
graders. We had already gone over the lesson about Paul on
the road to Damascus, acting out his blinded-by-the-light con-
version. At one point I had a roomful of kids lying on the
ground as one of them read Christ's words, "Why do you per-
secute me, Paul?" But then things started to get rowdy.

    As the noise level increased, I raised my voice in exaspera-
tion. "Okay, I have a special assignment for today. I want you to
do two things. First, make as much noise as you can for two
minutes. Then be absolutely silent for two minutes. I dare you
to do both."

    Gleefully they met my challenge. First they made an unholy
racket, yelling, shouting, clapping. (Fortunately, our classroom is
in a distant corner of the parish house.) The odd thing was,
they couldn't keep it up at top volume for very long. After a
minute they began to look expectantly at me. "Can we stop
now?" I shook my head. Finally, after two minutes, I announced,
"Silence."

    Eyes closed, heads bowed, hands came down, and they were
blissfully quiet. No snickering, no kicking, no guffawing. Two
minutes of such silence I think I could hear their hearts beat.
When time was up I asked, "Which felt more natural? Which
was more comfortable? Which was closer to God?"

    Take two minutes and find out for yourself.

*God, I worship You not only with joyous noise but also with
blessed silence.* —RICK HAMLIN

SHE SEEKETH WOOL, AND FLAX, AND WORKETH WILLINGLY WITH HER HANDS. —*Proverbs 31:13*

The astonishing thing about Guideposts knitters is their stamina. As I sit knitting a small yellow sweater with gold trim, I try to imagine two hundred thousand sweaters. What would it look like? Would it be a brightly colored pyramid, perhaps even a mountain?

The sweaters are all different, even though the Guideposts Knit for Kids pattern is very simple. It's not fancy knitting, unless you choose the Aran version posted on the Web site (www.dailyguideposts.com/help/sweater.asp). But our knitters don't get bored; time and time again they cast on the stitches that begin yet another sweater in different colors, with stripes or without, large or small.

I got a phone call the other day from a knitter in Manitoba, Canada. She sounded rather frail, but she had remembered my name and wanted to know if her box of sweaters had arrived safely. I was about to tell her that I no longer handled the Guideposts Knit for Kids project, but what I actually said was, "I'll give them a call and check for you." My caller was delighted. "Well, then," she said, "I'll start another sweater." And so it goes all over North America and beyond: Hands move and needles click.

It would take a whole book to recognize all these hundreds of faithful knitters. But you know who you are, and as you read this be sure that not a stitch of your work goes uncounted. After all, since "the very hairs of your head are all numbered" (Matthew 10:30) and not one sparrow is forgotten by God, I have no doubt that He has counted every stitch of every sweater, even the occasional dropped one. I think my next one will be green with yellow stripes.

Lord, thank You for warm sweaters for cold children and for the generous people who knit them. —BRIGITTE WEEKS

FEED ME WITH FOOD CONVENIENT FOR ME. —*Proverbs 30:8*

"You've gained three pounds," Dr. Serafin said without even a hint of a smile.

"Oh, no problem," I answered, perched on the examining table for my annual physical. "I'll lose it in a flash."

My first plan was simple: no snacks. That lasted until I went to a party with particularly tasty hors d'oeuvres.

Okay, a new scale. I'll weigh myself every day until I lose the weight. The new scale said I'd gained two more pounds. I increased my morning exercise and started carrying weights when I walked. *I am woman. I can do this.* Six months later, I was still five pounds overweight.

One day, over coffee, a friend of mine told me about her struggles with alcohol. "So many of us have the notion that the solution to our problems is within ourselves," she said. "Thanks to Alcoholics Anonymous, I've learned that the only way I can solve my problems is to turn them over to God."

My problem was certainly a tiny one compared to my friend's, but the principle was the same. "God," I prayed, "could You show me how to lose those pounds and fill the space they leave with something better?"

Once I asked, things started happening. We traveled to Africa, where I discovered that most of the people in the world get by on one meal a day. After we returned, I read three articles that emphasized that our bodies need half as much food in the second half of our lives. I developed the habit of never taking more than I needed. God had given me the motivation to start looking at food differently.

I thought losing weight was all about me. But as soon as I bothered to ask, God started showing me it was about something bigger. And as for Dr. Serafin, I can't wait for my next appointment. I think he's going to be surprised!

Father, I hunger for the satisfaction of following Your ways.
                                                          —PAM KIDD

NOW TO THE KING ETERNAL, IMMORTAL, INVISIBLE, THE ONLY GOD, BE HONOR AND GLORY FOREVER AND EVER.
—*I Timothy 1:17 (NAS)*

I love books and coffee. After a long day at work, I sometimes drop by a favorite bookstore and spend thirty minutes with a hot espresso, browsing through the stacks of books. These moments clear my mind and restore my spirit. They also put a dint in my wallet!

Not long ago I was leafing through a book on English history and discovered a story about King Canute, the battle-hardened Viking who ruled England from 1016 to 1035 and built a North Sea empire that stretched from Greenland to the Baltic, and from England to Russia.

One day Canute ordered his nobles to gather on the seashore. He had his throne carried to the beach and placed where the tide was advancing across the sand. Sitting on the throne, Canute commanded the waves of the ocean to advance no further. Sternly, he glared at the surf as it continued to rise, covering his feet with salt water. Finally, thoroughly drenched, Canute ordered his throne returned to his palace and stomped away in sodden disgust.

Several days later a wise Canute declared, "Let all the world know that the power of kings is empty and worthless. There is no king worthy of the name save God, by whose will heaven, earth and sea obey eternal laws." Canute never wore his crown again.

As I sat in the bookstore and drank my coffee, I could see myself in that imperious king. I've had moments when I commanded the waves of my life to advance no further. Every time I've gotten my feet wet, God's waves remind me that there is no king in all this universe save God.

Lord, help me to take the crown from my hard head and give it back to You. Amen. — SCOTT WALKER

I TRUST IN THE MERCY OF GOD FOR EVER AND EVER.
                                                               —*Psalm 52:8*

More and more these days I find myself thumping my chest with the palm of my hand and saying, "Mercy!" This was my mother-in-law's regular expression of faith. Whether she'd spilled a cup of coffee or heard of a major disaster, she rallied her ability to cope with a series of chest-thumping "mercies." Conversely, upon finding her misplaced glasses or getting a phone call from a long-lost friend, her string of "mercies" was more hand-fluttering than thumping and had a jubilant cadence that put a smile on her gentle face, all of which, I'm sure, brought joy to the heart of God.

When I heard the good news that my grandchild who had spent the semester struggling at school had received the President's Award for good citizenship, I could barely contain my hand-fluttering string of "mercies." Likewise, on hearing of the automobile accident of a friend (fortunately not hurt), one huge chest-thumping "Mercy!" said it all.

The dictionary says *mercy* is "a blessing that is an act of divine favor or compassion." I find myself constantly putting my prayerful concerns under the mercy of my Lord, knowing that what I am unable to do, He is able to do for me.

"I will sing of the mercies of the Lord for ever: with my mouth will I make known thy faithfulness to all generations" (Psalm 89:1). —FAY ANGUS

"LORD, LET OUR EYES BE OPENED." —*Matthew 20:33 (RSV)*

Just last week I gave a talk on creativity, urging the audience to open their eyes and to hone their insights. "Creative people can recognize repeating patterns and see similarities among things," I said knowingly.

So much for being the expert. This morning, for the first time ever, I recognized a home-décor pattern that was utterly unintentional. Inside my front door hangs a round, rust-colored plate featuring a golden angel trumpeter. On the kitchen door-frame is a white-china angel holding a harp. Above the light switch in my office, I've put a mauve-and-teal angel plucking a lute. And on a nail just inside my bedroom, there's an angelic horn player, maybe Michael, molded from plaster. I'd put up these angels ages ago, without making the connection that all serve as doorway guards, minding my room-to-room comings and goings. And all four are musicians, poised to fill my home with heavenly chords.

The day is young. What other creative insights—angelic or otherwise—does the Lord have in store for this "expert"?

Lord, open my eyes to new creative insights that enrich my spiritual life. —EVELYN BENCE

*"MARTHA, MARTHA," THE LORD ANSWERED, "YOU ARE
WORRIED AND UPSET ABOUT MANY THINGS, BUT ONLY ONE
THING IS NEEDED. MARY HAS CHOSEN WHAT IS BETTER. . . ."*
—Luke 10:41–42 (NIV)

My wife Kathy and I had been up late chatting with Maria and
John, friends who were with us for the weekend, so we were
still in bed when the phone rang. It was our son Ryan, calling
to see if he, his friend Jennifer and her children could come for
a visit at ten.

Kathy and I shifted into high gear. After breakfast with Maria
and John, we loaded the dishwasher. There was plenty of time
for showers and a trip to the recycling center.

"Kathy, could you take a load of laundry down when you're
finished with your shower?" I called as I headed downstairs to
load the garbage and recycling bins into our car.

Kathy's arms were full of laundry when everyone arrived fifteen minutes later, so she gave Ryan and Jennifer and Mandy
and Jim a one-handed hug and a kiss.

"Mom, can we talk to you in the kitchen for a minute?" Ryan
asked.

"You bet, Ryan, but let me get this load of laundry started
first."

It was while she was in the basement, pouring detergent
into the washer, that it struck her. *I think Ryan asked Jenn to
marry him!*

Kathy went charging back upstairs. Ryan and Jennifer were
standing alone in the kitchen when she turned the corner.
"Now, what was it you wanted to talk about?" she asked. There
was no answer. "Is there a ring I should see?"

When I walked into the family room, there was a spot on
the sofa saved for me. I hugged and kissed everyone. Then,
while talking over my shoulder, I went into the kitchen and
began unloading the dishwasher.

"Ted, come in and sit down," Kathy said. "We have a Mary
moment for you, and it shouldn't wait any longer."

*Lord, please help me recognize when I need to stop being
Martha and enjoy the Mary moments in my life.* —TED NACE

I CALL TO REMEMBRANCE MY SONG IN THE NIGHT: I COMMUNE WITH MINE OWN HEART. . . . —Psalm 77:6

I was awake again at 3:00 A.M. *Quick, Marion, before those troubling thoughts attack your mind. Sing!*

Singing the old hymns I learned as a child keeps away the "what ifs" that like to attack in the middle of the night. I don't sing out loud, just silently in my spirit. After a while I can usually get back to sleep.

I sang my last song several times as I hovered on the brink of sleep:

> *Jesus is the sweetest name I know*
> *And He's just the same as His lovely name.*
> *That's the reason why I love Him so.*
> *Oh, Jesus is the sweetest name I know.*

Right then I was ambushed by an unexpected attack: *Jesus doesn't care about you or your stupid songs!*

Oh, Lord, don't let that thought stay with me and make me doubt. Somehow, show me that You care.

"The piano tuner will be here by nine," my husband Gene reminded me the next morning. Neither Gene nor I play the piano, but he cherishes our baby grand. It's about ninety years old and has been in his family forever.

When Bobby Howington finished his work, he gave us our annual miniconcert. Gene and I sat side by side on the sofa listening intently as music from the perfectly tuned piano filled our living room and our souls. Bobby's skilled fingers lovingly played,

> *Jesus is the sweetest name I know*
> *And He's just the same as His lovely name.*
> *That's the reason why I love Him so.*
> *Oh, Jesus is the sweetest name I know.*

Your faithfulness amazes me, Father, time and time again.

                     —MARION BOND WEST

"HE MOVES MOUNTAINS WITHOUT THEIR KNOWING IT. . . ."
                                              —Job 9:5 (NIV)

I received my doctor of ministry from Reformed Theological
Seminary in Jackson, Mississippi. During the three years I studied at the seminary, I developed a good relationship with a
classmate of mine who happened to be white. In fact, he gave
me wise counsel on several occasions.

One day, on a "Grace Is Greater Than Race" tour, I traveled
to the city where that old classmate is pastor of a church and
met him for lunch. "Dolphus," he said, "I know you're trying to
bring about unity within the body of Christ, but because of
the attitudes of the people in the congregation I serve, I can't
invite you to preach. I'm sorry."

"Well," I said, "keep working to educate them and one day
they'll be open to my coming." My friend looked doubtful.

Three years later I walked into that very church and
preached at an evening service. My message was received
warmly. Now my friend wants to invite me back for a Sunday-
morning service! The same people who were opposed to my
preaching there are now leading the effort to get me back.

I need to be faithful in doing the work God gives me and
remember that it's God Who moves mountains, not me.

*Lord, thank You for Your faithfulness in moving the mountain
of racial division.* —DOLPHUS WEARY

THIS IS THE DAY THE LORD HAS MADE; LET US REJOICE AND BE GLAD IN IT. —Psalm 118:24 (NIV)

I was sipping a cup of coffee while leafing through my album of antique postcards when the cup slipped from my hands and spilled hot coffee all over the cards. My sister Rebekkah ran to get a roll of paper towels. As she sopped up coffee from the drenched pages, she said softly, "Don't let it ruin your day, Roberta."

Don't let it ruin your day. Almost always, that's just what would have happened. I would have let that little accident color every remaining moment of the day. *Why did you have to have that coffee in the first place?* I'd have berated myself. How many days had I sacrificed to such pointless regrets?

The cards cost little more than a dollar apiece and were replaceable. But a day the Lord has made? Absolutely priceless—there would never be another one exactly like it in all my life. A day full of things to see and hear and do, a day touched with the presence of God in every moment of every hour.

Thanks to Rebekkah and a cup of coffee, I'll never look at an ordinary day in the same way again, including the ones that don't go quite the way I'd like.

Today, Lord, is part of Your divine design. Help me to treat it as the gift it truly is. —ROBERTA MESSNER

A MAN THAT HATH FRIENDS MUST SHEW HIMSELF FRIENDLY:
AND THERE IS A FRIEND THAT STICKETH CLOSER THAN A
BROTHER. —*Proverbs 18:24*

People often ask, "Where did you get your dog Shep?" I like to
tell them about one man, a long time ago.

I was a partner in a little publishing firm. We were about to
fail, with all sorts of debts that only money could remedy—
and there was little chance of getting that. Even a bank was out
of the question. We paced and worried until Harold, my partner, said, "Come on, we've got to try."

"Okay," I said lamely. We walked to the big bank on the
corner, with me shaking and praying. Before I knew it, we were
sitting before a young man, several years my junior, and I set
forth our troubles. Somehow his attentiveness made me feel at
ease. Somehow, talking to him, I was unafraid to paint a dour
picture of what those troubles were. And somehow I wasn't
surprised when we got the loan.

We paid back the loan all right, but it was just the beginning
of our relationship with the banker. He became our wise
friend, mine especially. There are no major decisions, personal
or business, that I've made without his counsel. He's been a
quiet conscience of mine, God-inspired, I have no doubt.

Over the years I discovered that I was not the only one.
Dozens of people have been helped by him, including an elderly lady he has telephoned every morning just to check up on
her. One day she told him she had taken in a homeless dog, but
she was too infirm to walk him and didn't know what to do.
My friend hung up and called me, saying, "It's been years since
your dog Clay died. . . ."

Father, thank You for my friend, and for Shep. —VAN VARNER

THE BLESSING OF THE LORD MAKES RICH, AND HE ADDS NO SORROW WITH IT. *—Proverbs 10:22* (RSV)

Elizabeth's voice sounded troubled on the other end of the line. "Mom," she said, close to tears, "I got the things you asked for, but now I can't find the money!" I'd sent her off to the shop around the corner to pick up a few groceries, and she was calling on my cell phone.

After asking a few questions, it became clear that the twenty-five dollars I'd given her had fallen out of her pocket. I made my voice sound unflustered. "Put the groceries back, honey, then walk through the store and back home the way you came. Maybe you'll see the money on the ground."

While I waited for Elizabeth, I reflected on the day many years ago when a friend and I went into New York City to go to the planetarium. Glowing with newfound independence, I reached into my jeans when I got home to give my mom the twenty dollars that was left over. It was gone.

In that moment I knew I was far from grown up; I felt irresponsible, unreliable and foolish. My mother must have sensed that, for although money was tight she said nary an angry word. Her silence was a balm and a blessing. Now was my chance to be wise like her.

"I'm never going to the store again!" wailed Elizabeth as she walked in the door. I sat her down and told her my story. Then I gave her another twenty-five dollars and sent her back out for the groceries.

Lord, make me a good steward of the blessings my mother gave me. —JULIA ATTAWAY

PEOPLE WHO WANT TO GET RICH FALL INTO TEMPTATION AND A TRAP AND INTO MANY FOOLISH AND HARMFUL DESIRES. . . . —I Timothy 6:9 (NIV)

If God is serious about leading me not into temptation, He shouldn't let my neighbors put so much good stuff out on the curb on garbage day. The other day I was stopped in my tracks on my morning prayer walk by a pile of custom draperies and valances. When I got home, the hard testing began. *Maybe I'll just hop in the van and go get them.*

The bargain-hunter in me was avid: *Those drapes are still good, and my neighbor paid lots of money for them.*

Then my conscience said, *They may be free, but they probably don't fit your windows and you don't have the time to fix them. Besides, you have curtains on every window already and these don't even fit your color scheme.*

I had an answer for that: *Well, if I took them off the rods they'd fold up and wouldn't take up that much space.*

I got out my van keys and paused just long enough to hear my conscience whisper, *What would Jesus do?*

I knew what Jesus would say. "Karen, you have hundreds of unfinished projects right now. Time and mental energy are resources. Spend them on the things that matter."

I went back into the house, put away the car keys, and sat down and prayed:

Lord Jesus, help me to know when I ought to be redoing my attitudes instead of my surroundings. —KAREN BARBER

TURN, O LORD, SAVE MY LIFE; DELIVER ME FOR THE SAKE OF THY STEADFAST LOVE. —*Psalm 6:4* (RSV)

Like any adult of a certain age, I've had my share of existential crises: Who am I? What am I doing here? Why does my car always break down?

This last question came to me beneath my beat-up minivan. The way I figured it, even if I found a way to liberate the starter and revive the van, I'd only be breaking even. The van wouldn't run better; it would simply run.

"What's the point?" I said aloud.

As I turned the drive shaft to get a better angle for my ratchet, I heard it: the sound of the car moving . . . off the ramps . . . on to me.

Luckily, I had blocked the back wheels, so I'm still here to tell you this story. One false move—say, *forgetting* to block the back wheels—and my wife is picking out my funeral suit.

Breaking even is not, I repeat, not a bad thing. Life is a struggle, but it beats the options. Life is an opera full of joy and tragedy and swift scene changes and amazing, unexpected arias. And—get this—we're not the audience. We figure out the script as we go, singing our roles (no rehearsal) as best we can. And it isn't over till the fat lady sings . . . or the jack slips.

In my particular scene from my unique opera, I replaced the starter. It was the most joyful, blessed, break-even thing I have ever done.

Whether I'm at the footlights or in the wings, from the overture to the final curtain, my life is in Your hands, Lord.

—MARK COLLINS

WHERE WILL YOU LEAVE YOUR WEALTH? —Isaiah 10:3 (NAS)

SMALL CHANGE FOR BIG CHANGE! read the sign over the large plastic bottles placed along the front of the church.

In each of the six bottles was a cardboard mailing tube, and on the tubes smaller signs that read: PENNIES FOR PROCLAIMING, NICKELS FOR NURTURING, DIMES FOR DISCIPLING and QUARTERS FOR CHRIST'S KINGDOM.

It was Missions Outreach month at our church, and the idea was to emphasize stewardship by encouraging the Sunday school children to come forward and drop their offerings into the appropriate bottles.

On Sunday the children trooped up the aisle while an enthusiastic nine-year-old thumped out the offertory on the piano. She was soon accompanied by the sound of dozens of coins popcorning into the plastic bottles.

As the children milled about, a tall awkward teenage boy stooped to help a toddler whose pennies were clasped in sweaty little hands. An older sister directed her kindergartner brother toward the nickel bottle. A mother slipped out of her pew to go up front and suppress the unbridled enthusiasm of two siblings, each determined to donate to the same bottle at the same time. A grandfather showed his tiny grandson how it was done by dropping a coin into the quarter bottle.

Even as "the people were restrained from bringing any more" (Exodus 36:6, NAS), a dawdler plunked in one last dime and walked back down the aisle with a satisfied grin.

The missionary speaker smiled as he addressed the children. "You start by giving your pennies to the Lord, and then one day we hope you will give Him your lives."

Lord, I dedicated my life to You years ago, but have I short-changed You in the stewardship department? Help me to be a more cheerful giver. —ALMA BARKMAN

"IN YOUR ANGER DO NOT SIN": DO NOT LET THE SUN GO DOWN WHILE YOU ARE STILL ANGRY, AND DO NOT GIVE THE DEVIL A FOOTHOLD. —*Ephesians 4:26-37 (NIV)*

The first night of our weeklong icon painting class, the instructor announced, "We're done for tonight. Finish your last area, then head to bed. But don't forget to thoroughly clean your brushes!" After painting all morning, afternoon and evening, I yearned to head to the guesthouse lounge, pop some popcorn and relax.

At the sink I turned on the water full force and pushed my thumbs through the bristles. A fellow classmate, Bessie, offered me some of the cleaner she was rubbing into her brushes. "No thanks," I said. "I think I've got mine all done." Quickly tidying up my work area, I headed out. When I passed the sink, I was surprised that Bessie was still scrubbing her brushes.

The next day we began the most important painting of the week: the flesh tone of the face and hands. As I worked, flecks of the dark, mustard yellow I'd used the previous day speckled the face. *Now where did that come from?* You guessed it, my hastily cleaned brush. Back I went to the faucet to do the scrubbing I should have done the night before.

Today at home, I was fuming over something I would normally have shrugged off: My husband hadn't started the dishwasher after dinner and I was delayed cleaning up the kitchen in the morning. *Now where did all that anger come from?* Then I remembered something else that had happened the night before: We had disagreed about disciplining our son, and I'd gone to bed upset instead of working out the conflict. Just like my dirty brushes, my unresolved anger had colored my whole day. It was time for a good clean.

Dear God, please remind me to turn to You for help to sort out a problem or mend a relationship before the sun goes down. —MARY BROWN

*THEREFORE ENCOURAGE ONE ANOTHER AND BUILD ONE
ANOTHER UP. . . . —I Thessalonians 5:11 (RSV)*

Last year, when Johnny Carson's death was reported in the
national media, I couldn't help noticing on *The New York Times*
Web site that it was also the anniversary of the death of
Winston Churchill.

No two people could have been more unalike: One was a
great national hero who seemed to have led his suffering country single-handedly through the darkest days of World War II;
the other was an enigmatic entertainer from the Midwestern
plains, an icon of pop culture, who was known by almost every
American but not really known by anyone at all. Churchill res-
onated; Carson was an echo.

Yet were they so dissimilar? It can be said that Churchill
changed the course of history through the sheer force of his
oratory. He articulated the angst of the British people, stirred
their courage and restored their fortitude. Carson was no orator
in the classical sense. Yet he, too, used language—plainspoken
but with a comic edge that could be razor sharp.

I remember watching film clips of Churchill in school and
being inspired. I also remember the thrilling rite of passage of
being allowed to stay up late and watch Johnny. And through
some of America's darkest times—Vietnam, Watergate, the oil
embargo, the Iranian hostage crisis—Johnny was there, in his
own way bucking us up and getting us through it and tucking
us into bed. Much of history can be imagined without most
people; I have trouble imagining 1940s Britain without
Churchill or postwar America without Carson.

That neither man was perfect is pretty well known.
Churchill was, shall we say, intemperate in his habits, and
Carson was aloof—some said cold—and hard to know. Still,
each was imbued with a unique presence, a gift that lifted
us all.

Lord, let me be open to whomever You send to encourage me.
                                        —EDWARD GRINNAN

I HAVE LEARNED THE SECRET OF BEING CONTENT IN ANY AND EVERY SITUATION. . . . —*Philippians 4:12 (NIV)*

Several years ago I entered a contest and was thrilled to receive an honorable mention certificate and notification that I'd finished in twenty-second place. I certainly hadn't expected to win, and placing in the top thirty encouraged me for the future. But my daughter Maria had a different take on it.

"Twenty-second! Oh, poor Mommy!" You see, when you're in a first-grade class of only twenty-five kids, finishing twenty-second doesn't sound too good. I had to laugh at Maria's wonderful honesty. Her perspective was different from mine, to be sure. But it started me thinking about how powerful a simple change in attitude can be.

I'd taken on a job at the kids' school, organizing the once-a-month mailing of information to the school's six hundred-plus families. In spite of all my planning, last-minute problems with the first mailing created chaos. But I stopped myself from voicing my frustration when I realized that it could have gone even worse if not for all the help I got from friends and other parents. So I tried to take a positive attitude into the next mailing. It also wasn't perfect, but things ran more smoothly, perhaps because this time I didn't expect perfection.

It sounds like a cliché—things could have been worse—but so often that seems to be true. Something may be difficult and not go as planned, but when I choose to see that it turned out better than it might have—often thanks to the help and support of others—I feel blessed.

Lord, give me an appreciative heart, to know that sometimes good enough is just perfect. —GINA BRIDGEMAN

THEY HAVE EARS, BUT THEY HEAR NOT. . . . —Psalm 115:6

I just read an article about the options that will be available on cars of the future, and I'm fighting back yawns.

Why don't carmakers give us something we really need? I don't want windshield wipers that sense moisture and turn themselves on. I can tell when it's raining, and I don't like "options" that take away the most important option of all, my control of the car. I'd like to see them design things like:

1. A heater that I could leave on low while I shop, so I could return to warm seats and clear windshields.
2. A horn for the rear bumper, so I could beep at the children playing behind me in the driveway or warn the tailgater to back off.
3. A foot-operated dimmer switch, so I don't have to take my hand off the wheel to dim the lights. My first car had this, back in the fifties.
4. Radio knobs bigger than raisins.
5. A thinner steering wheel, so I don't feel like I'm wrestling a boa constrictor when I turn the wheel.

What applies to carmakers applies to me, of course. Before buying that expensive gold watch for my wife, maybe I should ask her what she really wants. It could be that she'd rather have a new sewing machine.

How nice that we have a Father in heaven who urges us to tell Him our needs and wants, even though He already knows what they are.

Thank You for respecting our wants and needs, Lord.
                                                    —DANIEL SCHANTZ

FOR ANYONE WHO ENTERS GOD'S REST ALSO RESTS FROM HIS OWN WORK, JUST AS GOD DID FROM HIS.
—*Hebrews 4:10 (NIV)*

"What do you think God is saying to you in all this?" Pastor Tom asked as he stood beside my hospital bed. Tom and I have asked each other that same question numerous times while discussing spiritual matters.

I'd been in the hospital for two weeks already, and in two days I would undergo more abdominal surgery. Coincidentally, just a couple of evenings before, I had asked God a lot of questions: Why did I have to go through the pain of diverticulitis, two surgeries and a lengthy recuperation? Couldn't He heal me miraculously and instantly? God gave me an answer that surprised me.

So I told Tom, "God said, 'This is a time of rest for you.' It kind of shocked me, because surgeries and sickness aren't what I think of as rest. But then God said, 'Don't worry about anything. Trust Me. I'm taking care of everything. Just rest.'"

That's what I did for the remainder of my thirty-three-day stay in the hospital. Despite long nights of sleeplessness, I took God at His word. I rested, focusing my mind on Him. I didn't think about work or finances or the bathroom faucet at home that needed to be repaired. And during those long days and nights an experience that could have been an ordeal became an occasion of intimate communion with God.

Father, thank You for showing me that I can rest in You no matter what difficulties I'm going through.
—HAROLD HOSTETLER

THAT THE SOUL BE WITHOUT KNOWLEDGE, IT IS NOT GOOD. . . . —Proverbs 19:2

My son Andy looked at me with his bright, blue, nine-year-old eyes. "Why do we die of old age?"

"Well," I stumbled, "as we age, we grow slower and slower, and then God decides it's time to stop."

"Oh." Then, without a pause, "Why do we taste with our mouth?"

"Because we have taste buds."

"Then do we have smell buds in our nose and hear buds in our ears?"

"I don't think so."

"Why not?"

I handled that one as well as I could and made a quick exit. Andy was in "why mode" and I knew it could go on for hours.

There seems to be an appropriate form of "why" for each stage of growing up. At three or four years old, Andy loved to ask "why" just for the pleasure of asking.

"Time to come indoors."

"Why?"

"Because dinner is ready."

"Why?"

"So we can eat."

"Why?"

It was during one of these long back-and-forths that my wife quipped that every child is born with a "why" chromosome.

As Andy grew, we enjoyed the increasing complexity of his questions. They revealed a real desire to learn and sometimes they challenged us too. Meanwhile Andy's older brother was asking even more profound "whys": Why is there evil in the world? Why must we die before attaining eternal life?

I guess I have my own "whys" too. And that is as it should be. God wants us to ask why. These endless questions enlarge our understanding and bring us closer to the one true Answer to them all.

Lord, help me to acquire knowledge and understanding to strengthen my faith and nourish my soul. —PHILIP ZALESKI

***PRIDE GOES BEFORE DESTRUCTION, AND A HAUGHTY SPIRIT
BEFORE A FALL.*** —*Proverbs 16:18* (RSV)

I was still in college when I married a serviceman. I hadn't yet
met his family, and because I'd heard stories about the in-law
problems of other Army wives, I was plenty apprehensive
about meeting mine.

After my husband's discharge, we'd settled into our own
home for a month or so when my mother-in-law phoned. "I've
invited the relatives to Sunday dinner so you can meet them
all," she said.

"How nice," I politely answered, then stunned myself by
adding, "I'll bake a cake to bring for dessert."

I say stunned because my kitchen experience was nil—we'd
lived in room-and-board Army quarters all our married life. But
I'd spotted a recipe on a sugar sack that said, "Impress guests
with this elegant cake." *How hard can it be to measure ingre-
dients?* I thought.

Well, I was so busy concentrating on how impressed my
mother-in-law and all the guests would be with my cake that I
unknowingly turned the sack and finished the second half of
the recipe before I had finished the first half, printed in a com-
parable spot on its opposite side.

When I pulled the cake from the oven an hour later, its top
looked like a mini-mountain range. *What'll I do now?* Then I
had an idea: *Frosting will cover the flaws.*

It worked. At least it did until dessert time, when we discovered the cake's center had collapsed. There was stunned
silence at the table . . . until someone giggled, precipitating a
chain reaction, with me joining in.

True enough, pride goes before a fall, but laughter is the
best medicine. And laughter was the surest sign that I was an
accepted member of my in-laws' clan.

Give me the ability, Lord, always to laugh at myself.
                                              —ISABEL WOLSELEY

*I CAN DO ALL THINGS THROUGH CHRIST WHICH
STRENGTHENETH ME.* —*Philippians 4:13*

I was working out at the gym with a weight that usually had
me trembling when I got to the fifteenth repetition. This time,
as I was approaching that fifteenth rep, for some reason I told
myself I was going to go for twenty.

And the strangest thing happened: As soon as I told myself
that fifteen reps wasn't my boundary, passing it wasn't a problem. All of a sudden, sixteen wasn't nearly as difficult as fifteen
had been all the other times. *Well, how do you like that?* I
thought. *Fifteen wasn't my limit after all.*

And wouldn't you know it, while I was having this little
inner celebration, I heard myself say, "Twenty-one!"

I think it's true that when I give myself limits, my body
tends to agree. And I think the same principle applies outside
the weight room. It's true on the job, in my relationships with
others and in my prayer life. I'll never know how far I can go
unless I stop telling myself what I can't do and start swinging
for the fences. You never know, I might hit a home run.

And the next time I'm at the gym, I'm going for twenty-five!

*Lord, please give me the positive thoughts that help me to do
my best.* —DAVE FRANCO

WHEN HE SAW THE CROWDS, HE HAD COMPASSION ON THEM, BECAUSE THEY WERE HARASSED AND HELPLESS, LIKE SHEEP WITHOUT A SHEPHERD. —Matthew 9:36 (NIV)

Chad walked into my American history classroom five minutes after the tardy bell, slammed his books to the floor, fell into his desk and put his head down. Amanda, my young student teacher, jumped up, ready to reprimand him. "Leave me alone!" he yelled.

"That's it," Amanda said. "Get your books. We're going to the office." She returned a few minutes later. "He'll be spending tomorrow in detention," she told me.

After class I turned to Amanda. "Let's talk at lunch. I have a story to share with you."

Over lunch in the teacher's lounge, I began my story. "I took a flower arranging class years ago. The instructor taught us to decide on the shape we wanted first, use an uneven number of flowers and begin with the tallest flower as the focal point. I made my arrangement and called the instructor over.

"'Your arrangement is nice, but too crowded,' she said. 'Remember that the empty spaces are part of the arrangement too.'"

I paused, looking up at Amanda. "In other words, what we don't see is sometimes as important as what we do see."

I was grading papers at my desk after school when Amanda stopped by. "I talked with Chad before school let out today," she said. "His parents were arrested last night during a drug raid. He came to school this morning, not knowing what to do." She paused, her voice softening, "I spoke with the principal, and Chad will be back in class tomorrow."

The next morning Amanda called me over to her desk. "Today I have a new way of seeing flower arrangements. But most importantly," she said as she looked across the classroom of students, "I have a new way of seeing my students."

Father, help me to treat others as compassionately as You treat me. —MELODY BONNETTE

AND WHOSOEVER WILL, LET HIM TAKE THE WATER OF LIFE FREELY. —Revelation 22:17

It happened fifty-five years ago, but I thought of it today as I looked at my prayer list: healing, guidance, help of all kinds for the needs of more than twenty people, myself included. How could I ever repay God if He granted so much? Then I remembered.

My husband John and I were students in Paris, getting along on a single meal a day. The magazine pieces with which we hoped to support ourselves had so far failed to sell. This latest idea, though, was our best yet: tracing the progress of an escargot from harvest to restaurant.

We had spent weeks documenting the snail's progression. Now came the final stage. The restaurant we chose was one we passed every day, wistfully scanning the gold-bordered menu posted outside. The proprietor was graciousness itself: He would be delighted to represent the culmination of the snail's saga.

And so at four o'clock on a winter afternoon, we arrived at Prunier and were ushered by a tuxedoed waiter to chairs upholstered in red velvet. Utensils for holding and extracting snails were already on the table, along with a basket of crusty rolls, which we hungrily devoured, refolding the damask napkin to conceal the empty container.

The waiter reappeared with two dozen escargots sizzling in garlic butter. We took pictures of the waiter, the snails, ourselves eating them, and in the doorway, as we departed, a photo of the proprietor himself. "But won't you stay and have dinner?" he asked.

Kids that we were, we didn't recognize this as an invitation to be his guests. Thinking only of the prices on that gold-bordered menu, we shook our heads. "We had a late lunch," John said. "We couldn't eat another thing." And away we went, down the cheerless sidewalk, famished in the midst of abundance.

Of course you can't pay for My blessings! God said with that memory. *Ask anything. Health, peace, guidance, wisdom, joy— the invitation to My table is always open.*

Faithful Lord, help me keep my eyes today not on my poverty but on Your boundless wealth. —ELIZABETH SHERRILL

*THAT WHICH IS FAR OFF, AND EXCEEDING DEEP, WHO CAN
FIND IT OUT?* —*Ecclesiastes 7:24*

"You and your nostalgia," my wife Rebecca has said to me more
times than I can count. She's right too. My affection for the
past—in particular, *my* past—borders on the obsessive. From
the plastic dinosaurs and cartoon characters that sit on my
desk at work to the kids' books that crowd in with the adult
ones on my bookshelves, I'm clearly someone with a greater-
than-average interest in times gone by.

Or am I? More and more lately, I've discovered that quite a
few of my fellow adults share this infatuation. While working,
I'll suddenly think of some old cartoon show I haven't seen
since I was seven or eight. I'll go on the Internet and discover
that the whole series is available on DVD and is selling
briskly—to grownups!

My office isn't the only one graced by little plastic toy figures either, though it certainly has far and away the biggest
population of them. Most people, I've come to see, have at least
a little of the nostalgia bug, and I think I understand why. Those
little knickknacks from years past are like compass points,
reminding us of who we once were, even as we journey on to
what we have yet to become. When I look at all the little
objects scattered on my desk with that in mind, they don't
seem so childish after all.

*Lord, thank You for the gifts of the past that keep me mindful
of the glories of the future.* —PTOLEMY TOMPKINS

KNOW YE THAT THE LORD HE IS GOD: IT IS HE THAT HATH MADE US, AND NOT WE OURSELVES; WE ARE HIS PEOPLE, AND THE SHEEP OF HIS PASTURE. —Psalm 100:3

The reason my dog Perky must live in my office was brought home to us in no uncertain fashion when our vigilance failed and Perky and Jessif encountered each other for the first time in two years. My husband Keith got his hand slashed so badly that he couldn't wear his wedding ring for weeks, and I lost my voice yelling at them to get away from each other. I still can't sing the high notes at services, and it's been months since the battle occurred.

Perky is an Australian shepherd mix, about forty pounds, and should probably have been an only dog. Jessif is a German shepherd/greyhound mix, about sixty-five pounds, and refuses to let anyone else be the alpha female, which is a role Perky wants to fill. As a result, when they are in the same place at the same time, they fight.

We tried obedience classes, individual work with a trainer and puppy tranquilizers. Nothing worked. Perky was aggressive, and Jessif would not let herself be dominated. We finally resigned ourselves simply to keeping the dogs apart.

Most of our friends don't understand why we don't give one of the dogs away. After all, they were strays when we took them in. Why should we be inconvenienced?

I always answer that they are our responsibility, and we love them, flaws and all. They have a home with Keith and me for as long as they live.

I think God sees us in much the same way. We fight for dominance of one kind or another in this world, and sometimes I'm sure it's more than an inconvenience. It's a very real disappointment to God. Yet we are His responsibility, and He loves us, flaws and all.

Thank You, God, for Your love that never fails.

—RHODA BLECKER

*BLESS THE LORD, O MY SOUL . . . WHO HEALS ALL YOUR
DISEASES. . . . —Psalm 103:2-3 (RSV)*

Several years ago, my son Chase went on a church ski trip.
None of the other youth from our little church skied; they were
on the trip to meet kids from other churches and maybe frolic
in the powder. Not my son.

A couple of years earlier, he had convinced me to let him
try ski lessons. Chase is a natural athlete and always game for
adventure. Soon he was going up higher and higher mountains.
Snowboarding was his choice, and I alternately covered my
eyes and opened them to watch him swooshing downward,
white powder flying behind him.

My daughter Lanea and I were about to go out for dinner
when the phone rang. "He hit face first," the voice on the
phone said. "It's not too bad. He's had a mild concussion." It
was my worst nightmare. Chase's father had died of head
injuries in an accident. Thank God Chase was alive!

I spoke to Chase at the hospital. "I'm fine. Stop worrying
and go to dinner, Mom. I'm getting a ride home."

When Lanea and I got back from dinner, there was Chase,
sitting at the computer. Half his face was bandaged, swollen
beyond recognition, the outer layer of skin gone.

"Oh, Chase!" I cried.

He shrugged. "I told them not to tell you so you wouldn't
worry. I'm okay, Mom," he said. But he wasn't okay. The wounds
were deep and the doctors gave me directions to treat them
like third degree burns. There could be infection and serious
scarring.

We prayed. *Trust God*, I reminded myself.

Within days, spots of my son's own ebony pigment began to
dot the pink wounds. Within a couple of weeks, he was back at
school. Today, if you looked at my handsome son, you'd never
know it happened. When I look at him, I see a miracle.

Lord, thank You for Your healing touch. —SHARON FOSTER

*I WILL PROCLAIM THE NAME OF THE LORD. OH, PRAISE
THE GREATNESS OF OUR GOD! —Deuteronomy 32:3 (NIV)*

"Please, Lord!"

I often find myself praying this little prayer. When I'm scheduled for a check-up or biopsy, I pray, "Please, Lord!" when I think of the upcoming test. If I'm working on something important, I write, "Please, Lord!" in the margin of the paper. I think of it as a way to keep my hopes constantly before God, a way of continually praying, "Please, Lord, let this happen for me." Until recently, I never thought of it as selfish.

Then I met Maryann. She's a ninety-four-year-old convalescent home resident who still speaks with the Irish brogue she brought to America as a sixteen-year-old girl. She has a fierce faith and is given to her own muttered prayers. When she's upset about anything, from rubbery meatloaf on her dinner tray to a distressing story on the news, she exclaims, "God bless us and save us!" When something goes particularly well, from perfectly cooked fish on her dinner tray to the election of her favorite candidate, she says, "Thanks be to the Man above!"

At the end of every visit, I tell Maryann when I'll be back, and she always says a fervent "Please God!" At first, I thought that she was making this small prayer in the same spirit I made mine. But Maryann's prayer is entirely different. My prayer amounts to "Please, Lord, please me." Her prayer is "Lord, I hope this pleases You."

You can learn a lot from a ninety-four-year-old if you really listen.

Please, Lord, teach me to please You! —MARCI ALBORGHETTI

BE YE OF AN UNDERSTANDING HEART. —*Proverbs 8:5*

I rushed into work, running to punch the time clock. "I had to defrost my freezer," I told my co-workers. "I nearly flooded the kitchen."

"What does that mean?" a twentyish colleague asked me. "I know what a freezer is, but how do you defrost one? Do you mean you had to pull the plug out of the wall?"

I had a feeling that this conversation was going to make me feel old, and I was right.

As another older co-worker stood by me for moral support, I explained to the wide-eyed girl that when ice built up in a freezer, you put a pan of hot water inside and wound up with a big mess on the floor. Sometimes you got a knife or an ice pick and chipped out huge chunks of ice and ran them across to the sink. And sometimes you didn't make it to the sink and wound up with all your towels on the floor sopping wet.

I wouldn't have felt so bad if she hadn't said, "You're joking, right?"

When I assured her I wasn't, she said, "Well, why don't you just use a blow-dryer?"

"Huh?" My response wasn't elegant, but it expressed my confusion quite well. "My hair's not wet."

"No, instead of all that hot water and stuff, just plug in your blow-dryer in the kitchen and aim it at the ice in the freezer."

My mouth opened so wide you could have popped an ice cube into it. "Why, that sounds like a good idea. I'll have to try it." I did. It worked.

Maybe I need to open my mind to new ideas, no matter what the age of the person who's giving them!

God, thank You for new things like frostless freezers and blow-dryers, and for clever co-workers and good new ideas.

—LINDA NEUKRUG

AND YOUR EARS SHALL HEAR A WORD BEHIND YOU, SAYING,
"THIS IS THE WAY, WALK IN IT" . . . . —Isaiah 30:21 (RSV)

It's been nearly twenty years since we last met in the pages of
Daily Guideposts. Back then, I was young, athletic, newly married, still trying to find my way in the world. Now I'm closing
in on fifty—a life filled with work and family, mortgages and
milestones. Lynn and I have just sent our oldest off to college;
our youngest is nearly ready for high school. We're as busy as
ever, perhaps more so.

Maybe because I'm so busy, I never took the time to think
about how things were changing as I grew older—tighter muscles, shorter breath, thinner hair. Then one day recently my
doctor told me, "You've lost twenty-five percent of your hearing in both ears. And we don't know how quickly you'll lose
the rest."

For a while, I fell into a funk, focused on brooding over my
lost hearing and what that might mean. Then a friend looked
me straight in the eye and said, "What will happen is God's
business. Remaining faithful, no matter what happens, is yours."

Those were just words at first, but in the year since I've had
my hearing aids, I've heard the truth in them nearly every day.
Yes, I still miss parts of conversations, but in straining to hear
I've strengthened relationships by having to pay closer attention to people. I'm using my other senses more carefully, and
I've developed a deeper sympathy for others who have experienced loss. I hear less, but I think I understand more.

Am I happy about growing older and the accompanying difficulties? Not one bit. But I know now that I don't always have
to be happy to be faithful to God's calling.

Grant me ears to hear, and understand, the wisdom of Your
leading, God. —JEFF JAPINGA

BLESSED ARE THEY THAT MOURN: FOR THEY SHALL BE COMFORTED. —Matthew 5:4

John, a businessman in our town, served with me on the three-member audit committee at a local bank. He was industrious, dependable, available whenever needed and absolutely trustworthy. I came to care for him deeply. Then one August morning, the bank president called and said, "Oscar, John died last night very suddenly." I was devastated. Grieving for my friend and his family, I did all I could to comfort his widow Mary, but I didn't know her well and could only barely conceive of her pain.

At the first anniversary of John's death, I ran into Mary on the street. "I'm not doing well," she said, her eyes filling with tears. "I want to talk about my grief, but friends don't seem to hear. They say, 'You'll get over it, Mary. You'll do all right.' But I can't get over it."

Her words touched me. I sent her a copy of *Daily Guideposts* and once a week I wrote her a note. I didn't have anything particularly profound to say. I'd give her some news, recall something that John had once said, let her know that she was in my prayers. For weeks I never heard from her. Had she even read my notes? Had I overstepped my bounds?

Then one day my wife and I ran into Mary at the supermarket. She was looking better and greeted me warmly. She gave Ruby a hug and said, "You don't know how much your husband has comforted and helped me."

I beamed, because Mary's words had comforted me too.

Dear Lord, sometimes just being there is Your answer.
—OSCAR GREENE

FOR UNTO US A CHILD IS BORN, UNTO US A SON IS GIVEN. . .
                                        —Isaiah 9:6

Okay, I admit it. It's February and I still have Christmas music
in my car's CD player. Why? Maybe because I can't remember where the CD cases are. Or because I'm too lazy to haul
another handful of CDs out to the car and do the great
switchover. Or perhaps it's because I'm mostly a radio kind of
girl when I'm in the car. Or maybe it's because listening to
Christmas music in February is a very good thing to do.

   Today I was driving home from work, surrounded by the
bleakness this time of year always brings to my part of the
country: gray skies, gray tree branches, gray snow banks, icy
gray highways. But into the midst of that came a hundred-voice
choir singing "Emmanuel, God is with us!" And I realized that it
was true. Not just in the fir-decked, red-bow days of December,
but all year long. In the nitty-gritty, day-in-day-out routine of
life, God is with us! So why pack away the wonder and joy of
Christmas with the jingle bells and holly berries? "Oh come, let
us adore him—Christ the Lord!" It seemed the perfect thing to
do on a chilly February afternoon.

   When I got home, I kissed my husband on the cheek and
said, "Merry Christmas!" Gary—who has known me a very long
time—didn't even seem surprised.

Holy Christ Child, be Lord of my life 365 days a year!
                                        —MARY LOU CARNEY

WITHHOLD NOT GOOD . . . WHEN IT IS IN THE POWER OF
THINE HAND TO DO IT. *—Proverbs 3:27*

When my son Jeff was in the ninth grade, he got into a scuffle
with another student, and they were both suspended for three
days. On the morning Jeff was to return to school, I was filled
with fear. *What will happen when the boys meet again?* It was
rumored that the other boy was a member of a gang. *Will the*
gang seek revenge?

As the schoolbus lumbered down the road with Jeff on it, I
said a prayer for his protection, then went in search of consolation. I selected a book at random from my bookshelf and
flipped open the cover. On the flyleaf, written in an unfamiliar
scrawl, were the words, *With a childlike trust, I lovingly place*
myself and all my affairs in the hands of the Father. That
which is for my highest good shall come to me.

I had found the book at a flea market, but I'd never gotten
around to reading it. Now, all these months later, a stranger
was assuring me that if I placed Jeff's problem in God's hands,
all would be well. And so it was.

Since then, I've made it a habit to write something encouraging in the books I turn in to the secondhand bookstore. I
know the words I write today may not be read for months or
years to come. But I have faith that when the time is right, God
will find a way to use my message of encouragement to help
the person who needs it most.

Father, show me how to share a message of hope with some-
one in trouble. —LIBBIE ADAMS

HOWEVER, OUR GOD TURNED THE CURSE INTO A BLESSING.
                                        —Nehemiah 13:2 (NKJV)

Saturday was my parents' sixtieth wedding anniversary. My four
siblings and I reserved the fellowship hall at their former
church in Dallas for a come-and-go reception in their honor.

I prayed it would be more than a nice little reception. Since
moving from Dallas to east Texas, Mother and Daddy had suffered several years of serious health problems in a new town
with few friends. Mother deeply needed to reconnect with her
old ones.

Unfortunately, that Friday our plans came unraveled. An
ambulance ushered my father to a hospital fifteen miles away,
and clouds threatened a rare snowstorm. *How can we go on
with it?* I thought. Yet how could we not? Family members
were already en route from five hundred miles away.

So not only did I talk to God about the snowstorm, I talked
to the storm itself. I took authority over it; I rebuked it; I spoke
peace to it in the name of Jesus. After all, He calmed a storm
and He *did* say believers would do greater works than He did.

You can probably guess what happened.

It snowed all Friday night and most of Saturday—four inches.
Mixed with my discouragement was this one mental reminder
from God: *Trust Me. I know how to bless my children.*

We decided to go on with the reception without Dad and
hoped somebody would show up. Amazingly, almost seventy
people did! Our come-and-go turned into a come-and-stay; for
three and a half hours friends and family ate, talked, laughed,
hugged my mom and wrote notes to Daddy in the hospital.

God, indeed, knew how to bless His children. The glow of
the evening stayed with Mother longer than the flowers they
received. And the snow was a bonus that will continue to bless
her every time she remembers how people loved them enough
to come in spite of it.

*Father, help me to trust that You know best how to bless Your
children.* —LUCILE ALLEN

"AND AS YOU SAY, OLDER MEN LIKE ME ARE WISE. THEY
UNDERSTAND." —Job 12:12 (TLB)

When I drive U.S. Route 11 back home from Harrisonburg,
Virginia, I pass a gray metal historical sign in the curve just
before Lacey Springs: BIRTHPLACE OF ABRAHAM LINCOLN'S FATHER.
Here in the heart of the South was born the father of the man
who would write the Emancipation Proclamation and the
Gettysburg Address.

When I did some research, however, I found that Lincoln
wasn't close to his father Thomas; he didn't attend his funeral
in 1851. Thomas was a farmer through and through; he may not
have understood his son's intense desire to read and learn
more than was necessary to run a farm.

But whatever Lincoln thought of his dad as a child and
young man, Thomas Lincoln did at least a few things that
affected his son's life in wonderful ways: He married two excellent, God-fearing, loving, laughing women (Nancy, Abe's mother,
and Sarah, his beloved stepmother), he gave himself to his
community in service (as a jury member, road-petitioner and a
guard for county prisoners), and he chose as his church one
that renounced slavery.

In 1860, when President-elect Lincoln made his last visit to
Sarah in Illinois, they went to the cemetery where Thomas was
buried. I like to think that whatever had been amiss between
Abe and his father was healed then, and that the good Thomas
had brought into his son's life was freed to work for America's
good in the years just ahead.

Lord, thank You for Abraham Lincoln, who held us together as
a nation in the roughest of times. May the healing he hoped to
begin be accomplished in our lives. —ROBERTA ROGERS

HE SHALL GATHER THE LAMBS WITH HIS ARM, AND CARRY THEM IN HIS BOSOM. . . . —Isaiah 40:11

The early morning phone call surprised me; my friend Laurie was on the verge of tears. "Gail, I'm beside myself. Nicole got her driver's license yesterday, so she's driving to school today—without me! I'm so worried. You've done this before. . . ." She paused, helpless. As if on cue, Nicole, who is her oldest child, drove up, and Trina, my youngest, bolted out the door of the house for her ride.

I flashed back to Tom at sixteen learning to drive. Would I ever forget the near miss with the cottonwood tree? "Just start braking *way* before you want to stop, honey," I said as I dug my nails into the armrest.

Then I thought of Trina's recent icy spin that had sent her into a snowbank. No injuries, just minor dents. Oh yes, I'd done this before. How my prayer life had revved into high gear once my kids started driving!

"I know how you feel," I told Laurie. "Believe me! But Nicole's a cautious driver. She's not wild or reckless, right?"

"Right."

"She has a new car and good tires, right?"

Fewer sniffles now. "Right."

"She's even got a cell phone and her little brother watching the gauges with her."

"But *I'm* not with her . . ."

"Look, Laurie. Do what I did—give her to God. I mean, really picture it. See yourself holding Nicole in your arms. Got it? Now hand her over to God. He's holding her now. She's safe in His arms. We all are."

Laurie seemed to be thinking this over. "I feel better now."

"Good. Call me again when she gets home."

Good Shepherd, teach me to share the ways You comfort me. Amen. —GAIL THORELL SCHILLING

LOVE ONE ANOTHER DEEPLY, FROM THE HEART.

—*I Peter 1:22 (NIV)*

For more than fifty years now, I've been saying good night to my helpmate with three little words: "I love you." So I don't need a special day on the calendar to remind me to tell Shirley that she's supercalifragilisticexpialidocious. But just to make sure she knows, I'll pledge my troth once more. I usually write her a poem, and I'll share this year's verse if you promise to keep it a secret.

> *Thank you, Shirl, for your love sublime,*
> *For putting me first, time after time,*
> *For your patience and faith and infectious laughter,*
> *That I pray will go with me all of this life and after.*

How often do we need to say, "I love you" to those we hold dear? Obviously, more often than every February 14. And obviously more often than Golde told Tevye in *Fiddler on the Roof.* You remember his insistent question in song: "Do you love me?" Finally, Golde answers yes, and her dairy farmer husband trills, "After twenty-five years, it's nice to know." It's always nice to know.

> *Teach us, God, when our love is expressed,*
> *We receive a blessing and others are blessed.*
> —FRED BAUER

"O LORD, FORGIVE! . . . FOR YOUR SAKE, O MY GOD, DO
NOT DELAY, BECAUSE YOUR CITY AND YOUR PEOPLE BEAR
YOUR NAME." —Daniel 9:19 (NIV)

Bible study was over, and I rushed out to buy some food for a
funeral luncheon. If I hurried, I'd just have time to get it there
by noon. I zipped through the store, aware that the peace I'd
felt during the Bible study was slipping away and impatience
was surfacing.

   I was barely able to restrain myself and slow down behind
the wobbly old lady in front of me in the prepared foods aisle.
Tense and anxious, I finally arrived at the checkout line. I was
tempted just to write my check in silence without greeting the
checker, but I forced a hello and a smile. It wasn't until I
jumped back into my car that I knew my battle to behave was
worth it: I still had my Bible study name tag on! What if I'd let
my impatience be known along with my name?

   Contrite, I realized that, with or without a name tag, there's
Someone I'm always representing. In my hurry to do a good
deed, I could have undone something just as important: my
witness.

Lord Jesus, as Your disciple, I bear Your name. Help me to be
a good witness to You in every part of my life.
                                        —MARJORIE PARKER

WE ARE MORE THAN CONQUERORS THROUGH HIM WHO
LOVED US. —*Romans 8:37 (NIV)*

The idea hit me one day in the shower, and within minutes I
was on the phone with a few of my friends, asking if they
wanted to help put together a devotional book for other young
people. Two of them said yes. Soon we were soliciting stories
from high school and college students from around the world,
and within six months we were holding our first book signing.

I expected teenagers to be knocking down the doors to the
bookstore, demanding copies by the thousands. Unfortunately,
reality did not live up to my delusions of grandeur. We sold a
few books that day and a few more at another signing the next
day. In the first month we sold a couple hundred, but after that
sales dropped off almost entirely.

It's now been a year since my idea hit me, and sometimes I
see the whole project as a failure. Financially speaking, I haven't
recouped half of the money I invested in the book's publication.

But just yesterday I picked up a copy from my shelf and
flipped through it. I thought about the forty people who had
contributed a piece of their lives to the project. I thought about
all I'd learned in the process of writing, editing and finding a
publisher. And I thought about the new stories that trickle in,
the ones about teenagers who have been encouraged by reading the book.

I smiled. In God's business, success isn't about numbers, is
it? It's about people: those we influence and those we become.
That's all the grandeur I could ever ask for.

Lord, thank You for shaping me into the person You want me
to be, whether I succeed or fail. —JOSHUA SUNDQUIST

SO DO NOT THROW AWAY YOUR CONFIDENCE; IT WILL BE RICHLY REWARDED. —*Hebrews 10:35 (NIV)*

Everything I thought about on my morning walk made me worry. The day before, our son Chris had called from school in California in a quandary over a Spanish class that seemed way over his head. Today was the deadline to decide whether to drop the class, and the outcome could alter our summer plans. Then my husband Gordon had come home saying that he wanted to put his name in the hat for a job in another city. Everything inside of me screamed, *No, I don't want to move again! I don't have the time or energy for it!* "It would disrupt my whole life," I told him. We had suspended our discussion at an uncomfortable impasse. As I rounded the curve and headed home, I tried to lift my problems to God, but somehow it didn't seem to do any good. I arrived home feeling just as depressed and powerless as ever.

I collapsed in the living room and opened my Bible to where I had been reading the day before. All at once, a sentence in Hebrews electrified me. I hurried upstairs to copy it down in my journal in capital letters. "DO NOT THROW AWAY YOUR CONFIDENCE."

"Is that the only way confidence can be lost—if I throw it away myself?" I wrote. "That's an amazing thought. Usually I think that overwhelming circumstances or my own lack of ability or the way others have treated me rob me of my confidence. What if confidence is really mine and mine alone either to keep or throw away?"

In the past, I'd often mentally substituted the word *self-confidence* for *confidence* when reading the Bible. Self-confidence is not always possible or practical, because there are many things beyond my ability and control. But Hebrews tells me to place my trust and reliance on God, "for he who promised is faithful" (Hebrews 10:23, NIV).

The next morning, as I rounded the same curve in my morning walk, I smiled. What an amazing turnaround my attitude had taken because of that one sentence I'd read the day before. Every time worry or depression crept in, I would simply remind myself, "Don't throw away your confidence." I went about my day with assurance and optimism.

Chris decided to stick with the Spanish class and eventually earned a B in it. I began praying for whatever God thought best concerning Gordon's future job, even if it meant laying aside my desire for stability. And I prayed with confidence because I was sure that whatever God's plan, it would be so much better than mine.

Lord, instead of throwing away my confidence, help me to throw my whole heart into trusting You. —KAREN BARBER

"IF YOUR EYES ARE GOOD, YOUR WHOLE BODY WILL BE FULL OF LIGHT." —*Matthew 6:22 (NIV)*

I don't like shopping for eyeglasses, so I brought my husband and son with me to help me find the best pair. We'd been there for almost an hour, and the frames seemed "too something"— too big, too serious, too round. Squinting into the brightly lit mirror, I put on a cute pair of wire frames and turned to my husband. "What about these?" He shrugged and made a face.

"Go! Go!" Two-year-old Solomon pointed to a toy store on the other side of the mall.

I picked up a bright blue pair that seemed a bit adventurous. "I'll always look happy in these."

My husband nodded. "Those are good. Come on, it's getting late."

"Which do you like better?" I put on a tortoise-shell pair and then the bright blue pair. "These . . . or these?"

"They both look good."

"Go! Go!" Solomon yelled.

"Fine." I stood in line at the counter with the blue frames in my hand. *Maybe I should get a more traditional pair*, I thought. *Something brown or black.* As the man in front of me collected his things, my eyes wandered to a poster on the far wall behind the counter: Two children were dressed in mismatched clothing, their bright eyes lit up behind large adult-sized glasses. The caption read, "GIVE A CHILD THE JOY OF SIGHT—DONATE YOUR OLD GLASSES."

My happy blue frames in my hand, I couldn't get over the smiles on those children's faces. Here I'd been thinking about glasses as something to be seen in, when they were really something I should be thankful I was able to see through.

Thank You, Lord, for the wonderful world You show me through my happy blue glasses. Help me to remember the good I can do with all the things—like old glasses—I no longer need. —SABRA CIANCANELLI

HE SAID TO THEM, "GO INTO ALL THE WORLD AND PREACH THE GOOD NEWS TO ALL CREATION." —Mark 16:15 (NIV)

Our pastor described the guest speaker visiting our church as "a true visionary." And he was right. Vernon Brewer of World Help is taking the Gospel to the forgotten people of the world. He explained to us the principle that guides such a daunting task: "Every day I try to live my life in such a way that I accomplish at least one thing that will outlive me and last for eternity."

That sure put a new spin on my Sunday afternoon to-do list. Should I attend the local tour of homes or call that friend who just lost her husband? *If you accomplish only one eternity-minded deed every day, Roberta,* God seemed to be telling me, *you'll change your life and the course of eternity. You don't have to do it all in one day. Just one thing each day.*

When I was growing up, we had a little plaque hanging in the entry of our house that read "Only one life, 'twill soon be past. Only what's done for Christ will last." Over the years I'd forgotten the powerful simplicity of that maxim, but thanks to a true visionary, I'm remembering it afresh.

Help me to keep eternity's values in view, Lord.

—ROBERTA MESSNER

***THERE IS NO AUTHORITY EXCEPT THAT WHICH GOD HAS
ESTABLISHED. . . .*** —*Romans 13:1* (NIV)

Election year is a terrible time to live in Washington, D.C.
Everyone gets caught up in politics, and often the rhetoric gets
downright ugly. Friends who normally talk about everything
with good humor get into heated arguments over the latest
"talking points" or poll results. And because the federal gov-
ernment is here and employs so many of the residents, the
local news is always about what is happening on Capitol Hill or
in the White House.

My wife Joy and I serve as volunteers for the National Prayer
Breakfast, which is a completely nonpartisan event. Like the
military, our group is supposed to respect and serve to the best
of our ability whoever is elected president. Often that's not
easy.

On the Thursday before the last national election, some
prayer breakfast volunteers were at lunch together. Everything
was fine until someone mentioned a story from that morning's
newspaper. Suddenly, battle lines were drawn and tempers
started to rise.

Rapping his spoon loudly on the table, the senior member
of the group got everyone's attention. "Look," he said, "everyone calm down. There are two things we know for sure about
the election. First, after all the uproar next Tuesday, we'll be
back here next Thursday eager to do our best. And second,
whoever is elected, God will still be in charge."

*Lord, help me to remember that You are above all rulers and
authority, and to trust Your hand even when I cannot see
Your purpose.* —ERIC FELLMAN

To every thing there is a season, and a time to every purpose under the heaven. —Ecclesiastes 3:1

Several years ago, on a trip to China, my husband Robert learned that the Chinese think of life in twelve-year segments. Age sixty is considered a complete lifetime, and the sixty-first birthday represents the beginning of a new life. Worldly responsibilities are complete, so it's an ideal time to develop the life of the spirit.

Of course, we're living longer now, so many of us are still quite young at sixty and continue our earlier responsibilities. But now that I'm in my seventies, I've consciously chosen to accept my elderhood. I'm beginning a new life in which I'm free to make spiritual growth my top priority. I consider it to be the most valuable stage of life. Sure, I have plenty of aches and pains and other physical nuisances, but in prayer and meditation I sometimes glimpse a reality that is so vast and so glorious that those minor physical ailments shrink into insignificance.

So today this elder with the graying hair and thinning bones would like to leave two thoughts with you. If you're in the earlier life stages, think of each failure as a stepping-stone to wisdom. And if, like me, you're in your autumn years, you have fully lived your wisdom and your foolishness. It's now time to harvest the spiritual wonder of your life.

Awaken my spirit, Holy One. As my body weakens, may my spirit grow stronger in You. —MARILYN MORGAN KING

NOW IT IS REQUIRED THAT THOSE WHO HAVE BEEN GIVEN A TRUST MUST PROVE FAITHFUL. —I Corinthians 4:2 (NIV)

When I was twenty years old, I moved away from my home in Ohio and found work in Colorado. What I lacked in experience, I tried to make up for in dependability. I saved enough money for tuition and went to college, but I always returned to the same job. I didn't miss a day of work until my third year with the company. I got some kind of flu over the weekend and had to call in sick. My boss said, "It figures. Most workers tend to get sick on a Monday." His remark inspired me to find another job.

I thought about that old boss of mine the other day when I read a letter the sixty-five-year-old George Washington wrote describing his daily routine: "I begin with the sun. . . . If my hirelings are not in their places at that time, I send them messages expressive of my sorrow for their indisposition." He didn't accuse them of playing sick.

Much has been written about Washington's leadership qualities, but I think kindness and trust are two of his most overlooked traits. I imagine that Washington showed the same kindness and trust to his wife, his wife's children, his troops, his colleagues and his constituents. He trusted them, and the people he trusted proved faithful.

Dear Lord, thank You for giving us great leaders to follow so that we might learn to lead those who follow us.

—TIM WILLIAMS

FOR YE KNOW THE GRACE OF OUR LORD JESUS CHRIST,
THAT, THOUGH HE WAS RICH, YET FOR YOUR SAKES HE
BECAME POOR. . . . —II Corinthians 8:9

When we moved to the Twin Cities, my husband Terry and I
lived at first in a rented townhouse. We had sold our home in
Alaska, and though our resources were far from unlimited, we
weren't as pinched as we had been. We had all sorts of fun
going out to dinner, exploring local attractions and taking in
concerts and theater performances.

Then we had the opportunity to buy acreage and build a
house. Expense after expense piled up, until soon we were
struggling to keep the bills paid. We couldn't go out as much as
before, but we had an attractive, nicely furnished home to com-
pensate for it.

One day I observed to my husband, "It seems to me that
there are two types of people—the 'havers' and the 'doers.'
Havers are willing to do less in order to have more, and doers
would rather have less and be able to do more. So which
are we?"

The question had no sooner popped out when a gently
chiding voice within me said: *Aren't you forgetting another
kind of person? Some people are givers.* I'd completely ignored
people who neither have nor do as much for themselves as
they might, because they're busy giving. Maybe they're sup-
porting overseas missions projects or helping those in need at
home or keeping their local churches financially afloat.

For me, the temptations to have more and do more are very
strong, and I don't always win out over them. But I'm determined to become more of a giver—of money, of time, of heart.

God, You are such a giver! May my willingness to give be a
blessing to You. —CAROL KNAPP

TRAIN A CHILD IN THE WAY HE SHOULD GO, AND WHEN HE IS OLD HE WILL NOT TURN FROM IT. —*Proverbs 22:6 (NIV)*

My daughter Katherine is very bright, but she's not very fond of homework. Often she'd tell me she had none, only to remember it the next morning. I felt she should do her schoolwork on her own, and this frustrated me. So I encouraged her to be more responsible and reminded her what would happen if she wasn't.

One morning Katherine had "forgotten" three assignments, and there wasn't time for her to complete them without being late for school. "You'll have to tell your teacher that you didn't do them," I said.

On the way to school, Katherine burst into tears. "My teacher will be mad at me, and it's all your fault!"

I couldn't believe that she was blaming me—I'd told her for weeks that this would happen—and then I thought of how often I blame God for what I do to myself. I needed to answer my daughter in the same way the Lord answers me.

"I love you, Katherine," I told her as we reached the school, "but I can't make your choices for you. You did this. You have to face the consequences. Tell your teacher the truth and apologize."

My daughter flounced out of the car, hesitated, and then ran back and hugged me. "I'm sorry, Mom," she said.

Lord, You are my Father and my teacher. May Your patience and love always inspire me. —REBECCA KELLY

I WILL GUIDE THEE WITH MINE EYE. —*Psalm 32:8*

Wandering around the house on a Saturday when my wife and
children are elsewhere for a while, I begin to see holy places
that I never quite noticed before: the infinitesimal indent made
by ten years of left hands as woman and man and children lean
against the wall while adjusting the thermostat with their right
hands; the tower of penciled height marks marking toddler to
teenager; the ancient cracked cup holding five toothbrushes
like fingers in a fist; the dent in the couch where it bore children thousands and thousands of times; the muscular oak table
where meals have come and gone for a decade; the spaded soil
by the door where fish and hamsters are buried; the rattling
chair we have always meant to fix and never have and never
will; the lawn that has held us all in its green embrace in every
season. . . .

For a moment I'm overwhelmed. This afternoon, in the
small warm house where for a moment no one brawls and
bawls, I'm given the immense gift of seeing, for an instant, the
true shape of my life. I'm a man rich in children, rich beyond
imagining, rich beyond calculation, and I'm so moved by this
epiphany that I sit on the floor, and an instant later the back
door bursts open and two sons tumble in fighting like cougars.
For once I do not roar and rage, not immediately anyway, for
their savage verve is still a verb and not a memory, for which I
am awfully glad.

*Dear Lord, thanks for what is, which I hardly ever see with
sharp enough peepers.* —BRIAN DOYLE

I, EVEN I, AM HE THAT COMFORTETH YOU....
—*Isaiah 51:12*

Patricia, a member of our church, announced one Sunday that she had shingles and asked for prayers. I dutifully prayed and extended my sympathy when she said she was having a lot of pain.

But it wasn't until I got shingles myself that I understood the pain she'd been talking about. My shingles had advanced enough before I discovered them that our doctor wasn't sure we could get them stopped. But strong doses of an antiviral medication, plus the prayers of our church members, including Patricia, set me on the road to recovery.

When Patricia said to me during the worst of it, "I know what you're going through," I knew she did, and that was a comfort. When other members of our church who had never experienced shingles touched my hand and said, "I'm sorry," that was a comfort too. But the greatest comfort of all came from the Friend above, Who listened to my prayers and held my hand at night when I couldn't sleep.

Lord, help me reach out to someone today who is suffering, even if I don't fully understand his or her pain.
—MADGE HARRAH

"HE IS ABLE TO HUMBLE THOSE WHO WALK IN PRIDE."
—*Daniel 4:37 (NAS)*

Our two daughters were perfect little girls, born just over two years apart. Friends and family called them angels. I dressed them alike and made sure to coordinate hair bows and socks with their outfits. Almost everywhere we three went, strangers praised my parental skills. I thought I deserved it. *They're never rude in public or talk back, thanks to me.*

I prided myself on my mothering ability. I didn't work outside the home, never shouted at my children and drew smiley faces on their lunch bags every day. We went to church three times a week. When I'd see other parents struggling with their children, I'd think, *If you try hard enough like me, it works! Simply follow my example and there'll be no problem children.*

Then, at eighteen, each of my daughters started rebelling. It wasn't the quiet kind of rebellion, the kind to sweep under a rug. And the same friends and relatives who'd praised my mothering skills now called to tell me about the girls' bad behavior.

God, I prayed, *how could this happen? Other parents may have messed up raising their children, but my children should be different. I tried as hard as I knew how. I don't deserve this.*

My daughters' rebellion showed me the truth: Puffed up by my own supposed success, I'd passed judgment on other parents. Now my embarrassment had exposed my sin of pride. It was a hard lesson, but I trust God has used it to make me a better person—and a better parent.

Father, Your Word puts it best: "When pride comes, then comes disgrace, but with humility comes wisdom" (Proverbs 11:2, NIV).
—JULIE GARMON

WHATEVER YOUR HAND FINDS TO DO, DO IT WITH ALL
YOUR MIGHT. . . . —*Ecclesiastes 9:10* (NIV)

Working as a registered nurse with seniors in assisted-care
homes, I found two types of residents. The angry ones didn't
want to be there and, in a way, I didn't blame them. They'd lost
so much: hard-earned homes and possessions, independence,
privacy, good health. And then there were people like Mr. and
Mrs. Epp, who radiated quiet acceptance. What secret had they
found to keep discouragement at bay?

One morning before breakfast I entered their room with
their medication. At first I didn't see the couple. They were sitting together at a small table sipping coffee from Royal Albert
china cups. "Mugs from the home won't do," said Mrs. Epp,
smoothing the lace tablecloth, "nor will the coffee from the
dining hall."

Mr. Epp nodded. "This is how we've always done it," he said
proudly.

There's comfort in our simple routines, in the ordinary tasks
of life. When I feel frazzled, I consider the Epps and enjoy a hot
cup of tea, take a stroll in the park or write a letter to someone
I love. Sometimes the smallest things can make the whole day
better.

Dear Lord, thank You for the familiar things that brighten
my day. —HELEN GRACE LESCHEID

THEN WILL I SPRINKLE CLEAN WATER UPON YOU, AND YE SHALL BE CLEAN. . . . —Ezekiel 36:25

My Maggie is an artist; she likes to draw. Being the exuberant soul she is, she prefers larger surfaces. A big white wall is irresistible; tabletops are attractive too. In a pinch Maggie will draw on herself if indelible markers are available.

Maggie's fascination with drawing is unique in my parenting experience. When she executed her first large-scale masterpiece, I used the technique that had worked with my other children: I handed her a sponge and made her scrub the wall. It was a big job for a two-and-a-half-year-old, and Maggie didn't like it at all. But the next day she rushed up to me eagerly and said, "I need a sponge, Mommy! I drawed on the floor!"

Such persistence is not a matter of mere stubbornness. For Maggie, the joy of swirling a crayon in full-arm rotation is so immense that it has nothing to do with the idea that she's only supposed to draw on paper. She doesn't realize she's being disobedient. Since she's only two, I don't find that particularly surprising. She has time to learn.

I'm a long way from being two. I no longer draw on walls, and I manage to avoid a lot of bigger no-no's. But there are still many times each day when I do what I feel like doing, without considering what God wants me to do. All too often it's only when I'm in bed mentally reviewing the day that I even realize that I was disobedient.

Unlike Maggie, I'm not always cheerful about saying I'm sorry. I'm never quite as willing to admit I've done wrong or as eager to get back to the drawing board. But maybe that will come with time.

I've done it again, Lord. Come, wash me clean.

—JULIA ATTAWAY

THOU ART MY FATHER, MY GOD, AND THE ROCK OF MY SALVATION. —*Psalm 89:26*

I saw my father angry at my mother only once.

Dad was a private detective with an office in New York City, twenty-five miles from our home in the suburbs. To a child, it seemed fun and glamorous, knowing behind-the-scenes stories about kidnappings or murders. What I didn't know about was Dad's perpetual fear that someone he had helped send to prison might seek revenge on our family.

On the day I remember so well, Mother answered a phone call. "He's not here," I heard her say.

"That's funny," she said as she replaced the receiver, "the man just hung up."

A family rule was that unidentified calls be reported to the office. Mother called Dad, then turned to me. "Lock the front door! I'll get the back one. Then help me lower the shades."

Thirty minutes later I heard a car slow and stop, then footsteps on the walk. Peeking from an upstairs window, I saw one of Dad's operatives station himself at the front door. Minutes later Dad himself arrived. The locked doors, the drawn shades, the sentinel at the door, none of it made such an impression on me as Daddy's voice raised to Mother: "Never, never, *never* say, 'He's not here'!"

She never did again, I'm sure.

But don't I say that, too, anytime a problem overwhelms me? Don't I hear God telling me now, "Never, never, *never* say, 'My heavenly Father is not here'"?

Faithful Lord, teach me to say when trouble calls, "My Father is right here." —ELIZABETH SHERRILL

LET HIM HAVE ALL YOUR WORRIES AND CARES, FOR HE IS ALWAYS THINKING ABOUT YOU AND WATCHING EVERYTHING THAT CONCERNS YOU. —*I Peter 5:7* (TLB)

The bridge to nowhere crosses a steep gorge of the East Fork of the San Gabriel River in California, high in the mountains several miles from where we live. The concrete span extends 230 feet from a rock buttress to the ridge on the other side. Designed to connect a proposed highway between ski resorts, the bridge was completed in 1936 and has never carried a single car. In March 1938, torrential rains raised the river to a forty-foot churning disaster. Roads under construction were destroyed and the project abandoned. Only the bridge remained, useless, leading nowhere.

Over the years I've spent hours building such bridges, brooding on what could've—would've—been, if only I'd done this, that or the other. Most recently I felt smug satisfaction in booking a travel package at a reduced rate. Four days later another special came up for two hundred dollars less! It was too late to switch. I grumbled about the injustice to a friend. "Your fretting is getting you nowhere," she said. "Go and enjoy your trip." She was right.

I'm resolved to abandon useless bridges that take me nowhere. Instead I'll build bridges of trust, faith and confidence in the common sense the Lord has given me with which to map my daily life.

Holy Spirit, I trust Your guidance on the roadways of life. How I rejoice that Jesus is the bridge that leads me to the heart of God! —FAY ANGUS

*THE LORD WILL WATCH OVER YOUR COMING AND GOING
BOTH NOW AND FOREVERMORE. —Psalm 121:8 (NIV)*

Just when I thought I had a good grip on the wisdom of the
saying "Let go and let God," our twenty-six-year-old daughter
Sanna moved to Tennessee to live with Whitney and me. She
had a job, she paid her bills, she was mature and delightful to
have around. But the guy she was dating . . . well, there's where
I lost my grip.

All my efforts to steer Sanna away from him and into a
church with a singles group backfired, forcing me to "let go and
let God." In time, the relationship ended without my help.

"I really want to find the man God has in mind for me,"
Sanna said.

"I want that for you, too, honey," I said, swallowing the urge
to steer. She was about to move into a large apartment complex. Lord knows what influences awaited. *Let go and let God,
Shari.*

As moving day approached, Sanna decided to switch from
an upstairs to a downstairs apartment. "But, Sanna, the upstairs
has more light," I said.

"But the ground floor feels like where I'm supposed to be,"
she replied.

Time passed. Sanna began seeing someone new, a gem of a
man. She joined his church. "I know he's the one for her," I said
to Whitney.

"Let go and let God, Shari," he said.

Finally, on an evening I'll never forget, Glen and Sanna gave
us the news: "We're engaged!"

At their wedding reception, Glen toasted Sanna as the girl
he'd been praying and hoping for. "And then she moved in next
door!" he said.

Lord, even when I lose my grip, You never lose Yours.
                                                —SHARI SMYTH

"AND IF YOU GREET ONLY YOUR BROTHERS, WHAT ARE YOU DOING MORE THAN OTHERS? . . ." —Matthew 5:47 (NIV)

For all of our married life, Shirley and I have been part of Sunday school classes, probably because we got the habit as kids. But it's more than habit; we go to discuss faith questions with others who study the Bible for the insights it gives about living meaningful lives.

One question recently posed to our class was "Why are so many churches losing members?" One older member thought that the message of salvation wasn't preached enough. Another opined that the church had become irrelevant in people's lives, that it didn't provide solutions to daily problems and that it wasn't involved enough in the community's needs. A third suggested that many were too busy to give up an hour on Sunday morning, that after working all week, people were exhausted and wanted to rest. I had heard all of these reasons before, but then a young woman spoke. She had a nonattending friend who said she found her neighborhood bar "warmer and more friendly" than the churches she had visited.

That doesn't describe the churches I've known, but maybe she's on to something. The TV show *Cheers* featured a cast of characters that formed a caring community in a Boston tavern "where everybody knows your name." I'd like to think that churches are just as welcoming. But one thing I know for sure: At church on Sunday, I'm going to start writing down every newcomer's name.

> *Lord, school us in the art of reaching out to others,*
> *Of treating all Your kids like sisters and brothers.*
>   —FRED BAUER

AND BECAUSE YE ARE SONS, GOD HATH SENT FORTH THE
SPIRIT OF HIS SON INTO YOUR HEARTS, CRYING, ABBA,
FATHER. —*Galatians 4:6*

Julia and I were tired last night. We'd had a hectic weekend of
ballet recitals, museum visits and soaking rain, and the work-
week had been a busy one. We were desperate for sleep;
fifteen-month-old Stephen was not. He climbed up into our
bed, lay down next to me and patted me with his hand.
"Daddy!" he said.

"Yes, it's Daddy," I mumbled. "I'm right here. Go to sleep."

Stephen smiled. "Daddy!" he said and patted me again.

"Night-night, Stevie," I said, putting my head back on the
pillow.

"Daddy!" he said, as if he had discovered something wonderful. "Daddy! Daddy! Daddy! Daddy!"

I turned toward him, looked into his eyes and stroked his
cheek. Suddenly I didn't feel so tired.

Stephen didn't want me to play with him or read him a
board book. All he wanted was to be with me and to let me
know how happy that made him.

It made me happy too. And it made me think: Usually I
come to my heavenly Father burdened with needs—for forgiveness, for healing, for strength. And it's good that I do that.
But how often do I just let myself rest in His presence and tell
Him I love Him?

I turned out the light, and Stephen settled down. As sleep
came, I prayed:

Abba, Father! Daddy! Daddy! Daddy! —ANDREW ATTAWAY

SHE LOOKETH WELL TO THE WAYS OF HER HOUSEHOLD, AND
EATETH NOT THE BREAD OF IDLENESS. —*Proverbs 31:27*

When I see previews of some of the movies and TV programs
that target children, I marvel that today's kids don't turn into
bundles of goosebumps. I certainly would have when I was
their age. In fact, mere words could frighten me back then. For
example, whenever my father thought my mother had spent a
penny too much on anything, he'd direly predict, "We're going
over the hill to the poorhouse!" Thus each time we crested a
hill—especially if it had a house on top—I'd cower on the floor
between the car seats convinced, "That's the poorhouse . . .
it'll get us now!"

Another apprehension-causing phrase came when Dad
warned, "If you keep scowling and the wind changes, your face
will stay that way until the wind changes back again." I'd
secretly find a mirror to see whether whatever grudge I was
nursing was worth the look on my face.

A character flaw my mother spotted was my lack of gumption. "If you had any gumption," she said, "you'd get your homework done now instead of wasting time on the funnies." If that
didn't cause me to put down the Katzenjammer Kids and open
a textbook, she'd ominously add, "Idle hands are the devil's
playground."

As I look back on my early years, what I felt for my parents
wasn't fear but healthy respect. The "poorhouse warning"
keeps me watching money, not wasting it. Putting on a smile
wards off anger whether or not the wind blows. And the gumption Mom taught is the impetus to get needed tasks done first
for more pleasure in whatever comes later. It's never too late to
learn that.

Thank You, heavenly Father, for whatever gumption You have
given me. And thanks especially for parents who cared enough
to instruct, discipline and lovingly train me in Your way.
                                          —ISABEL WOLSELEY

CLOTHE YOURSELVES WITH COMPASSION, KINDNESS, HUMILITY,
GENTLENESS AND PATIENCE. —*Colossians 3:12 (NIV)*

My dear friend Helen Morrison died last year. I met her at my
first job when I came to California twenty years ago. Helen
never had a bad word to say about anyone. When I felt like
having a good gossip about a co-worker with a snappish attitude, Helen would say, "Oh, maybe he was having a bad day" in
her lilting British accent. When I started to tell her about the
carpool driver who leapt out of the van to chat with a friend
and made me late for work, she said, "Isn't it nice to unexpectedly meet a friend?"

I once tried to get Helen to admit that a former boss we'd
all found controlling and manipulative was . . . well, controlling and manipulative. "Come on," I coaxed, "you're not going to
say you liked him!"

"Well," she said, "at times he could be a tiny bit difficult."

"A tiny bit difficult?" I exploded. "He tried to get his best
friend fired! Helen, isn't there *anyone* you don't like?"

Helen seemed surprised by my question and considered
it for several long moments. Finally she said, "When I moved
to America by myself all those years ago, I knew no one. So
I couldn't afford to be picky and choosy about my friends.
That habit has stayed with me all these years, and it's served
me well."

I must have looked skeptical because she lowered her voice
and whispered in a conspiratorial tone, "Besides, Linda, everyone
brings joy—some when they come and some when they go."

God, today let me say a prayer of thanks for those friends
whom I loved when they came and cried over when they
went. —LINDA NEUKRUG

BUT GODLINESS WITH CONTENTMENT IS GREAT GAIN.
                                              —*I Timothy 6:6* (NIV)

"Oh, Lord, I am so thankful for this _____, but I just wish
this part of it were _____."

I find myself praying these "grumbling with faint praise"
prayers a lot. But I'm old enough to know that the only real
antidote for it is true praise. It's getting to the true praise that's
the problem.

A few weeks ago, I was in the middle of a grumble-praise
when the phrase "zero-based budgeting" popped into my head.
It was a concept I'd learned sitting through endless Board of
Education meetings as a reporter back in Maryland. The idea
was to throw out everything in the budget and start with the
absolutely essential items, such as buildings, teachers, basic
maintenance costs. It is a useful way to prioritize needs and
wants.

Hmm, I thought, *what if I applied that idea to my negative
thoughts and found the things I can honestly and totally
thank God for at this moment?*

So I ignored every thought where I might be tempted to
thank Him for something and then add "but," and started at
the bottom, thanking Him for things I was genuinely glad for,
like my husband Bill's cute new mustache, the outline of
Massanutten Mountain against the sky, the hummingbirds on
the feeder, the wind blowing through the open porch windows, having gas in my car and energy to fix dinner . . . the list
grew and grew. And instead of grumbling, soon I was laughing
with joy for my "zero-based blessings."

Lord, today I thank you for _____;
                                   (FILL IN THE BLANK)

                                              —ROBERTA ROGERS

REMEMBER THE LORD IN A DISTANT LAND, AND THINK ON JERUSALEM. —*Jeremiah 51:50 (NIV)*

My mother moved into an assisted-living home after Alzheimer's made it impossible for her to live alone. She'd only been there a week when I got a call from the supervisor. "I hate to tell you this, but your mom's been swiping things from other people's rooms. Socks, candy bars, T-shirts. Nothing big, except that one lady's cross is missing."

My mom? Stealing? This was the most honest person I knew, who once drove twenty miles back to a store where the clerk had given her too much change—less than a dollar and considerably less than it cost in gas to return the overage.

The next time I visited, I gently chided her for the pilfering. "You've got to cut that out, Mom," I said, sitting with her in the lunchroom. "Did you take that cross?"

She shook her head, her curly gray hair bouncing.

"Sure about that?" I pressed.

Mom turned away, then reached into her purse and pulled out the small silver cross. She set it down on the table gingerly and stared at it. "I wasn't trying to steal" was all the explanation she gave.

Later I turned over the cross to the supervisor, apologizing. "Don't, don't," she said. "Your mom's a charmer. She's just trying to hang on to the things that mean the most to her."

The next time I came out I brought Mom a small silver cross. She stopped stealing after that.

Eventually we had to move Mom to a facility where she could receive more care and where, of course, she charmed everyone. She even led prayers on Friday morning. She had forgotten almost everything else, yet the prayers came to her lips as if she had freshly committed them to memory. And when she died, the saddest people of all were the people she prayed with on Friday morning with that little silver cross I gave her clutched in her hand.

Lord, Mom is with You now. Teach me never to forget You, just as You never forgot her. —EDWARD GRINNAN

I HAVE SET BEFORE YOU AN OPEN DOOR, AND NO ONE CAN SHUT IT. . . . —Revelation 3:8 (NKJV)

I grew up in Yakima, Washington, with a large extended family. We cousins were as close as brothers and sisters; we lived in the same neighborhood, attended the same church and school, and often vacationed together.

After I married Wayne and moved to Kent, just a few miles south of Seattle, my cousin David, who was closest to me in age, developed leukemia. His doctors sent him to Seattle's Fred Hutchinson Cancer Research Center. Although I didn't often venture into the big city, I was determined to visit David.

Somehow I ended up at Swedish Hospital, which is connected to Fred Hutchinson by a sky bridge. Lost and confused, I wandered down a number of corridors without finding the bridge. Finally, I stopped a doctor and asked if he could give me directions.

"It's simple," he assured me. "All you need to do is walk down this hallway, take the first right and walk through the door marked ABSOLUTELY NO ADMITTANCE." Those directions did more than show me the way to my cousin.

Somehow, that experience has given me the courage to walk through other doors: my dyslexia that I feared would keep me from working; my terror of speaking in front of people. God has met me at the door marked ABSOLUTELY NO ADMITTANCE and held it open for me.

Father God, thank You for the obstacles You send into my life that have taught me to rely only on You. —DEBBIE MACOMBER

AND [JESUS] SAITH UNTO THEM, IS IT LAWFUL TO DO GOOD ON THE SABBATH DAYS . . . ? —Mark 3:4

I was feeling anything but peaceful as I inched forward for communion. That morning, my husband Gary had left early to go work on someone's septic system. And on a Sunday! His dump truck, with bulldozer in tow, had rumbled down the road just after sunrise. Why did he have to take this job? It wasn't even for one of the contractors he regularly works for, just a friend of a friend of our son Brett.

Back in my pew, I bowed my head to receive the blessing. Then I moved quickly toward the door, watching other couples linger to visit. How I hated going to church alone.

Hours later, Gary came home, covered in dirt from head to toe. "How'd it go?" I asked.

"Pretty rough," he said, kicking off his caked-with-mud boots. "I had to dig under the front porch to find the pipe that was causing the problems. But I was able to fix it." He looked at me with those eyes I'd loved for all of my adult life. "You should have seen how happy the woman and little girl were. Their plumbing hadn't been working right for weeks."

It's good and right and proper to be in the house of God on the Sabbath. But sometimes His work takes you to other places. Sometimes it challenges you to rise above your own abilities. And sometimes, just sometimes, doing God's work means rolling up your sleeves and tackling a hard, dirty job . . . even on Sunday.

Lord, You went about doing good. Make us like You—seven days a week! —MARY LOU CARNEY

DO NOT FEAR, FOR I HAVE REDEEMED YOU; I HAVE CALLED YOU BY NAME; YOU ARE MINE! —Isaiah 43:1 (NAS)

Beau is my ninety-pound golden retriever. Every day we greet the new morning together and each night we take long walks. I guess you could say we're best friends.

Tonight as I write these lines, Beau is sprawled on the study floor next to my desk. Outside, a thunderstorm rages, and Beau is fretful and nervous. Bad weather releases the ancient wolf in Beau, and he seeks shelter and security. Twice in the last five minutes he has stood up and placed his wide muzzle on my leg, demanding that I ruffle his ears and pat him on the head. And when I stop, he lifts his paw for me to hold. He can't be touched enough.

I guess I'm a lot like Beau. When I walk through my own storms, God just can't be near enough to me. I, too, want to be touched and feel God's big hand grasp mine. I need reassurance that God is bigger than the storm.

Tonight as I help Beau through his troubled moments, I'm reassured that God's love and care for me dwarfs my own compassion. Though sometimes I don't feel God's hand on my shoulder, He's always there. And He has promised me that there's no storm He and I can't live through together.

Dear God, help me to feel Your presence this day. Amen.
                                              —SCOTT WALKER

*BUT LET NONE OF YOU SUFFER . . . AS A BUSYBODY IN
OTHER PEOPLE'S MATTERS.* —*I Peter 4:15* (NKJV)

My friends are killing me with kindness. Each morning the
deliveryman tosses my beloved newspaper in front of the college building. If I don't run down and pick it up within five
minutes, some student or staff member will bring it inside,
trying to be helpful.

Trouble is, I never know where they'll put it. I've found my
paper all over the campus: in the cafeteria, the library, the
offices, by the mailboxes. Sometimes it disappears altogether.

I've made chapel announcements: "Please leave my newspaper where it is, thank you." I put notices in the school paper:
"Thanks for being so thoughtful, but the best thing you can do
is leave my paper where it is." I've even taped notes to the
paper itself: "Please leave this paper here, so I don't have to
search the building for it."

Being the "victim" of kindness has caused me to examine
my own methods and motives. Am I really helping students
when I provide them with all kinds of services and resources,
or am I teaching them to expect to be waited on, hand and
foot? When my grandson is trying to learn a new craft, I've
learned to keep my hands off and let him struggle with the
project. The look of joy on his face when he figures it out for
himself is ample payment for my patience.

*I thank You, Lord, for giving me just the right amount of help
in life so that I can know the joy of learning on my own.*

—DANIEL SCHANTZ

WE DO NOT KNOW HOW TO PRAY AS WE SHOULD . . .
                            —*Romans 8:26 (NAS)*

For the past several years a few of us from our small congregation have made a point of gathering on Wednesday evenings
for a time of prayer. Two couples are retirees, there are one or
two singles, the pastor, a couple of church deacons, and a
young family with six children. We meet in the church lounge,
where we read some Scripture, sing a couple of hymns and
share prayer requests.

Being young and restless but well taught, the children usually say their short prayers first and then quietly slip downstairs where they amuse themselves without disturbing us
oldsters.

But one evening little Sarah, about two years old, decided
she would stay with the grown-ups. I confess I peeked at her
once or twice. Her blonde curly head was reverently bowed,
her eyes tightly shut, her chubby hands clasped across the front
of her pinafore. When there came a slight pause between sup-
plications, Sarah herself began to pray. Although we couldn't
understand her childish babble, she seemed so sincere that
when she finished, the grandfatherly deacon responded with a
hearty "Amen!"

Content that she had contributed her little bit, Sarah
skipped off to join her siblings.

What was the gist of Sarah's prayer? Only God knows, and
that's all that matters.

*Thank You, Lord, that "He who searches the hearts knows
what the mind of the Spirit is" (Romans 8:27, NAS).*
                            —ALMA BARKMAN

OPEN THOU MINE EYES, THAT I MAY BEHOLD WONDROUS THINGS. . . . —Psalm 119:18

Along with cursive script, geography and mathematics, the fourth-grade students at our local school learn to play chess. The school year concludes with a gala round-robin tournament in which everyone participates.

Andy, our nine-year-old, has been looking forward to the great event. To give him a head start, I've hauled out our battered chess set a couple of times a month. He's mastered the basics, learned to advance and defend his more powerful pieces, even memorized one or two of the simpler openings. Andy clearly enjoys the game but displays none of the single-minded devotion that characterizes great players.

I have to admit that I'm a little disappointed. I've never been good at chess myself, and it would be nice if Andy could do better. At the same time, the last thing Carol and I want is a chess prodigy on our hands. Human intelligence works in many ways, and Andy shows great skill in other areas, like drawing and music.

One night, watching him make what seemed to be more than his quota of wrong moves, I reminded myself that you don't need to master chess to master life. Just then Andy looked up at me and cheerfully exclaimed, "Checkmate!" While I'd been musing over his lack of chess skills, he had outfoxed me, wedging me into a corner with no escape. "Better luck next time, Dad," he added.

Maybe Andy will shine in chess after all. But whether he does or not, he taught me a lesson over the chessboard that night: God has surprises in store for us all.

May I always make room for Your gifts, Lord, no matter how unexpected. —PHILIP ZALESKI

*"BUT WHEN YOU GIVE TO THE NEEDY, DO NOT LET YOUR
LEFT HAND KNOW WHAT YOUR RIGHT HAND IS DOING, SO
THAT YOUR GIVING MAY BE IN SECRET. THEN YOUR FATHER,
WHO SEES WHAT IS DONE IN SECRET, WILL REWARD YOU."*
—*Matthew 6:3-4 (NIV)*

Despite my Irish heritage, St. Patrick's Day was always just a day
to wear green and decorate the wreath on our front door with
shamrocks. But that changed when my beloved Uncle Pat died
suddenly of a heart attack. It was then that I learned about the
life of my uncle's patron saint, who introduced the people of
Ireland to Christianity.

As friends paid tribute to my uncle, they pointed out a par-
allel between the lives of these two men who shared the same
name. Though separated by nearly fifteen centuries in time,
both were examples of caring, Christlike service.

Stories of Uncle Pat's secret acts of kindness—many
bestowed on people who couldn't do anything for him in
return—surfaced for the first time. I noticed, too, that the
small, gentle gestures to which he never gave a second thought
were remembered with great clarity by those whose lives he
touched. The lady who wrapped his meat at the butcher shop
recalled fondly how he always took time to inquire about her
family. The glasses of ice water on hot summer days were
remembered by the mail carrier.

The clerk at the local deli, her gray hair coiled tightly in a
bun, was the first of many who shared the same wistful memory. "He bought me chocolates," she confided. Uncle Pat's trade-
mark chocolates, I discovered, were a gift that elevated many a
hardworking gas station attendant or stock boy to a position of
prominence.

Today, as I don green and celebrate my Irish ancestry, I'm
reminded anew of the legacies of St. Patrick and Uncle Pat.
People are most attracted to Christianity by the love that drives
our deeds.

Help me, Lord, to serve You in secret, loving ways.
—ROBERTA MESSNER

JESUS SAID TO HIM, "JUDAS, WOULD YOU BETRAY THE SON OF MAN WITH A KISS?" —Luke 22:48 (RSV)

The machine for the audio tour at the Metropolitan Museum of Art looked a little like an iPod, but the guide assured me that all I had to do was punch in the right numbers and I could hear about hundreds of works of art in the collection.

I tried it, delighted by the information the machine gave. For instance, who knew that the little man staring out of a huge Tiepolo is the artist Giovanni Battista Tiepolo himself? Or that in a large painting of the chemist Antoine-Laurent Lavoisier, his wife is depicted with a portfolio of drawings because she was an artist too?

Then I came to a medieval sculpture with a familiar scene, Christ's betrayal. It was easy enough to identify the characters: Peter raising his sword; Judas with his back to the viewer; Christ gazing on with compassion. I wondered what the audio tour would have to say about it. I punched in a number.

"This poignant scene," the voice on the tape said, "was part of a choir screen in a cathedral. No one could really see the back of it, but it's worth looking at today." I walked around to the back of the sculpture. "Here you can see Judas's face. Now compare him to Christ. You'll notice something startling: The sculptor has given them both the same features." Was this the artist's joke? Or was he making a statement that could only be read when the sculpture was put on the floor of a modern museum?

I thought of the subject again—Christ's betrayal. But wasn't it Judas' betrayal too? In betraying his Lord, he betrayed himself and all that was Christlike about him.

I returned to my tape, with a lot on my mind.

Forgive me, Lord, when I forget You. —RICK HAMLIN

THOU, O LORD, ART A GOD FULL OF COMPASSION, AND
GRACIOUS. . . . —Psalm 86:15

Some time back two people in our church wrote a long list of
all my husband David's and my real and imagined failings and
put it in all the mailboxes in the church office. Although our
church's ruling elders demanded an apology from the writers,
none was offered.

Church had always been my refuge and now it was torture
to make myself go. And then one Sunday, sitting in church, I
was sure I heard God speaking to me: *I want you to write
those people a letter in the spirit of forgiveness.*

The mere suggestion was incredible to me. *Surely You're
kidding, God!* But the words stuck in my head and refused to
budge.

Two days later I sat down at my computer just to get rid of
the wild notion that God wanted me to write the letter. But
when I raised my hands over the keyboard, they shook so
much I couldn't type. *Okay, God, if You really want me to do
this, I'm going to need Your help.* This time when I raised my
hands, I typed away.

The letter was short, to the point and was written in the
spirit of forgiveness just as God had asked. I dropped it in the
mail and let it go.

The next Sunday my chief critic approached me at the coffee machine. He hinted that I'd written just to ingratiate myself
to him, then turned and left. It was clear that my letter had
missed its mark.

That's when a miracle happened: A perfect peace descended
around me; my fear was gone. Church was beginning to feel
like home again. God hadn't really meant the letter for my crit-
ics; He'd meant it for me. I was free.

Father, help me always to be a messenger of Your grace.
                                                    —PAM KIDD

*THE AIM OF OUR CHARGE IS LOVE THAT ISSUES FROM A
PURE HEART AND A GOOD CONSCIENCE AND SINCERE FAITH.*
                                              —*I Timothy 1:5 (RSV)*

I received an e-mail from a friend with this odd subject line:
Mark—is this true? Before I opened the message, I knew its
contents: "Children's television host Fred Rogers served as a
sniper during the Vietnam War. He always wore long-sleeved
sweaters to conceal the tattoos."

Because I co-edited a book on Mister Rogers, I'm often
asked questions about him. This one was easy: Not true. No, no,
no. (I'm trying to imagine Fred Rogers, in his cardigan, with a
gun. Boggles the mind.)

When I tell people I met Fred Rogers, I always get the same
question: "What was he *really* like?"

He was just as he appeared. Seriously. I guess it's amazing
that someone could live a life without pretense; it's more amazing that we can't believe it—that we feel the need to make
up stories about the saints in our midst. What does that say
about us?

Fred Rogers would have been seventy-eight today. It's a
good day to remember his very simple, very difficult advice:
"You are special just the way you are. There's no one else like
you."

No one like you either, Mister Rogers. Happy birthday, Fred.

*Lord, when I'm tempted to be cynical, help me to see and love
the good in the people around me.* —MARK COLLINS

"IF YOU ARE WISE, YOUR WISDOM WILL REWARD YOU. . . ."
                                        —Proverbs 9:12 (NIV)

Before my daughter Lindsay and her new baby were discharged
from the hospital, her doctor came to check her out. Her husband was taking a load of flowers down to the car, so she and
I listened together as he reviewed some precautions for
Lindsay's first week at home. Then he sat on the edge of her
bed and gave her one last piece of advice.

"Let your husband take care of the baby—and let him do it
his way," he said. "If you always tell him how to change her or
dress her or burp her, he'll simply stop helping. Babies adjust.
And in most cases, the difference doesn't really matter."

Lindsay nodded, probably not yet understanding the wisdom of his words. I nodded knowingly. After all, my husband
Lynn and I have been married for thirty-seven years.

A few days later I was back home, watching Lynn cut a cantaloupe in half—the wrong way. Everyone knows you cut a
cantaloupe the short way, through the fat middle, like a lemon;
not the long way, end to end, like a watermelon. I told him so.

He paused, looking at the cantaloupe. "Why does it matter?"

That's when I remembered the doctor's advice. The circumstances change, but the challenge to accept each other's differences remains the same through all the seasons of marriage.

*Lord, help me to see what doesn't matter, which will help me
know what matters most.* —CAROL KUYKENDALL

BUT GRACE WAS GIVEN TO EACH OF US ACCORDING TO THE MEASURE OF CHRIST'S GIFT. —*Ephesians 4:7 (RSV)*

Around my office, I'm known as the "process guy"—a person who pays a lot of attention to the way meetings are run and who participates. I've read scores of books and gone to a plethora of workshops on how to lead good meetings. But the best advice I ever got didn't come from some high-priced expert. It was from a plainspoken graduate of a six-grade country school in South Dakota.

Alma was on a national, church-wide committee I was staffing. Eager to impress some of her colleagues, I pulled out my best techniques that day: a carefully constructed agenda, attention to rules of order, a focus on outcomes and accountability. We efficiently tackled the list of problems to solve and made lots of important decisions. I was feeling quite satisfied. And then Alma was at my arm. "I think you forgot something," she said.

I quickly scanned the agenda. Everything was checked off. "What?" I asked.

"I think you forgot that all of us might have something important to contribute," Alma said quietly. "You only seemed interested in some."

I learn new techniques for decision-making every year from some of the best-known writers and leaders in the business. But the nonnegotiable foundation of every meeting I coordinate remains grounded in that piece of advice I got from Alma: Everyone holds a piece of God's wisdom. Everyone has something important to say.

Give me ears to hear Your leading, God, in the voices of those whom You created. —JEFF JAPINGA

BELOVED, LET US LOVE ONE ANOTHER: FOR LOVE IS OF GOD. . . . —I John 4:7

Conversations with my six-year-old granddaughter Olivia resemble the old game of Twenty Questions. This one took place while we waited for my hamburger and her chicken strips at a local café.

Olivia: "Who are your children?"

Me: "Your mom Rebecca and your uncles Patrick and Michael. You know that."

Olivia: "Are Emilee and Aaron your children?"

Me: "No."

Olivia: "Is Katie your child?"

Me: "No. Katie is your mom's birth mother, and Emilee and Aaron are her children. You know that too."

Olivia: "Well, my mom is adopted, you know!"

Me: "Yes, I know."

Olivia: "How did you decide who got her?"

Me (thinking quickly): "I got her because I was older."

Olivia: "Who loved my mom more, you or Katie?"

Me: "We both loved her the same."

Our food arrived. Olivia stopped talking to dip her fries in ketchup. I spent the momentary silence thinking about love. Despite what I'd told Olivia, surely I loved Rebecca more than Katie did! After all, Katie wasn't part of her life for twenty-three years.

But love is a two-way street. In order for Rebecca to be a beloved part of our family, Katie had made the heart-wrenching decision to place her for adoption. I'd told Olivia the truth after all: Katie and I loved Rebecca the same, and that love had given us the added joy of knowing and loving each other. Love multiplied, because none of us can ever outlove our generous, giving, amazing God.

Loving Lord, thank You that we're all beloved parts of Your precious family! —PENNEY SCHWAB

Look, I am alive forever and ever! And I hold the keys of death and the grave. —*Revelation 1:18* (NLT)

I've been losing track of my keys recently.

Last winter, one set must have fallen from my coat pocket. I retraced my steps, but I never found it. Thank goodness it was a nondescript set, not those I kept on the heart-shaped ring my sister gave me twenty-five years ago. The heart-ring reminds me of her love and of the love of Jesus. He never said He *is* the key, but the book of Revelation twice says He holds one or more keys—which He surely minds better than I do mine.

Early this spring, I locked my favorite set in the car while dropping off newspapers at the recycling center. I had tucked the keys in the corner of the trunk for safekeeping. The instant the trunk slammed, I remembered where I'd stashed them. I groaned and walked home for a reserve set. Then, just last week, I left my heart-ring on top of a washing machine in the laundry room in the next building. I hadn't locked my apartment, so I didn't miss them until a neighborhood grandmother knocked on my door and dangled them before my eyes.

Hearing about these close calls, my friend Patricia offered to weave me a lanyard. That was a joke, but she did give me a wrist-coil. Now my heart-shaped ring is connected to this bracelet. My keys will be hard to lose, my heart-ring close at hand, like the love of which it reminds me.

Ever-living Jesus, each time I pick up my keys, remind me of Your everlasting love. —EVELYN BENCE

LET US THROW OFF EVERYTHING THAT HINDERS AND THE
SIN THAT SO EASILY ENTANGLES, AND LET US RUN WITH
PERSEVERANCE THE RACE MARKED OUT FOR US.
                                    —Hebrews 12:1 (NIV)

"Spit out that gum!" my coach yelled at me as I rounded the
third turn of the 400-meter dash at the high school sectional
track meet. She met me at the finish line to make sure her
words had gotten through.

"Not bad—sixty-three seconds—but what are you doing
with gum?" she cried. "Don't you realize that every effort you're
putting into anything besides moving toward the finish line is
taking away energy for the race?"

I argued right back. "I need the gum," I said. "It's nice to
have a distraction out there!" She walked away, shaking her
head.

For the state meet the next weekend I begrudgingly heeded
her advice, partly out of fear and partly because I'd do anything to shave even a tenth of a second from my time. This
race, I checked the clock after I'd crossed the finish line: sixty
seconds! I couldn't believe that I'd cut off three seconds, just
by eliminating one little thing. I wondered what else I was
doing in my life that detracted from my overall effort. Was I losing focus elsewhere?

Since then, I've been on the lookout for all the other things
that might be slowing me down and keeping me from my
goals. I always hesitate to give them up, thinking that, like my
chewing gum, they'll help me get through the tough times. But
every time, there's a better way.

God, help me conserve my energy and focus on You.
                                    —ASHLEY JOHNSON

TRUST IN HIM AT ALL TIMES; YE PEOPLE, POUR OUT YOUR
HEART BEFORE HIM. . . . *—Psalm 62:8*

When my husband Norman and I walked into the house after
a full Sunday of church and friends, we found a message to call
a doctor at the University of North Carolina Hospital. My heart
sank. Our son John was completing his graduate studies at the
university.

Norman picked up the phone to return the call, and I stood
next to him so I could hear what the doctor was saying. "Your
son came in today in great pain. He has an inflamed gallbladder
with possible pancreatic complications. We hope to reduce the
infection first and operate on him later."

"Well, doctor," I whispered, "John is in your hands, and he is
in God's hands. Do what you think is best." We began to pray:
for the doctor, for our only son and for strength from God to
help us through.

At 11:15 that night, the doctor called back to tell us John
hadn't responded to the medication. "Surgery will be very dangerous," he said, "but it might be more dangerous not to operate."

"Doctor," I repeated, "he's in your hands and God's hands.
We'll be with you in prayer."

The doctor had said he would call us after the operation.
Four hours passed without a call, then five, then six. We prayed
all night long, waiting for the phone to ring. At about 3:30 in
the morning, I had a strong conviction that John was going to
be all right. When I told Norman, he said, "Ruth, I had the same
feeling a few moments ago."

By six o'clock in the morning, the doctor finally called.
"John came through the operation successfully," he said. "I think
he's going to be all right."

It had been a long time since I had experienced such an
overwhelming sense of the greatness and love of God as I did
that morning.

*Lord, even in the midst of adversity, Your grace strengthens
my faith.* —RUTH STAFFORD PEALE

BE YE THANKFUL. —*Colossians 3:15*

"Hey, Brock, I'm just calling to thank you. You don't know how much I appreciate your help."

It was my Uncle Davey calling again. You'd think I'd paid off his mortgage or bought him a new car the way he's always calling to express his gratitude. The thing is, I haven't really done anything for him. It's usually the other way around.

By all accounts Uncle Davey is a very successful man. He's a brilliant engineer who built a fantastic company from the ground up. Through hard work, wise decisions and a solid reputation for honesty, he's made it a success. I've always had a lot of admiration for my uncle's many abilities, but especially for his simple way of saying thanks.

Back in my college days, when money was scarce, I worked for his company one spring break. On the construction site he treated everyone the same, from the foreman to the cleanup crew. He had a smile for all and always a "thanks for the good work you've done." At payday he handed me my check and said the same words—just when I should have been thanking him!

I do a little work for him now, and I confess I can never catch up. He's always one step ahead, thanking me. So what do I do? I thank the cleaning lady and my assistant and the CEO of our company and my clients. And I thank God for the example of Uncle Davey. I have a lot to be grateful for.

Father, what can I say but thanks. —BROCK KIDD

I HAVE COME INTO THE WORLD AS A LIGHT, SO NO ONE WHO BELIEVES IN ME SHOULD STAY IN DARKNESS.
—*John 12:46 (NIV)*

There are difficult decisions that I've had to make in my life, but one of the hardest was the decision to come back to Mississippi. When I left as a young man, I vowed never to return. But I felt that God was calling my wife Rosie and me back to Mendenhall. We had to put our own wishes aside and answer that call. Even after twenty-five-plus years of working in this impoverished rural community, it's a decision I have to renew often.

Recently, someone asked me, "Dolphus, do you ever feel like leaving Mississippi?"

"Yes," I replied, "I think about leaving from time to time."

"How often do you think about leaving? Once or twice a year?"

"No, I feel like throwing up my hands and quitting about once a week."

"Then why do you stay?"

"Because my heart tells me that God wants me to stay," I answered. "Whenever part of me feels like giving up, in my spirit I know that being faithful to Him is far more important than my personal desire to escape problems and frustrations."

Lord, even when I'm sure I've had enough, give me the strength to keep on going and to keep on trusting You.
—DOLPHUS WEARY

THE SOVEREIGN LORD IS MY STRENGTH; HE MAKES MY
FEET LIKE THE FEET OF A DEER, HE ENABLES ME TO GO ON
THE HEIGHTS. . . . —Habakkuk 3:19 (NIV)

I learned to rock dance when I was a boy, following my
younger brother Greg as we went fishing on the banks of the
Kawishiwi River in northern Minnesota. The banks are lined
with moss-covered rocks ranging in size from footballs to dinner tables. Rock dancing is the art of stepping quickly from
rock to rock without slipping and getting your feet—or anything else—wet. Some of the rocks looked solid but would shift
under my weight; the dampness of some of the others gave
their moss a banana peel-like quality. It took balance and
rhythm to reach the places from which the best fish could
be caught.

   Balance and rhythm have been on my mind a lot this year.
With our boys grown and gone and not yet producing grandchildren, I have many more options and choices in life. Yet, like
those old river rocks, some of the choices I'm facing seem safe
and solid but are really quite slippery. An invitation to invest
in a new company that seems promising can take days, weeks
and months of effort to produce results. A new friendship
might open my mind to new horizons, yet weigh me down
with the demands of a new relationship. And once I've made a
decision, I need balance to keep my footing and rhythm to
know when to move and when to stay.

   After thirty-some years, my balance on the rocks isn't quite
as good as it used to be, so I slow the rhythm down a bit. It
takes longer, but I still get to the good fishing.

Lord, give me Your strength to keep my balance and Your
wisdom to sense the right rhythm for this season of my life.
                                             —ERIC FELLMAN

YOUR LOVE HAS GIVEN ME GREAT JOY AND ENCOURAGEMENT. . . .
                                              —*Philemon* 7 (*NIV*)

My son walked slowly from the swing with his head down. As
he got closer, I couldn't help but notice his wrinkled brow and
curled bottom lip.

"What's the matter, Solomon?" I asked. "What happened?"

"They won't let me swing," he whispered, pointing to his
older cousins.

"Oh, it's okay. You can sit here with me." I scooted over on
the lawn chair and made room for him.

"No!" he said firmly. His eyes filled with tears. "My feelings
hurt."

"I'm sorry, honey." I said. "Sit with me. We'll have fun."

"No!" He stomped his boots in the leaves. "Kiss my feelings.
Make it better."

I must have looked confused because he pointed to his
elbow.

"Here, Mommy!" He thrust his elbow forward. "Kiss here."

Leaning over, I gave him a hug and kissed his elbow through
his corduroy jacket.

"Better?" I asked.

His eyes brightened and he was off, running toward the
swing set. "Thank you, Mommy!"

Now that I think of it, aside from the elbow part, it makes
perfect sense: If a kiss can make a scraped knee feel better,
how much more can it do for hurt feelings?

*Lord, when people around me are hurting, let me never forget
the healing power of love.* —SABRA CIANCANELLI

AND HE SAID UNTO THEM, TAKE HEED, AND BEWARE OF
COVETOUSNESS: FOR A MAN'S LIFE CONSISTETH NOT IN THE
ABUNDANCE OF THE THINGS WHICH HE POSSESSETH.
                                                    —Luke 12:15

I am a collector: books, pictures, clothing, programs, records
and every copy of the weekly *Blood-Horse* magazine since
1965. Recently these magazines have caused a problem. I've
stashed copies of them in closets and in the kitchen cabinets
that reach up to the high ceiling. One day I noticed that the
cabinets were pulling away from the ceiling. A crash involving
foodstuff, glassware and pottery was imminent. Quickly and
back-breakingly, I got down all the copies. It took four men and
four hundred dollars to reattach the cabinets.

My friend Daniel found me sitting amid stacks of magazines,
wondering where I could put them. "Shouldn't this be a lesson
to you? Throw them away," he said.

"No. They're valuable for research," I said. "For an article.
Someday." To be truthful, I had no idea what that article would
be. "Anyway, I can't."

I think he realized their desperate, sentimental hold on me.
"Come on, Van. Take your religion seriously. Jesus Christ wasn't
burdened with belongings, was He? What about St. Francis? He
gave everything away."

And that's when I began to think.

And that's how I began to shed things. I took old suits and
books I'll never wear or read again to a charity. Old programs,
letters, bills, you-name-it are being recycled.

I'm just beginning to let go but, honestly, do you know of
anybody who would like forty years' worth of *Blood-Horse*?

Father, I am trying. I need Your help regularly. —VAN VARNER

THIS ONE THING I DO. . . . —*Philippians 3:13*

It was my usual end-of-day confession of failure. Letters I hadn't written, phone calls I'd intended to make, opportunities for kindness I hadn't seized upon. God must be as tired of hearing these bedtime laments, I thought, as I was of making them.

That's when some drawings I'd seen that morning popped into my mind: a two-page spread in a volume of cartoons in the dentist's waiting room. There were no captions, just thirty black-and-white drawings tracing a day in the life of a cymbal player. The musician wakes up, shaves, dresses, eats breakfast, studies his score. Finally he puts his cymbals in their case, travels to the concert hall and takes his place in the percussion section of the orchestra.

He waits quietly through most of the program. As his time to perform approaches, he seizes the cymbals and stands up, breathlessly watching the conductor's baton. The big moment comes! He clashes the cymbals together, one ringing, reverberating, perfectly timed note.

His allotted role accomplished, he leaves the stage, puts on hat and coat, travels home, enjoys dinner, yawns, puts on his pajamas, brushes his teeth, and goes to bed supremely content.

The cymbal player has done the one thing required of him. And was I, I wondered, remembering that picture-story, so capable and important—so central to God's plan—that He asked more of me? Maybe in the multiplicity of each day's events there was a single assignment for me. Maybe if I watched the Conductor more closely I would discover what it was.

Faithful Lord, what one thing have You for me to do this day?
                                                            —ELIZABETH SHERRILL

*AND AFTER THE EARTHQUAKE A FIRE; BUT THE LORD WAS
NOT IN THE FIRE: AND AFTER THE FIRE A STILL SMALL
VOICE.* —I Kings 19:12

My husband Keith and I finally bit the bullet. We bought a cell
phone. We took it with us for our weeklong stay at a monastery
in the Pacific Northwest, and I switched it on and forgot about
it. The isolated serenity among the pine forests was the very
opposite of the noise and bustle we'd left behind in Los
Angeles, where every third person in any setting anywhere—
and every fifth person driving on the freeways—is chattering
into a phone, ever "connected." I've always believed that one of
the reasons for monastic silence is that God is quieter than we
are, and if we stay silent and peaceful, we can hear that divine
whisper.

On the third day of our visit, I took out the phone to see
if it needed recharging. But we hadn't been connected all
along—there was no antenna coverage over the area. I shut off
the phone and went to tell Keith. We looked at each other with
abrupt understanding and left the guesthouse to walk down
the dirt road into the coolness of the pines. Every so often,
with perhaps more than polite glee, we called out, "Can you
hear me now?" We were confident that the connection we
wanted to make was there, and Someone could hear us very
well indeed.

*Thank You, Lord, for always being at the other end of the
line.* —RHODA BLECKER

PRAY WITHOUT CEASING. —*I Thessalonians 5:17*

"Mom, there's something wrong with this book!" My son John sounded irritated, in the way that tells me something bothers him at a very deep level. I glanced up from what I was doing and asked what the problem was. "I'm not sure, Mom. Here, you read it!"

John flipped through the storybook and found the offending page. I read it and understood. The story warbled on passionately about how all peace and happiness comes from being one with nature. That didn't ring true with John. I was pleased he could sense it. It was time for a talk.

I spend a lot of time talking with my son. This is partly because John is an auditory learner and retains information best if it's discussed. It's partly because John asks good questions that need elaborate answers. And it's partly because my eight-year-old is plagued by very strong feelings, which he often needs help sifting through.

So we talk. We talk about school things, we talk about ideas. We talk about fears and confusing thoughts. We discuss, question, analyze and probe. We talk and talk and talk. It's through all this talking that I have come to know my son and to sense his needs, interests and concerns.

Which is, I suppose, the reason God wants us to pray without ceasing. If I talked with Him half as much as I talk to others, I'd know His will a whole lot better.

Lord, build in me a great desire to know You best of all.
—JULIA ATTAWAY

THUS SAYS THE LORD: "HEAVEN IS MY THRONE AND THE EARTH IS MY FOOTSTOOL. . . ." —Isaiah 66:1 (RSV)

A couple of years ago when I turned fifty, my friends at work gave me an old globe dating to 1953, the year I was born. It's a floor globe nestled in a nice wooden stand. And it lights up, just like the one at St. Dennis, my Philadelphia grammar school, where the nuns stressed, rather forcefully at times, basics like geography. Prestatehood Hawaii is labeled "The Hawaiian Islands"; Burma sits where Myanmar is today; Rhodesia is there, but Bangladesh is not. And, of course, there's the vast expanse of the Soviet Union, a craggy giant at the top of the Earth.

There's one problem with the globe: It's cracked. I told myself I'd fix it, but I haven't got around to it yet. In fact, I've grown fond of the crack, which cuts through Siberia and Newfoundland.

I suppose it's an obvious metaphor: The world is a broken, imperfect, ever-changing planet. Geologists know, for instance, that Europe is moving away from North America at the rate of about an inch a year. The island of Maui and South America scamper about three inches a year in opposite directions. Measured by single years, these are infinitesimal distances, but over the enormous scope of geologic time—God's time, really—the world is a fast-moving place with whole continents on the run.

Countries disappear and new ones take their place, landmasses shift, governments rise and fall, everything changes. And I think I'm going to fix it with a bit of glue?

I've changed, too, in my fifty-odd years. We all do, just like the imperfect world we live in. We try to do better. We try to do good. And amazingly, we sometimes succeed. But as that crack in my globe reminds me, we have a long way to go.

Father, our world is a broken and often chaotic place. Only You and Your perfect and unchanging love keep it whole.

—EDWARD GRINNAN

OUR FATHER WHO ART IN HEAVEN. . . .   —Matthew 6:9 (RSV)

My father Harry J. Thorell served with the legendary 10th
Mountain Division of the U.S. Army during World War II. In
April 1945 he survived a perilous assault on Mt. Belvedere
in the Italian Alps thanks to fog, which obscured him and some
of the other skiing soldiers who were resupplying ammuni-
tion. Dad escaped death, but some of his buddies did not.

Now, at age eighty-six, Dad was having a harder time
dodging a new enemy—Alzheimer's disease. As the fog of for-
getfulness blurred the present, Dad found himself transported
more and more frequently behind enemy lines. Each time he
wept for his lost comrades.

"I used to pray—how does it go?—'Our Father, Who art in
heaven . . . Our Father . . .'" He looked at me helplessly.

"Hallowed be thy name," I coaxed.

"Our Father, Who art . . ." Tears welled up in his eyes. I
could give him the words, but he'd forget them again. What
could I do to help? Then I spied a pen.

"Here, Dad." I grabbed the pen and printed the words of
the Lord's Prayer on an index card. "The next time you want to
pray, hold this card. The prayer is right here."

Dad looked at the card and then wiped his eyes. "Yeah . . .
okay, I can do that." Then he tucked the prayer in his pocket
and smiled.

Even if we forget our prayers, we won't forget You, God.
                                           —GAIL THORELL SCHILLING

THE TEACHING OF THE WISE IS A FOUNTAIN OF LIFE....
—Proverbs 13:14 (RSV)

The other day, back in Princeton, New Jersey, the town where I lived for more than half my life, I passed the McCarter Theater, a place that provided many hours of theatrical enjoyment for my wife Shirley and me. One of its claims to fame is that Thornton Wilder's Pulitzer Prize-winning *Our Town* was first performed there in 1938.

In the play's third act, we hear from the people buried in the Grover's Corners, New Hampshire, cemetery their reprises of how they spent their time, what in retrospect was important and what was not, their mistakes, their disappointments, their joys and pleasures in ordinary things.

Whenever I visit the "Our Town" in my life, my hometown in Ohio, I always go to the cemetery where many of my loved ones are buried—my dad, grandparents, aunts and uncles. And because it was a small town, I know many of the other people who were laid to rest there. I say *know* rather than *knew*, because they are still alive in my mind: pastors, Boy Scout leaders, teachers, postmen, customers on my newspaper route, the banker who gave me a loan when I had no collateral, the grocery store owner who hired me while I was still in high school, people at the newspaper where I started writing at fifteen. Each of them helped shape me, my faith, my values; each of them made some contribution to my life, and I am greatly indebted to them for their gifts—as I'm sure you are, for the people who selflessly gave you a piece of themselves. Despite what some contend, there are no self-made men or women. Trust me.

> *Thank You, Lord, for the caring souls who*
> *Taught me right from wrong, false from true.*
> —FRED BAUER

"I [WISDOM] WAS HIS CONSTANT DELIGHT, LAUGHING AND PLAYING IN HIS PRESENCE." —*Proverbs 8:30 (TLB)*

Rusty is a purebred papillon, with large ears and long fur at his jowls that gives his face the look of a brown-and-white butterfly. He's the neighbors' dog, and they're away at work most of the day. Rather than whine and whimper at being left alone, Rusty has found someone to visit—us. Each time he crawls through the hole he dug under our fence, he brings fun and frolic into our lives. And that is often.

So much so that we're all agreed he's a time-share dog. If our neighbors aren't home when darkness falls, Rusty "sleeps over" with us. Whether he's running to catch a toy we've tossed or flirting with his own reflection in the swimming pool, he's our much-looked-forward-to entertainment. If I'm stressed or just plain down in the dumps, I follow Rusty's lead and take time to play, or I grab the leash and we go for a walk—tonics that lighten me up. And when I'm feeling lonely, like him, I visit a friend.

How lovely it is when unexpected blessings come into my life to cheer me up and put a smile into my heart. Help me to pass them on, dear Lord. —FAY ANGUS

JESUS . . . FOR THE JOY THAT WAS SET BEFORE HIM ENDURED THE CROSS, DESPISING THE SHAME. . . . —Hebrews 12:2

I helped my wife Tib empty the grocery sacks when she came back from the supermarket this afternoon. Milk, bananas, shredded wheat—one by one I set the standard items on the kitchen counter. In one sack, though, I found special things: jelly beans, a bag of green-plastic Easter grass, an egg-coloring kit—a reminder that our grandchildren would be coming again for Easter.

Oh, but between now and that best of celebrations lay the most wrenching days of the year, that almost unbearable span of time we call Holy Week. Betrayal, arrest, desertion by every friend. Then a mock trial, torture, humiliation, a public and agonizing death. To follow Jesus through these events is to know that He shared the worst any of us can ever experience.

We know, of course, how the story ends. We'll get through the week because we know the victory that follows. I had an aunt who always read the last chapter of a detective story first. "I enjoy the clues and plot twists so much more," she said, "knowing where it's all going." We know that too. We handle the sorrows of this week—Jesus' sorrows and our own—because we've read the final chapter.

What if I were to pull seven strands of this shiny green Easter grass from the bag, and as I go with Jesus through this week, tape a piece of the grass to a reminder of some hopeless time in my own life. What if with the help of these little Easter reminders, I learned to look at every seeming negative from the viewpoint of the story's end?

Risen Lord, help me to see Your empty tomb beyond the crosses in my life. —JOHN SHERRILL

*AND THE MULTITUDES THAT WENT BEFORE, AND THAT
FOLLOWED, CRIED, SAYING, HOSANNA TO THE SON OF
DAVID. . . . —Matthew 21:9*

His name was Henry Pitney Van Dusen, the author of twenty-five books and president of New York's Union Theological Seminary during the years my father taught there.

I visited the famous theologian a few months after he retired from Union—we'd kept in touch after my father died. When lunchtime rolled around, Dr. Van Dusen suggested we go to the seminary's refectory, where I'd often eaten with Dad. Together we walked from his apartment to the familiar cafeteria.

"May I see your identification?" asked a young lady standing by the tray rack. Dr. Van Dusen got out his wallet and produced his driver's license. "No, I mean your cafeteria card," she said. She looked at the license. "Are you with the school, Mr. . . . Mr. . . . Does-en?"

"Well, no longer, I'm afraid."

"I'm sorry, you can't just drop in off the street, you know."

On Dr. Van Dusen's face I saw a mixture of emotions: sorrow, I thought; nostalgia; wistfulness. But no trace of the reactions I might have expected. No injured pride. No "Do you know who I am, young lady?" In place of these, acceptance and humility.

As we walked to a delicatessen two blocks away, I thought Dr. Van Dusen had proclaimed as much theology in that moment as in all his books. Jesus chose to ride a donkey when He came into Jerusalem on the crest of His popularity. He was fulfilling Scripture, but He was also making a statement about the fleeting nature of success.

I carried the first strand of Easter grass to a photo that hangs in my office: Dad and other professors stand behind Dr. Van Dusen, who officiates at a graduation. I taped that strip of grass to the photo frame to remind me to ride the donkey of humility anytime acclaim comes my way.

*Risen Lord, the only acclaim that lasts would be to hear Your
voice say one day, "Well done, thou good and faithful servant"
(Matthew 25:21).* —JOHN SHERRILL

MY SOUL IS EXCEEDING SORROWFUL, EVEN UNTO DEATH. . . .
—*Matthew 26:38*

On the wall of my office, facing the photo of Dr. Van Dusen, is a watercolor of a village in the high, dry Altiplano of Bolivia. In the foreground, a group of Aymara Indians guide their llamas toward town. The focus of the painting is a church with white-washed walls and a massive bell tower looming above mud-and-wattle huts.

The watercolor takes me back to the year Tib and I spent as teachers in Bolivia, and especially to a car trip we made during Holy Week to explore the high desert country.

Though we were fourteen thousand feet above sea level, the peaks of the Andes rose high above us. Villages crouched in their immense shadows, always with a church like the one in the watercolor. The church interiors were simple, bare and beautiful—except for the Crucifix. Here was a writhing, agonized Jesus: blood streaming from real nails in hands and feet and from a savage circle of three-inch thorns.

Back in La Paz, I asked a longtime missionary about this emphasis on painful death. "Where's the victory of the Cross?" I asked.

"The Indians identify with pain," Ed Barber explained. "They're perpetually poor, often cold and sick. Not so long ago, the only life they knew was toil in the silver mines three hundred and sixty-five days a year."

Missionaries, Ed went on, were attempting to make the risen Christ real to the Aymara. "But they have a lot to teach us too: The joy of Easter has no meaning for any of us apart from suffering. Better than most of us, Indians have incorporated pain into their understanding of God."

So today I tape a strand of Easter grass to the frame of the watercolor, reminding me that when suffering strikes family, church, neighborhood, country, I can thank God that He has woven this into the very fabric of His story.

Risen Lord, help me to stay with You through the painful days of this week. —JOHN SHERRILL

AND JESUS . . . TOUCHED HIS EAR, AND HEALED HIM.
                                                    —Luke 22:51

My alma mater's newsletter came in the mail today, with a black-bordered photo of one of my professors on the cover— and with it a familiar sense of guilt. Dr. K was a brilliant and sarcastic man whose scorn was directed at anyone who believed in miracles.

At the time, I didn't believe in miracles either. Then, a decade after graduation, I experienced one. Two years after an operation for malignant melanoma, a new, larger lump appeared on my neck. My doctor at New York City's Sloan-Kettering Cancer Center scheduled immediate surgery. The day before the operation, our pastor laid hands on me and prayed for healing. Next day the operation revealed, where the lump had been, only a tiny, shriveled cinder.

Later I wrote about this experience and the transforming effect it had on my life. I sent a copy to Dr. K. It was a foolish gesture; I might have anticipated the dismissive letter I received from him.

In the fateful days before His Crucifixion, Jesus was challenged by the Sadducees, men, I imagine, much like Dr. K. Certainly they did not believe in anything as preposterous as resurrection from the dead. Matthew tells us that Jesus "put the Sadducees to silence" (Matthew 22:34). Not me! I didn't respond to Dr. K's letter. If I'd been more forceful in presenting my case, might this man, one day, have let his fine intellect be invaded by wonder?

The guilt was still there as I read his obituary. But holding the newsletter, I seemed to hear: *Salvation belongs to Me, not you.* How do I know by what route God may have worked to reach this gifted child of His?

With that in mind, I taped a strand of Easter grass to the newsletter to remind me of other friends who, like the Sadducees, have little room for the joy and mystery of the kingdom.

Risen Lord, give me the grace to be a faithful witness to Your love and then to trust that love for the outcome.
                                                    —JOHN SHERRILL

AND THERE AROSE A GREAT STORM OF WIND, AND THE
WAVES BEAT INTO THE SHIP. . . . —Mark 4:37

My strand of Easter grass today went on a ship model on a shelf in the TV room, reminding me of the trip we took last winter with Tib's brother. Donn is a former naval officer who lives on St. Croix, so he can sail year round.

We'd had many fine Caribbean cruises aboard the *Vive Violette*, but last year, as we headed toward Virgin Gorda, a storm blew up that tossed the yacht around and whipped diesel fumes back aboard. The combination of pitching, yawing and noxious air had everyone but Donn running to the railings.

I was hanging on to one of the supports on deck, thinking fondly of solid ground, when Donn looked down from the bridge and saw me. "Keep your eyes on the horizon!" he shouted over the wind.

To my amazement, it worked. I quieted my stomach and mastered the nausea by focusing on that distant steady point instead of the heaving seas close at hand.

The disciples, too, knew storms at sea, those sudden, boat-swamping winds that roil the Sea of Galilee. Now, as Jesus approached His final hours, a different kind of storm threatened. The disciples, He knew, would be buffeted and nearly overwhelmed by His betrayal and death. He helped them prepare for the coming storm by focusing their attention on the long-range picture, not on the terrors close by. "I go," He promised, "to prepare a place for you" (John 14:2).

When storms strike we, too, can keep our equilibrium by looking ahead to the final chapter in the unfolding story of Easter.

Lord, help me see beyond the present sorrow to the joy of the Resurrection. —JOHN SHERRILL

I, IF I BE LIFTED UP . . . WILL DRAW ALL MEN UNTO ME.
—*John 12:32*

I remember a snowy evening in an Austrian village, walking with Tib to the home of friends. The Schneiders had invited us to attend a house-church meeting in what was literally an upper room, their living quarters above their grocery store. It promised to be an interesting time, with a visiting American rabbi, who had accepted Jesus as the Messiah, explaining the Jewish roots of our Holy Communion.

We shook off snow and stepped into a room with antlers on the wall, embroidered runners on the tables and shelf after shelf of carved wooden animals. I knew one of the guests, a German whose family had perished in the firebombing of Dresden during World War II. Another man wore the collar of a Catholic priest. There was an African American woman—a staff sergeant from an Army base across the border in Germany. There were a number of Austrians in their thirties and forties who, our host whispered, were meeting a Jew for the first time in their lives.

Yet here we were, gathered together to celebrate the Lord's Supper: friends and former enemies, people of different nationalities, ages, races and denominations, breaking bread and drinking wine together in the celebration common to every branch of Christendom. This was a wonder not of man's organization but God's faithfulness.

When we left Austria a few weeks later, Herr Schneider had a gift for us, a four-inch-high bear carved in oak. That's where a strand of Easter grass went this morning. Jesus knew there would be sad divisions among His followers. The night before He died He gave them a commandment: "Love one another" (John 15:12). And because He knew we cannot love without His help, He gave us a sacrament stronger than all separation.

Risen Lord, teach us to love. —JOHN SHERRILL

Your Father knoweth what things ye have need of, before ye ask him. —*Matthew 6:8*

For years my dear Tib has lived with pain from herniated disks in her neck. Without success, she'd tried everything to relieve the discomfort. Then one evening we learned from Lucy Close, a friend who'd also lived with spinal pain, about an operation that "gave me back my life." The next day Tib made an appointment with Lucy's surgeon and, buoyed with hope, we drove into New York City to see him. "I'm sorry to tell you this," the surgeon said after examining her, "you wouldn't be helped by an operation."

On the way home, Tib talked for the first time in her seventy-seven years about slowing down and canceling an upcoming trip to France.

Waiting for us in the mailbox at home was a letter from a man we'd never met. Ron Glosser, a member of Guideposts' board of directors, knew us only as contributors to the magazine. The letter was about a visit Ron had some years ago with Guideposts' founder, Norman Vincent Peale.

"Norman's doctor wanted him to slow down," Ron wrote. "'I want to do that.' But Norman didn't. 'Every time you think of me,' Norman said, 'I want you to see me alert and productive because I believe I can be fully alive for many more years.'

"Norman lived productively till he was ninety-four," Ron concluded. "Now, my prayer for Norman will be my prayer for you."

I looked at the postmark. The letter had been mailed from California eight days *before* Tib and I visited the surgeon in New York City.

I taped Ron's letter to the frame of my computer, decked with a strand of Easter grass, where I can see it as I explore other ways for Tib to get relief from pain—and as we prepare for that trip to France.

When we're in a dark place, when all we see is failure and defeat, at that very moment our Easter is already on the way.

Risen Lord, today we call that dark Friday good. Give me the faith to look beyond my own defeats to the victory You are preparing. —John Sherrill

*ON THE SABBATH THEY RESTED ACCORDING TO THE
COMMANDMENT.* —*Luke 23:56* (RSV)

It's Saturday, one week since I first began attaching little promise-strands of Easter grass to a letter, a wooden bear, pictures.

Yesterday, at our church, there was a Good Friday service to attend. But today, Holy Saturday, Jesus is in the grave and by tradition there is no Eucharist. In my life, too, as in the lives of everyone I know, there are depressing times when Jesus seems to vanish. When this happens, I feel guilty. Where is my faith?

I walk around the house holding one last strand of Easter grass, looking for anything at all that I can deck with hopefulness. And there it is—a book.

Not the Bible, although Scripture is quoted extensively in it. This is the Book of Common Prayer, the little red volume used daily in the Episcopal Church for the cycle of worship, Scripture reading and prayer.

Routine? Of course. And that's the point. I thumb through the so-familiar pages: Morning Prayer, Evening Prayer, the Eucharist, Daily Devotions for Individuals and Families. At times when God seems far away, how great it is to do as Jesus did, follow a routine. Luke tells us that Jesus went into the synagogue "as his custom was" (Luke 4:16). His followers too—on this black Saturday—when their hopes were dead and buried, when faith was shaken, nevertheless observed the Sabbath. We, too, need customs to follow, routines to fall back on.

I open the Prayer Book and attach this final strand of grass to a petition that comforts me in such times as this. "Almighty God . . . from whom no secrets are hid. . . ." God knows all about my spiritual depression and He is there, too, just as surely as He is there when I'm elated.

Routine? Yes. But a better word is *rhythm*. Heartbeats and breathing we seldom think about either, routine functions of the body, all-important rhythms on which our lives depend.

Risen Lord, let me not despise routines but treasure them as the heartbeats of our spiritual life. —JOHN SHERRILL

SING . . . HIS PRAISE IN THE CONGREGATION. . . .
—*Psalm 149:1*

Easter morning! Hundreds of tulips and hyacinths, and the open trumpets of the Easter lilies spill down the steps from the altar of St. Mark's in Mt. Kisco, New York, proclaiming the gladness of renewal. The choir enters singing, "Christ is risen!"

The choir . . . for forty-five years I've sung with them, but following a recent throat exam I've had to resign. This is my first Easter sitting with Tib in the congregation. My once-fellow choir members process past our pew in their robes. How I would love to be with them, today of all days!

I hastily correct myself. A church choir does not *perform,* our director never tired of reminding us; our singing was an offering "for the glory of God." Still, it was difficult not to think of the music as somehow on display before the congregation.

Here comes the moment when I'm most going to miss being in the choir! Every year on Easter Sunday we lead the congregation in the "Hallelujah Chorus."

Now the organ launches into Handel's glorious music. The congregation stands. And suddenly my eyes fill with tears. Not because I'm not up front in the choir loft; these are tears of surprise and gladness. Suddenly I'm filled with gratitude precisely because I'm *not* up there with the trained voices and leaders. For the first time I'm not following the bass line of a score. I'm experiencing the shared joy of Easter, joining in the voice of the whole people.

Everyone around me in the pews is facing some sadness or stress. "Hallelujah! Hallelujah!" we sing anyway. I glance at Samuel, whose son is in the Army, and Phyllis, facing surgery, and Bailey, so long out of work. "Hallelujah!" we sing. We are people who share a great secret; people who come together today to proclaim that Christ is risen. We are people of the Resurrection, and this Easter I am part of the worldwide chorus.

Christ is risen! Hallelujah! Hallelujah! —JOHN SHERRILL

"I AM WITH YOU ALWAYS. . . ." —*Matthew 28:20* (RSV)

It's Monday, the day after Easter.

Yesterday, when the children and grandchildren left, Tib and I went through the usual post-holiday letdown. We coped with it as we always do—cleaning up. I collected left-behind jelly beans before they could be trod into the rug, picked up a ball of colored foil where someone had missed a wastebasket, found a half-eaten chocolate rabbit under one of the kids' beds. Tib gathered the wicker baskets and carried them up to the attic, then got out the vacuum cleaner and attacked the escaped Easter grass.

How did the shiny green strands get so far from the bedrooms where we had unpacked the baskets? I plucked a couple from the back of the sofa in the living room, found one on my sweater sleeve, even extracted one from the butter dish. But Tib and I didn't give up; we searched and swept until eventually we had picked up the very last one. And then last night, as I started upstairs to bed, a green sliver winked at me from the riser.

It's been the same this morning. I've found three strands already in places where I'd already looked. I was getting exasperated with the stuff until I thought, *Wait! Aren't these the little tokens I used all last week to assure me that—whatever the grief or frustration or disappointment—Easter will come?*

Maybe I should change my attitude about these elusive strips of grass mysteriously popping up at unexpected times and places. Last week I chose the spots to tape these forecasts of the Easter message. Suppose I let the grass choose for me now. Suppose in the future, each time I catch sight of a piece of it, I let it remind me that Easter is not a day. It's a promise.

Risen Lord, keep the glory of Your Resurrection before me all the year through. —JOHN SHERRILL

FOR GOD, WHO COMMANDED THE LIGHT TO SHINE OUT OF
DARKNESS, HATH SHINED IN OUR HEARTS. . . .
                                        —*II Corinthians 4:6*

Our church had just dedicated a new stained glass window in
the sanctuary, high above the altar. In the center is the risen
Jesus on a bright, cobalt blue background, His arms outstretched, a golden crown on His head. His robe shimmers with
vibrant stripes of emerald, crimson and deep purple.

I was particularly anxious to see the window at night
because several other churches in town have stunning windows that are lit after dark. So the first time I drove to church
in the evening, I was disappointed to see nothing at all. The
lights on the outside of the building didn't illuminate the window. But the following week, when lights were installed on the
inside to shine outward, the stained glass revealed its beauty.

I think of the people I know who shine with the same kind
of beauty, most alive with faith: the sisters at a nearby retreat
center who maintain the prayer garden I've come to cherish, or
the man at church who puts in so many hours organizing volunteers and donations for the downtown soup kitchen.
Through their service, the light of Christ shines directly out
from their hearts—you can't miss the glow.

At times I might have on all the outside lights, such as
attending church and going to Bible study, but can anyone see
Christ in me? It's not until I turn on the light of Christ's love
inside my heart, through serving someone else, that the full
beauty of that love can be seen.

Lord, bless the faithful whose first thought is to serve You by
serving others. Daily they inspire me to do the same.
                                        —GINA BRIDGEMAN

PRAY ONE FOR ANOTHER, THAT YE MAY BE HEALED. . . .
—*James 5:16*

Log on.

PASSWORD.

"Dadshealth," I typed. Dad had had a bad cold lately. Maybe the symptoms indicated something more serious. I'd been worried about him. That's why I'd made "Dadshealth" my password—a reminder to pray for him.

YOU HAVE TWELVE DAYS TO CHANGE YOUR PASSWORD. DO YOU WANT TO CHANGE IT NOW? my computer asked me.

"No," I told the computer. Dad wasn't out of the woods yet. He was doing better though. The doctor had run some tests. We'd find out if it was serious.

Twelve days. That must have meant I'd been praying for him for eighteen days, because my password has to be changed every thirty days. Another prayer today, then I punched the ENTER key. Time for work.

Three-thirty in the afternoon. The work had been so involving I hadn't really thought about Dad. E-mails, phone calls, snail mail, memos, manuscripts—they came at a rate that made me think I'd never catch up. One more call. I answered it.

"Hi!" It was Dad. "Just wanted you to know that the tests all came out fine. The doctor says in another week or two I'll be well." *Two weeks. That's almost twelve days.*

"Good, Dad. I'll keep you in my prayers." I'd keep him in my password too.

Some years ago in *Guideposts* there was an article that claimed if you prayed for something for thirty days you'd get results. Thirty days. And you know what? In thirty days I've always found that the urgency that led me to the prayer in the first place has diminished.

An answer in thirty days? Well, yes, there is an answer. Try it. Just for thirty days.

*Starting today and for the next twenty-nine days, Lord, I will pray for*_____. —RICK HAMLIN
(INSERT NAME)

NEVERTHELESS LET EVERY ONE OF YOU IN PARTICULAR SO
LOVE HIS WIFE EVEN AS HIMSELF; AND THE WIFE SEE THAT
SHE REVERENCE HER HUSBAND. —*Ephesians 5:33*

My husband Gene and I had had an early morning spat. "Do
you want to ride with me to get your ferns?" he asked me
stiffly. "I'm going to pick up two truckloads of pine straw."

"Okay."

We drove to the store in silence. "I'll take twenty bails home
and return for another twenty," Gene explained when we
arrived, avoiding my eyes.

I nodded angrily. "Meet you here by the pine straw."

After making my selections, I returned to the two eighteen-
wheelers loaded with pine and wheat straw to wait. The morning sun became unbearably hot, so I moved to the four feet of
shade between the parked trucks. Then I got tired and
squeezed myself underneath one of the tall trucks. It felt just
like air conditioning. Sitting cross-legged under the truck, I
could only see people from their knees down. *No matter, I'll*
recognize Gene.

After almost an hour of waiting, I started to worry. After two
hours, I prepared myself to be a widow again. My cell phone
needed recharging, but I managed to call Jerry, our friend and
pastor. "Where are you, Marion? I'll come there," he said.

"Under an eighteen-wheeler at the garden center!" I
shouted as my phone went dead.

With my world falling apart, I came out from underneath
the truck to meet Jerry. "He's not in either hospital," our pastor
explained grimly.

Suddenly Gene drove up in his white truck and leaped out
like someone from a Western movie. We nearly knocked each
other down embracing.

On the way home, Gene explained that he'd been waiting
by the ferns while everyone else at the garden center—
including the police and the sheriff—searched for me. No one
had thought to look underneath an eighteen-wheeler.

Thank You, Father, for the fear that showed us our love was
still there. —MARION BOND WEST

PRAYING ALWAYS WITH ALL PRAYER AND SUPPLICATION IN THE SPIRIT. . . . —Ephesians 6:18

I hadn't paid much attention to them before, but now I notice them everywhere I travel—flowers placed along the side of the road in memory of loved ones who lost their lives in accidents there. One afternoon as I approached my exit on the interstate, I watched transfixed as a couple knelt on the ground at the roadside and set up three crosses covered with colorful silk flowers.

Dear God, did they lose children? Siblings? Friends? That weekend, I noticed several more memorials on the highway as I traveled to Cincinnati. And so I began a new habit of prayer. Whenever I come across one of those makeshift memorials, I pray for the rest of the day for all who've been touched by the tragedy it commemorates.

I've discovered since then that such opportunities for prayer are everywhere if I look closely, like the Christmas tree in my neighbors' bay window that stayed lit until their son came home from Iraq last February. And if I keep alert for the signs of need that are all around me, I can come closer to following Paul's instruction to pray always.

Father, keep my heart in a continual state of prayer.
—ROBERTA MESSNER

THEN SHALL ALL THE TREES OF THE WOOD REJOICE.
—*Psalm 96:12*

I've always loved trees. As a child, I had a favorite neighborhood tree in which I'd sit to read my book. I can't remember what my college professors looked like, but I can describe the autumnal pinkish-orange of a glowing young maple on campus. As a young mother, I admired an elegant fir holding court in a bare field. My children and I called her the "Queen Tree." Today I can show you where a gnarled old soldier of an apple tree used to grow near our Minnesota home before a country road was widened.

Trees have always been friends, but on one particular day they offered me a special comfort. It was time to leave my home in the Alaskan woods. For ten years, as the children grew to young adulthood, I had waved them off on their adventures from this sturdy sheltering house.

Now my husband had gone ahead to a new job in another state. I was the last one to leave our home. As I locked its doors and paused in the rutted drive for a final look, I thought forlornly, *Who's going to wave good-bye to me?* I felt suddenly overwhelmed by the new path my life was taking.

Just then my eyes were drawn to the tall, supple birch trees encircling me. They were bending and swaying in the wind, dozens of them, waving their leafy boughs in a group farewell. My trees, in God's perfect timing, were the ones to wave good-bye.

Loving God, Maker of all things, make me aware of Your presence through the things You have made. —CAROL KNAPP

BLESSED BE THE GOD AND FATHER OF OUR LORD JESUS CHRIST! BY HIS GREAT MERCY WE HAVE BEEN BORN ANEW TO A LIVING HOPE THROUGH THE RESURRECTION OF JESUS CHRIST FROM THE DEAD. —I Peter 1:3 (RSV)

The Sunday after Easter, I stood in our church basement looking at the lilies that had adorned the sanctuary. Like the blossoms turning brown, the joy of Christ's Resurrection that I'd experienced last Sunday was fading. After the spiritually uplifting services of Holy Week, the past week of the daily grind had left me feeling listless. Pointing to the wilting lilies, I lamented to another parishioner, "What a shame to throw them away."

"We don't throw them out," she responded. "I'm going to plant them around the church grounds where they can bloom again each summer."

"That's a great idea!" I exclaimed. The bulbs would be nourished underground for months, then send up new shoots and flower again.

I began thinking about how I could do the same thing. How could I plant the Resurrection joy of Easter in my heart and keep it flourishing? Maybe I needed more quiet times for prayer and Scripture reading. Or perhaps I could be like St. Seraphim of Sarov, who greeted everyone at all seasons with "Christ is risen!" and called each "my joy."

There was no need to feel listless. Easter wasn't so far away at all. It was ready to bloom at all times. All I needed was the nourishment from God's Word, some regular doses of prayer and the willingness to see people as "my joy."

Oh, Lord, open the eyes of my heart to see Your gifts. Please remind me of the triumph of Your Resurrection in my daily struggles. —MARY BROWN

*THOUGH I WALK IN THE MIDST OF TROUBLE, THOU WILT
REVIVE ME. . . . —Psalm 138:7*

Two years ago, during my freshman year of college, I agreed to
participate in an all-night walkathon to raise money for charity.
One team member had to be walking at all times; the others
could hang out or take a nap at the tents set up near the track.

Our team of eleven women and four men was doing just
fine. But a little after midnight all the women retreated to their
dorms for a good night's sleep. That left just us four guys. By
4:00 A.M. I didn't think we were going to make it. How would
we manage the next three hours? I was exhausted and so were
the other three.

"If we're going to finish, we've got to walk together the
whole time," I said. "If we walk individually, we'll never stay
awake until seven."

The others agreed, and soon we were heading into the
night. We quickly grew bored of the track and headed out on a
tour of the campus and then the entire city, talking the whole
way. As the sun began to rise, we slogged through a swamp in
the woods, making plans to build a cabin there or camp out
someday. At seven o'clock the rest of the team joined us and
we completed the walkathon.

Now, two years later, I am sitting at my desk, looking at a
picture on the wall of four exhausted guys standing arm in arm
just after sunrise. That night we became friends and now we're
roommates. And just as we did that sleepless night, we're still
accomplishing the impossible by walking together.

*Thank You, Lord, for the friends who provide companionship
during the long, dark nights.* —JOSHUA SUNDQUIST

I HAVE PLANTED . . . BUT GOD GAVE THE INCREASE.
—*I Corinthians 3:6*

Every spring, I steal a bouquet of lilacs.

Okay, maybe *steal* is too strong a word. But the lilac bush isn't mine. Still, I load my arms with the fragrant purple blossoms.

The flowers bloom just barely in sight of the highway. I park my car on the shoulder of the road and wade through neglected grasses, past the foundation of a long-gone house and through a small patch of cactus to the purple wonder, bent and splendid, offering itself to me in polite submission. I gather the blossoms in my arms and walk back to my car.

I'd like to think that whoever planted my secret lilac bush would be pleased that I seek out this annual bouquet. Perhaps she watched it grow from her kitchen window. Perhaps, long before the highway was here, her mother planted a small, gangly twig. And with sun and rain and time it became a lilac bush of extraordinary beauty.

Later, as I inhale the heady scent of my bouquet, I'm reminded that good things take time. And that, in ways we can't begin to imagine, the seeds we plant today will produce fruit. And maybe a few lilacs.

Oh, Master Gardener, thank You for the miracle of growth and the role I'm called to play in it. And thank You for lilacs!
—MARY LOU CARNEY

THE LORD IS GOOD, A REFUGE IN TIMES OF TROUBLE. HE
CARES FOR THOSE WHO TRUST IN HIM. —*Nahum 1:7 (NIV)*

It was a sorrowful day for my friend, who was moving out of her home following a divorce. "I'm trying to be cheerful, but I can't do it," she told me. "How can I face this cross?"

That evening I took my son to a youth meeting at our church. As the meeting began, the youth pastor announced, "We're under a severe weather watch. If the tornado siren goes off, we go to the bottom of the storage stairwell."

About twenty minutes later, the siren went off. As we stood up to head down the stairs, someone suggested we bring the pizzas and soft drinks. Once we were downstairs, we squeezed in amid the cardboard boxes of light bulbs and bathroom tissue, opened the pizza boxes, and started talking. After a while we weren't even aware of the siren.

Once the rough weather had safely passed, I realized that although it was the first time we had been in church when the siren went off, we weren't afraid because someone had a plan. A survey of the church building had been done, and the safest places had been identified beforehand. When we needed to know, the plan was communicated to us. All we had to do was grab the pizza and follow the plan.

Finally I had an answer for my divorced friend: It's not cheerfulness we need when we're faced with difficult things, but trust. In my moments of greatest need, I trust that God has a plan that will lead me to a place of safety. And that's why I can take heart on the very worst of days.

Father, on the most difficult of days I put my hand in Yours, trusting that even in this, You know where we're going.

—KAREN BARBER

*IN EVERY THING GIVE THANKS: FOR THIS IS THE WILL OF
GOD IN CHRIST JESUS CONCERNING YOU.*
—*I Thessalonians 5:18*

I thank God for a lot of things, for giving me a long life, for a family that loves me and, not the least, for Spare Ribs. I grew up with two brothers and five dogs, but all of the dogs were aristocrats compared with the mongrel that simply appeared one day and decided to stay.

"What's that awful-looking creature out there?" Mom said to us kids when she saw him. And he was pretty awful. Medium-sized, grizzled, he had a muzzle that was so scarred he looked like a punch-drunk fighter. When he was around for several days more, Mom took over. "We can't feed another dog," she said and, over our protests, arranged for a farmer in the country to take him.

He was back almost before Mom had delivered him. When he returned after a second trip to the farmer, Mom gave up. "I guess we have six dogs," she said with a laugh. And feeding him was no problem. He made the rounds of various butcher shops for scraps. He waited for someone he could join before crossing the busy Bardstown Road. He was always at Belknap School to walk us home. He finished any fights that a dog of ours was in, and the two came back, their tails wagging. He was top dog.

Spare Ribs had an effect on all of us. He was no beauty, but he was tough, loyal, persistent, self-reliant and smart.

Surely You don't wonder why I thank You, Lord, for Spare Ribs. —VAN VARNER

THE FRUIT OF THE SPIRIT IS LOVE, JOY, PEACE. . . .
—*Galatians 5:22*

Mhondoro is a tiny village in the southern African nation of Zimbabwe. On a country lane the dust rises in the last light of day to create a golden halo around a woman who balances a huge yellow bucket on her head. She smiles as she sings a Shona lullaby to the baby bound to her side by a bright woven cloth.

For days, with the help of resources provided by generous donors, I've worked with a group to establish a home here for AIDS orphans. The going's been rough; there's a lot of sadness in a country where one third of the population is dying of AIDS.

Our host is taking us on a walk through the winter wheat fields. Night wraps around us. The stars pop out one by one. Off in the distance, the village cows are making their way home, the sweet sound of their bells floating through the air. There's no electricity in the region, but the stars are enough to light our way back to the little thatched-roofed hut where we'll have dinner.

The night air is cool, and I welcome the warmth of the glowing wood fire inside the hut. As I find a comfortable spot on the hard dirt floor, a man kneels before me with a pitcher, a bowl and a cloth. He pours warm water over my hands, then gently dries them.

From the iron pot bubbling on the fire, I'm served a plate of *sadza*, corn mush with freshly ground peanuts stirred in. I eat with my hands. In the darkness it's impossible to count the people who are gathered with us, but there are many. There's no conversation. There's no need to entertain each other; tranquility prevails.

I came to this country to offer what I could. But God, being a God of grace, decided to give me something back. In a little African hut, God gave me peace. Whenever the world gets me down, I'll remember this night.

Father, anything I dare to give is but a pittance of what You give back to me. —PAM KIDD

*LET US NOT BECOME WEARY IN DOING GOOD, FOR AT THE
PROPER TIME WE WILL REAP A HARVEST IF WE DO NOT
GIVE UP.* —*Galatians 6:9* (NIV)

It never dawned on me when we bought our home in
Poughquag, New York, that living on the slope of what was
once pastureland would be a landscaping challenge, but it certainly was.

After a futile attempt to persuade grass to grow on the
steep incline directly behind our back deck, we created a garden of Russian olive, rug junipers, variegated barberries and
potentillas. Over the years our garden has improved dramatically. Pine bark nuggets have become mulch, earthworms have
gone where no spade at one time could penetrate, and seasons
of working the rocky terrain have made this once inhospitable
hillside quite lovely.

This year my wife and I decided to plant a few dozen perennials in our garden. Kathy laid out a design, and we began digging. The anchor trio of plantings needed to be done first. With
two down and one to go, I—*clink!*—hit what I thought had to
be the backside of the Rock of Gibraltar. I approached it from
a different angle and—*clink!* I tried digging from the other side
of the planned hole and—*clink!* I used a hoe instead of the
shovel and—you guessed it—*clink!* "Kathy, we've got a problem," I said. "This isn't going to work."

Kathy took the hoe from me, and I went to get an iced tea.
When I came back, she handed me a palm-sized flat stone, my
Rock of Gibraltar.

"How'd you do that?" I asked her.

She smiled. "Let me give you a life lesson," she said. "Like
most problems, this one wasn't as large as you'd imagined.
Since your first attempts didn't solve it, I worked around it and
enlarged the diameter of the hole until the edge of the problem
appeared. The rest was easy. Problem solved."

Life lesson, indeed.

Father, thank You for our beautiful garden and for a life lesson in perseverance for an easily frustrated gardener.

—TED NACE

WHO IS LIKE A WISE MAN? AND WHO KNOWS THE INTERPRETATION OF A THING? . . . —Ecclesiastes 8:1 (NKJV)

Before church services, my wife grabs my arm and says, "I've got to see Phyllis. Pick us a seat, anywhere, it doesn't matter where. I'll be along shortly."

"How about in the front row?" I call after her.

"No! I don't want people staring at my back."

"How about the back row?"

"I can't see a thing from the back row with my bad eyes."

"Okay, how about middle right?"

She shakes her head. "Not by all those noisy college students."

"Then how about the middle left?"

"Fine, that's perfect."

I roll my eyes. "Of course it's perfect. That's where we sit every Sunday. Why did you say 'anywhere' when you didn't mean it?"

She smiles. "Oh, I guess it's like when you stop at the auto parts store and you say you'll be in there three minutes, and it's always thirty minutes."

My turn to smile. Our conversation reminds me that there's more to communication than what people say. I have to listen for meanings. When a college student says to me, "I'll have that term paper to you this afternoon," he really means, "I forgot all about that paper. I haven't even started on it, but I'll bear down on it right after lunch." And he'll try, but his girlfriend will distract him, so he won't get it done till Monday, and his printer won't work until Tuesday. People don't always say exactly what they mean. I need to ask questions and, above all, to extend them a generous portion of grace.

Lord, give me the instinct to read between the lines—and patience. —DANIEL SCHANTZ

*AND THE CHILDREN OF ISRAEL DID EAT MANNA FORTY
YEARS. . . . —Exodus 16:35*

I use a lectionary for my daily Bible reading, and it's remarkable
how often these preset passages seem chosen especially for
my situation at that moment.

The Exodus account of manna falling from heaven, though,
fell on what seemed a wretchedly inappropriate time for me.
The Israelites are trudging across a bleak and barren landscape
longing for earlier, happier times—I could identify with that!
Both my husband and I had had surgery recently on joints crip-
pled by arthritis—old people's problems. Our house needed
repairs, too, but hospital bills were more than anticipated. Work
assignments were overdue, and I didn't know where the time
and the energy and the money were going to come from.

What does God do for the Israelites? Rains provisions for
them right out of the sky. Food they don't have to work for,
bread lying on the ground for the taking—exactly what they
need for each day.

Where was the manna for me? I demanded of the Exodus
verses. Where was my supply tumbling out of the heavens?

What was this miraculous manna anyway? Trying to make
twenty-first-century sense out of the passage, I got out my Bible
dictionary to see what the thing was.

But manna, it turned out, is not a thing. It's a question.
Manna means "What is this?" The Israelites had no idea what
those small round white things on the ground were. They certainly didn't recognize them, at first, as the answer to their need.

What unrecognized supply was lying at my feet too? I
wondered. How often I have regarded the new and unknown
with suspicion. A new form of worship, a new technology, a
new boss at work—only to have "What is this?" turn out to be
God's perfect provision.

*Faithful Lord, what unexpected shape will Your supply for me
take today?* —ELIZABETH SHERRILL

FOR YOU HAVE BEEN BORN AGAIN NOT OF SEED WHICH IS PERISHABLE BUT IMPERISHABLE, THAT IS, THROUGH THE LIVING AND ABIDING WORD OF GOD. —I Peter 1:23 (NAS)

By May spring had arrived here on the Canadian prairie. Tulips anxious to bloom had pushed their way up through the damp soil, their green leaves a welcome sight. Migrating songbirds had returned, including the pair of robins that usually set up housekeeping in the Virginia creepers that line our carport.

Leo and I came into the house after planting peas and carrots in our vegetable plot, only to hear the weatherman issuing repeated warnings about a heavy snowfall. At first I dismissed them. *Probably just for the high Arctic. And I know how unreliable those forecasters are, right?*

Wrong! The next morning we woke up to heavy, wet snowflakes pelting down, an unseasonable blanket of white covering the green lawns, burdening tree branches, eventually covering even the tallest tulips. *What about the birds?*

Tossing several cups of birdseed under the protective branches of the cedar shrubs, along with chopped apples and raisins for the robins, I waited. *If only they'll find them. . . .*

The storm grew worse. But then I noticed movement among the cedars and watched as a sparrow fluttered weakly down to the ground. I heard a faint *cheep*, and then another and another. Before long there was a chorus of birdsong reassuring me that they were weathering the storm.

The seed of Your Word has sustained me through many unexpected challenges, Lord. Help me to be as joyful as those sparrows in freely sharing Your faithful guidance with those who flounder in life's storms. —ALMA BARKMAN

PERFECT LOVE CASTETH OUT FEAR. . . . —I John 4:18

In the late eighties, my husband Larry and I enjoyed a close relationship with another couple, and the four of us did many things together. Then, quite unexpectedly, the other couple drew away, becoming distant and remote. It was obvious we had offended them in some way, but we had no idea what we had done. Our attempts to find out were met with the same answer each time: "No, nothing's wrong."

One evening, as Larry and I were rehashing the situation, we realized the tremendous hurt we both were feeling at having been mistreated. Finally, Larry angrily exclaimed, "I'm going to call them right now and find out what their problem is!" I agreed that a confrontation was called for, but I also felt a terrible rush of anxiety. Why was it that confrontations always upset me so?

At that moment, I recalled something I had read in Gerald Jampolsky's book, *Love Is Letting Go of Fear*: If we always approach a confrontation with the intention of helping the other person rather than attacking him, there will never be any fear. Rather, we will be acting from love and compassion. We have to realize that the person we're confronting is actually expressing great pain though it may manifest itself as anger.

When I shared this insight with Larry, he agreed that we should slow down and rethink our position. When he did make the call, I felt a wonderful sense of peace and rightness about it. We found out that our friends had felt hurt and neglected when our growing business placed new demands on our time, and we weren't able to be with them as often. Choosing not to place blame allowed us to see both sides of the issue, and with patience and love, we were able to restore a precious friendship that, many years later, still endures.

Father, help me always to choose peace over conflict.

                           —LIBBIE ADAMS

*AND SEEK THE PEACE OF THE CITY WHITHER I HAVE CAUSED
YOU TO BE CARRIED . . . AND PRAY UNTO THE LORD FOR IT:
FOR IN THE PEACE THEREOF SHALL YE HAVE PEACE.*
—*Jeremiah* 29:7

I guess I saw nearly everything in my eight years in New York
City: my car narrowly escaped being totaled by a van fleeing
the police and going the wrong way through a tunnel; I was
attacked in a subway car by a crazed person and was one of
many held hostage on an elevator by an enraged lady who
refused to let it descend; police chased a man through a playground where my son Julian was playing; my wife was followed
home by a strange man; and one day we walked right into the
middle of a fight between three men, all of whom were wield-
ing baseball bats.

Despite all the pain that causes people to do ugly things
to one another in the city, I believe that in some ways living
there is a very good thing. People all over the city are praying
—they can't help themselves. Ride a New York City subway
and you'll understand. The city is something that happens to
you every day.

I now live in Solana Beach, California. The coastline is pic-
turesque; the weather is consistently mild; the homes are spectacular; the lawns are manicured; the streets are clean; the cars
are new; the people are friendly. And I forget to pray for my
community. It's not because people aren't in pain—people
everywhere are. The needs are there. I simply can't see them
anymore.

*Lord, on this National Day of Prayer, show me the needs that
are hidden all around me.* —DAVE FRANCO

I DO REMEMBER MY FAULTS THIS DAY. . . . —*Genesis 41:9*

I live in a geodesic dome—a round two-story that some of our friends describe as "a big bran muffin on the plains." It's my husband Don's dream house. He drew the plans, helped with construction, built the huge front deck and laid a truckload of brick to make unique rosebush planters for the front yard.

The house is nearly perfect. The upstairs windows provide a panoramic view: miles of growing yellow corn, burnt-orange sorghum and bright green wheat. The wood-burning fireplace is vented to heat the whole house, so we stay warm during power outages. There's plenty of room for our six grandchildren, especially now that Don's completed the basement game room.

The house is *nearly* perfect. It has one big flaw: The roof leaks. During the past twenty-three years, we've completely replaced the roof, done five major patch jobs and regularly caulked the seams. It still leaks.

The forecast calls for rain tomorrow, so we caulked again today. Don climbed a twelve-foot ladder, carrying a five-foot ladder and the caulking gun. I held the big ladder steady when not running to fetch other tools.

"If we had an ordinary house we wouldn't have to keep doing this!" I yelled up to him.

"An ordinary house would be boring!" he yelled back. "It's the flaws that make this house interesting!"

"I'll remember that when I'm putting out the buckets tomorrow!" I responded.

And remember it I did, but not while putting out buckets; we're still waiting for that rain. I thought of it when I was tempted to give up on a friend I really liked—except for her irritating habit of always being late. And when a co-worker forgot to mail a time-sensitive letter. And when my (nearly perfect) husband again announced, "Rain in the forecast. We'd better do a little more work on that roof."

Lord, only You are perfect! Help me be as forgiving of other people's faults, mistakes and quirks as I am of my own.

—PENNEY SCHWAB

"ARE NOT TWO SPARROWS SOLD FOR A PENNY? AND NOT ONE OF THEM WILL FALL TO THE GROUND WITHOUT YOUR FATHER'S WILL." —*Matthew 10:29 (RSV)*

Birds have fascinated me all my life. I've hunted them with my binoculars all over the globe, but my best bird-watching takes place in the backyard around the birdbath and feeder. There are always new birds coming to my table, some for the season, others just passing through, like the flock of warblers that showed up today. They were myrtles or yellow rumps, so named because of the lemony swatch on their backsides.

A couple of them had the misfortune of flying into the kitchen window. When I heard the thud, I hurried outside and found two birds, both females, under the bushes, one out cold, the other stunned and drowsy.

Sometimes I've had luck reviving an injured bird by warming it in my hands, so I tried holding bird number one. I knew she was alive; I could feel her heart racing beneath the black and white feathers that had kept her from freezing during her high-altitude flight from South America. But when she didn't respond after five minutes, I turned to bird number two. She was now conscious and when I raised her on one finger, she left in a hurry without so much as a chirped thank-you.

The first bird would now sit on my hand, but nod and tip over, so I put her in a box to rest. Fifteen minutes later she was improved. Eyeing me suspiciously as if to say, "You're not my mother," she spread her wings and flittered off in the same direction as bird number two.

I'm always pleased to read the Bible passage that says not even a sparrow falls without God's knowledge. It reassures me that He knows of my movements, too, of my goings out and comings in, of my ups and downs, of my gains and pains. In other words, He cares. That's good news for all of us.

When I forget, Lord, to give life its reverential due,
Remind me that all things were created by You.
                                                                        —FRED BAUER

There are diversities of gifts, but the same Spirit.
—I Corinthians 12:4

"Why do you always read the wedding announcements?" I asked my wife Carol, who is studying the wedding section in the Sunday *Times.*

"There might be someone here we know."

"Our friends all got married fifteen or twenty years ago. If it's anybody, it's going to be the children of friends."

"See."

"I just don't know what's so important about the information you find there. Who somebody's parents are, who their grandparents are—why does that matter?"

"It interests me." It always amazes me that after eighteen years of marriage, with all the things we enjoy in common, we still have separate interests. Carol can't understand why I read the op-ed page. I can't imagine reading about weddings.

"Look," she says, delighted. "You know that young guy who lives downstairs? Here's his wedding announcement."

"We knew he was getting married. We met his fiancée. She's very nice. She already told you about her dress and bouquet and what the bridesmaids were going to wear."

"But look what it says about his family. This is an amazing coincidence. I worked for his grandmother the summer I was seventeen. Helped out at her summer home."

"How do you know it's the same woman?"

"It gives her husband's name and where she's from. Everything."

"Small world."

"Just think, we could have known the groom for years and I would never have known that about him. Not without reading the wedding announcements."

"Okay. From now on, tell me if you find something important in the wedding announcements."

"And you tell me what's on the op-ed page." It's a division of labor, as good a reason as any for God to bring two people together. The whole is always greater than the sum of the parts.

Help me grow, Lord, as I learn how little I know.
—Rick Hamlin

GOD'S LAWS ARE PERFECT. THEY PROTECT US, MAKE US
WISE, AND GIVE US JOY AND LIGHT. . . . THEY ARE MORE
DESIRABLE THAN GOLD. . . . —*Psalm 19:7–8, 10 (TLB)*

I am sorely tempted to buy a lottery ticket! The jackpot is
mega-millions of dollars, and I'm arguing with God. Just think
of the blessing. Not only for my family, grandkids and all, but
for the things I could do with the money for those in need
around the world. Try me, Lord. Test me. I could handle a million or two!

> *You've more than millions in blessings, dear child.*
> *Count all the stars on a clear, cold night,*
> *the diamonds of dew in the morning light.*
> *The smiles of friends, and strangers alike*
> *that gladden your days and make them bright.*
> *Gather the words of your answered prayers,*
> *more than millions through the years.*
> *The promises given in my Holy Book,*
> *thumb through the pages and take a good look.*
> *You're wealthy, dear child, way beyond measure,*
> *these are the blessings to share and to treasure!*

Guess I don't need that lottery ticket after all.

Thank You for the riches You have given me, Lord, that no
mega-million-dollar jackpot could ever buy. —FAY ANGUS

FORGETTING WHAT LIES BEHIND AND REACHING FORWARD
TO WHAT LIES AHEAD, I PRESS ON TOWARD THE GOAL FOR
THE PRIZE OF THE UPWARD CALL OF GOD IN CHRIST
JESUS. —*Philippians 3:13-14* (NAS)

Sometimes I think that my golden retriever Beau was born with
a tennis ball wedged in his mouth. His goal in life seems to be
to chase the balls I throw for him.

But there's one problem: Whenever Beau retrieves a ball, he
refuses to return it to me. He races back to me, proud of his
successful recovery, but determined not to surrender his prize.
He's eager for me to throw the ball again, but he doesn't understand that if he doesn't give me the ball, I can't throw it.

Sometimes I'm a lot like Beau in my relationship with God.
I want Him to zing that next challenge out in front of me, but
I don't want to let go of the security of my last accomplishment. I want to hold on to the past and race toward the future
at the same time. But to remain vital and alive, I need the exhil-
aration of another race, another challenge, another opportunity to do what I do best. And that means I must release the
victories of yesterday and trust God to throw the ball for me
one more time.

Father, help me to forget what lies behind and reach forward
to what lies ahead. Amen. —SCOTT WALKER

"I, JESUS, HAVE SENT MY ANGEL TO YOU TO GIVE YOU THIS TESTIMONY. . . ." —Revelation 22:16 (NIV)

Has God—or at least an angel—ever tapped you on the shoulder? I don't mean some gentle mental nudge or a deep feeling inside your heart; I mean a good, solid hand on the shoulder at 11:15 on a sunny May morning.

Last May, my business partners and I were working on the last details of a major client presentation. We had forgotten one small piece of equipment, which was due to arrive at my house, a mile from the meeting, at 10:00 A.M. Just after eleven, I called my wife Joy to ask if the package had arrived. She checked. Instead of a package, there was a note saying, "Delivery attempted at 9:30 A.M. Will try again tomorrow."

"What?" I exclaimed. "We must have that package! Where were you?"

"I must have been in the shower," Joy said.

Whereupon I launched into a tirade about how important this package was to our client and our future. Not wanting to be drawn into the brewing marital conflict, my partners walked quietly away.

Just as my voice started to get louder, they noticed a delivery truck making a stop across the street. Figuring there might be just one truck per area, they walked over and asked the driver if he had missed a delivery to Eric Fellman earlier that morning, which resulted in his tapping me on the shoulder and handing me the package. As I signed for it, he smiled, pointed to my still-open cell phone and said, "You should apologize to your wife too."

I'd better be more careful with my reactions. God is not only watching, sometimes He shows up. Or at least He sends an angel dressed like a delivery person.

Lord, thank You for the many times You have showed up in my life through someone helping, teaching or needing me.

                                              —ERIC FELLMAN

ALL SCRIPTURE IS GOD-BREATHED AND IS USEFUL FOR
TEACHING, REBUKING, CORRECTING AND TRAINING IN
RIGHTEOUSNESS, SO THAT THE MAN OF GOD MAY BE
THOROUGHLY EQUIPPED FOR EVERY GOOD WORK.
—II Timothy 3:16-17 (NIV)

Yesterday I wrapped a wedding present for my niece Elizabeth. Alongside some bedding, I packed a Bible—in which I underlined the above verse—to remind her of the night I babysat when she was five. I had insisted that she brush her teeth before bedtime.

"No," she retorted, "I don't have to."

"Well, we didn't brush after dinner, so, yes, you must."

We tussled verbally until she trumped me: "Does it say in the Bible that I have to brush my teeth before bed?"

"Well, *um*, no." I changed my tack and reached for my own toothbrush. "But it's what I do at night. I'll brush mine, you brush yours. How's that?"

Elizabeth sidled up to the sink and said, "Okay."

I learned a lot from the tooth-brushing incident. In a note with her wedding present, I'll refrain from insisting that my grown-up niece read Scripture every night before bed. Instead I'll use the tack that worked years ago. "I'll read mine, you read yours. How's that?"

Lord, help me and those I love to ground our lives in Your holy Scripture. —EVELYN BENCE

THE DESERT SHALL REJOICE AND BLOSSOM AS THE ROSE.
                                          —Isaiah 35:1 (NKJV)

Friday was the best day of the week in my childhood, the day
I went shopping with my mother at Woolworth's. Just walking
in the door was an overwhelming experience because of the
fragrance of roasted peanuts and fresh chocolate fudge that
drifted from the candy shop in the center of the store, circu-
lated by large, lazy ceiling fans. I'd get a half-pound of jelly
beans in a crisp white sack, then wander through the toy
section, drooling over rows of comic books, yo-yos and wind-up
cars.

My favorite part of the store was the booth where a kitchen-
knife salesman did live infomercials throughout the day. As he
gave his pitch, he'd pick up a potato and carve a perfect rose,
which he dipped in red food coloring and held up for us to
admire. I was hypnotized.

As I get older, I find that there are more potatoes than roses
in life. Life is not about what you can do with a trophy wife, lottery winnings or that dream job on a South Sea island. Real life
is about potatoes that have to be coaxed into roses. Many an
ordinary husband has learned to shine because he was loved
by a truly unselfish wife. The most basic apartment can be
photo-worthy with a few caresses of a paintbrush.

I don't need expensive tools or artistic talent to find the
glory hidden in ordinary things. I just need the eyes of God.

*Father, show me the roses all around me that are disguised as
potatoes.* —DANIEL SCHANTZ

"FROM EVERYONE WHO HAS BEEN GIVEN MUCH, MUCH WILL BE DEMANDED. . . ." —Luke 12:48 (NIV)

People in coastal Connecticut where we live are fiercely protective of their houses—or, more accurately, their views. I'm told this is typical of waterfront communities. Folks who've worked hard to acquire a home overlooking the water seldom take kindly to anyone blocking their view.

My daily walk includes a charming half-circle street with pretty double-lot properties overlooking the harbor and the town fishing fleet. I often stop to exchange a wave or a few words with an older woman who lives on this street as she tends her well-kept garden or sits in a lawn chair gazing out at the harbor.

Last spring a large house started to go up on the property across the street from her. It easily blocked three-quarters of her harbor view. I felt so sorry for her; she had seemed so content, looking out over the expanse of water only a few hundred yards from her door. I guessed that she'd lost whatever appeals she'd made to the zoning board and the town officials, and I wondered if she'd been able to afford a lawyer.

One day I stopped and commiserated with her. "Guess you couldn't put a stop to this," I said as I gestured across the street.

"Oh," she answered smiling, "I actually spoke up for the new owners to the zoning commission. I still have a nice slice of the water view, and they seem like people who will appreciate what they have."

When I got home that day, I didn't start working at the computer or cleaning the mildew in the tub the way I'd planned. Instead, I went out on our deck and looked out at the water and spent a few minutes just appreciating all the good things I have.

Lord, help me to remember that whatever I have, You've given me. Thank You. —MARCI ALBORGHETTI

"A WOMAN GIVING BIRTH TO A CHILD HAS PAIN BECAUSE HER TIME HAS COME; BUT WHEN HER BABY IS BORN SHE FORGETS THE ANGUISH BECAUSE OF HER JOY THAT A CHILD IS BORN INTO THE WORLD." —John 16:21 (NIV)

Mother's Day arrives at a great time for Louisianans. It's not too hot, the gardenias are blooming, and it's crawfish season. It's no surprise that many mothers here are being honored today with a crawfish boil and, if they're lucky, plump Ponchatoula strawberries for dessert.

It's a ritual around these parts to boil the crawfish yourself. That's part of the fun. The crawfish are sorted and rinsed while the fifteen-gallon pot of water heats up. Garlic and seasonings are thrown in, and when the water comes to a full, roiling boil, the crawfish, small red potatoes and corn on the cob are added. Before long, hot, steamy crawfish are dumped onto newspaper-covered picnic tables and everyone gathers around to peel and enjoy them.

My sons Christopher and Kevin were working hard, keeping their promise that I would not have to lift a finger for this Mother's Day meal. I got up from my chair on the patio and walked into the kitchen to refill my lemonade.

"Kev, don't worry about peeling the garlic," Christopher instructed. "They go in just as they are. And the bell peppers, hold them like this when you slice them and they'll be the perfect size for boiling."

Kevin looked on, nodding in agreement. "Okay," he said, "thanks."

There were my sons, twenty-three and twenty, joking and laughing together. As a young mother I'd wondered if such a scene would ever happen. I walked in, hugged them both, popped a strawberry into my mouth, and relished not only the sweetness of a perfectly ripe fruit but the gift of motherhood.

Patient Father, thank You for Your reminder that many of the gifts we receive take time to ripen. —MELODY BONNETTE

OUT OF ZION, THE PERFECTION OF BEAUTY, GOD HATH SHINED. —Psalm 50:2

Andrew and I sat up talking late last night. We talked about New Year's Eve twelve years ago, the night I agreed to marry him. Fondly we recalled what I'd cooked for dinner, the white roses he'd brought, the glow of candles and the happy certainty that we were called to a life together.

We paused in our reflections and fell silent. The warm memories drifted off, replaced by the realities of life with five kids and too much to do.

"What do you love about me?" I asked abruptly.

Andrew didn't hesitate. It was as if my husband had been waiting these past twelve years for me to ask him just that question. Out tumbled item after item, wonder after wonder. He finished his long list with, "And you're as beautiful as the day I married you."

This last comment made me smile. My husband tells me frequently that I'm beautiful. I know I should be flattered, but though Andrew is awfully sweet I tend to think he's also deluded. At best (on a particularly good day), I might pass for pretty. Most days I'm far from dazzling.

Still, last night I wondered if there might be a touch of truth in Andrew's claim. It's possible that my husband can see beauty in me that I can't see. I was, after all, made in God's image. And if Andrew has learned to see that in and through me, then who am I to say I'm just an ordinary kind of girl?

Creator of all, show me Your beauty in everyone I encounter today. —JULIA ATTAWAY

WHATSOEVER THINGS ARE LOVELY... THINK ON THESE THINGS. —*Philippians 4:8*

One of my favorite things to do is to climb partway up the mountain behind our home in this little valley village of eight hundred in Colorado, find a big boulder with a flat surface to sit on and just soak up the stunning beauty of this amazing, living world God has created.

I walk up Falls Avenue and leave the road just between Pine Shadows and Bear Run Cottages to start my climb. The lavender wild asters nod to me in the breeze as I pass. There are pinecones and ponderosa needles on the path and a rather large seashell! How in the world did it get here? I pick it up to bring home with me. The mountain is as generous as the Creator.

I hear a bird, but I can't see it. It seems to be singing, "Here, here, over here!" Maybe it's calling me. This boulder will be a good place to sit and be silent.

As I listen to the sound of the falls in the distance and the creek running down the mountain, bringing water to the thirsty land, I suddenly want to sing. I can feel the wonder of this place and the glory of God's Creation.

I feel sure there's a place of beauty near your home. Even in the midst of a bustling city, there are art museums, parks, gardens and old churches to feed the beauty-hungry soul. Maybe today would be a good time for a visit.

Thank You, Great Creator, for loving me so much that You provide sacred places to rest and refresh my soul.

—MARILYN MORGAN KING

HEAVEN AND EARTH SHALL PASS AWAY, BUT MY WORDS
SHALL NOT PASS AWAY. —*Matthew 24:35*

About once a week I hop onto the subway and go back to
Greenwich Village, where I first lived in New York City. I am
going to have dinner at Fedora. The restaurant opened in 1953,
the year after my arrival in the city. I was an early customer
and, along with many other souls, still am. The restaurant is a
survivor. It's impervious to rising rents because Fedora Dorato
owns the redbrick townhouse in which the restaurant has
always been located.

I walk down four steps to the door, then mind a sign "Watch
Your Step," and I'm there. The place remains unchanged, with
its dozen white-clothed tables, walls filled with pictures of customers and movie posters, and always fresh flowers. The food
is Italian, I guess, but long since Americanized.

"Hi, Van," Robert says, bringing me my usual Coke. "Don't
tell me, I know: antipasto, salad with Thousand Island, chicken
Tetrazzini, banana cream pie." It's true. I always eat the same
things. The pie especially, because Fedora makes it every day.

At about 8:30 P.M., the room erupts with applause. Fedora
herself enters. Lithe and lovely, she greets table after table. She's
a year older than I, but vigorous. Her husband Bill tended the
bar until his death a few years ago; she carries on.

"I believe in prayer," she said to me once, "it is so comforting." I take comfort in prayer, too, and in knowing that the
homey restaurant, Fedora herself and I have survived together.

Give us a few more years of dining, Father, just a few.

—VAN VARNER

I HAVE LEARNED, IN WHATSOEVER STATE I AM, THEREWITH TO BE CONTENT. —*Philippians 4:11*

My work as a writer for decorating magazines takes me into many homes. Although each of them is lovely, I'm usually happy to get back to my little log cabin that once served as a fishing lodge.

But when a packet of pictures taken at our latest prizewinning home arrived one day last year, the peaceful palette of pink, robin's egg blue and white was so captivating, I immediately transported myself there, enjoying an imaginary cup of coffee on the screened-in back porch that I was certain looked out on a lake.

The owner, Jan Giacalone from Flint, Michigan, proved as delightful as her cottage. "Tell me about the view from that porch," I asked during our phone interview, fighting a twinge of envy because a new housing development was going up beside my cabin.

"The view?" she answered with a chuckle. "The view is of a doctor's office. I'm smack dab in the middle of the city!"

Jan went on to tell me that she loved the water, too, and even moved to Florida a few years back to be able to enjoy her favorite vacation spot. "But I found out that paradise isn't paradise unless you have people to share it with," she said. The Giacalones lasted in Florida three months, and then Jan and her husband moved back to a place two doors down from where she grew up. She's close to her mother and sister, and her daughter lives on the same block.

And that spacious lakeside home of Jan's? It's all of nine hundred square feet. But like the little log cabin that I'm enjoying anew, thanks to Jan, it's paradise.

Wherever I am is paradise, Lord, as long as You and those I love are with me. —ROBERTA MESSNER

FOR WHEN I AM WEAK, THEN AM I STRONG.
                                    —*II Corinthians 12:10*

A little more than a year ago my husband Lynn suffered massive bleeding in his brain. He survived two critical surgeries and spent nearly two weeks on life support in ICU. At first the doctors didn't give us much hope for his recovery—or even survival. In spite of that prognosis Lynn has made a miraculous recovery and is now back at work in his law office.

I'm not sure my recovery has been as good. During that critical time a fear was born within me that I kept stuffing down to a hidden place deep within my soul, refusing to acknowledge its continuing presence. That fear has grown and spread, and it keeps bubbling to the surface when Lynn doesn't get home at his usual time, or when he disappears into another part of the house and is silent for too long, or when I can't reach him on the telephone. . . .

Over and over the Bible tells us we aren't supposed to worry, so admitting that I still face fears, in spite of Lynn's recovery, makes me feel unfaithful and weak. But acknowledging that weakness also makes me aware of my dependence on God. One by one, as I acknowledge these fears, I remember that God is in control . . . and is loving . . . and is always with me.

Lord, in my weakness, I am totally dependent upon Your strength. —CAROL KUYKENDALL

THOU DOST KNOW WHEN I SIT DOWN AND WHEN I RISE UP;
THOU DOST UNDERSTAND MY THOUGHT FROM AFAR.
—*Psalm 139:2* (NAS)

I'm a doubting Thomas. I recognize and admire faith in others, but to follow God myself, I want one more sign, one more confirmation. It's been the same with my career. *Are You sure, God?* I've found myself asking. *Do You really mean for me to do this work?*

This spring I attended a women's conference with five hundred participants. At the end of the conference many door prizes were given away—lovely artwork, gift certificates from fancy salons and ornate floral arrangements. *I never win anything,* I thought as the numbers of the winning tickets were called out. *And those flowers are too frilly for me anyway.*

Then the last gift was rolled out: a brand-new computer chair. I'd been borrowing a chair to work in from our twelve-year-old. I dug in my purse to find my crumpled up ticket: 433.

Father, I'm not asking for the chair as a sign. It's wrong. But I sure would love to work in that chair.

"Ladies, the winning number is four-seventeen. Are you still here, four-seventeen? Okay, we'll draw again." She jiggled the box. "Number four-twenty-two!"

Never mind, God.

A woman screamed and ran down to the front of the hall. "That's me, that's me!"

See, God. How silly of me to ask.

"Oh, I'm terribly sorry, but you're number four-twelve." Blushing, the woman left the stage.

"Folks, how about number four-thirty-three?"

"Woo-hoo!" I screamed cheerleader style, ran onto the stage and twirled in my new chair. My friends wheeled me out to the car.

Okay, Lord, I'll keep working. You knew I wanted the chair even before I asked. —JULIE GARMON

WE SHOULD SERVE IN NEWNESS OF SPIRIT. . . .
                                                        —Romans 7:6

Usually I'm a pretty happy guy, but lately I'd been out of sorts.
Every day it was the same old cycle: work, home, sleep. Even
the weekends seemed carbon copies of one another. I was
stagnating.

"When you're stuck in place," my father once told me, "it
helps to try something new—or something old that you once
enjoyed." As a child, I spent hours peering through a telescope
at the moon, planets and stars. These brilliant jewels filled me
with amazement at the mystery and beauty of God's creation.
It had been years since I'd used my telescope, but I remembered where it was stored. So I hauled it out and headed to the
backyard.

I began by peering at the waning moon, then at Jupiter.
They were bright, beautiful and, I had to admit, boring. If my
daily life was routine, how much more so the circling of the
stars? Up in the sky, nothing ever changes. I glanced at the Big
Dipper. Same seven stars as always.

Just then a streak of light approached the Dipper, cut
through the bowl and crossed the handle. A meteor! And a
bright one, with a hint of red in its trail. Meteors are anything
but predictable; you can never tell when one will appear, how
long it will last, where it will go or how bright it will be. It
was as if the skies were sending me a message: There's always
room for something new.

When I turned back to the telescope and looked again at
God's creation, it hadn't changed, but somehow it looked
brighter, warmer and more alive. I was seeing it with changed
eyes.

Help me, Lord, to see Your world afresh and to give thanks.
                                                        —PHILIP ZALESKI

BE NOT WISE IN YOUR OWN CONCEITS. —*Romans 12:16*

I paid the clerk with exact change and headed out the door of the discount store. I checked my pocket for my car keys. Nothing. *Odd*, I thought. I rummaged through my tiny hand-bag. Not a key in sight. By the time I reached my car, I was dreading what I would see when I looked through the window. Sure enough, my keys hung in the ignition.

I stood and stared at the inside of my car, the tightly locked doors an impenetrable barrier. And I'd only run into the store to buy a pack of gum! *What do people do in these situations?* Sure, I'd heard people tell stories about this happening to them, but I'd never really listened. After all, it had never happened to me. I was *always* careful to make sure I had my keys in my hand before I hit the lock.

Make that *almost* always.

Half an hour later, my mother-in-law arrived with the spare key she'd picked up at my house. And as I clicked open the door and turned the ignition, I made two promises. First, I would have an extra key made and keep it in my wallet. Two, I would listen closely—and empathetically—the next time someone told me about locking his or her keys in the car.

God of infinite love, keep me humble—even if it means locking myself out of my car from time to time.

—MARY LOU CARNEY

ASK NOW THE BEASTS, AND THEY SHALL TEACH THEE. . . .
                                                    —Job 12:7

I've had dogs all my life: my obstreperous boyhood beagle Sparky, Pete the high-strung poodle, my laid-back spaniel Rudy, the high-energy athletic Lab Marty and my current cocker Sally, a true princess. Yet despite their markedly different personalities, they all had one common trait: the exuberant display of happiness. (Marty used to wag his tail so hard that he'd occasionally fall over.)

Maybe you have just come through the front door after being gone for all of, say, oh, thirty-seven minutes. Or you pick up your canine companion's favorite toy and wonder aloud if it's a nice day to go outside. The mere mention of food will sometimes do it. Or perhaps you've been away for a long time, and when you get home you're treated like the prodigal son. You know the dog has done nothing but fret about you, and now that you're back all those worries are unleashed in a fit of delirium. And when his exertions are finally concluded, he'll just sit there and stare at you in utter relief.

Don't assume a dog is embarrassed by these outbursts, that he might be thinking, *Look at what a fool I'm making of myself!* or *Aren't I too old to act like this?* It doesn't cross his mind. A friend once remarked that she wished she could train her dog to stay put when she came through the door. Why would anyone want to train a dog to do that? It would be like training a flower not to bloom.

God, let me never forget to praise You, to raise my voice in joy, to give thanks for all Your blessings and to wag my tail like crazy when the Spirit moves me! —EDWARD GRINNAN

Is it a small matter . . . ? —Genesis 30:15

I had just gotten out of my car at the retirement home where I'd gone to visit a friend. A car pulled up in the driveway behind me, and a lovely older lady got out, dressed impeccably in a bright blue suit. As I got busy unloading my car, I suddenly heard a scraping sound, like something being dragged across the pavement. I glanced over to see that she had dropped a small box and was pushing it with her foot across the parking lot.

"Can I help you with that?" I asked as I walked over to pick up the package. When I handed it—a set of new lipsticks—to her, she couldn't thank me enough.

"Oh, you're such a dear to help me," she said. "You see, with this hip I just can't bend over." She then insisted I take one of the lipsticks as thanks.

I hadn't done anything, really, just bend over—something I do dozens of times a day and never think about. How very little effort it can take to help someone: taking a few boxes of macaroni-and-cheese to the food bank, or a bag of old baseball caps to the homeless shelter during the hot Arizona summer. It doesn't make a big difference, sure, but as I learned in that parking lot, a small difference can make all the difference to the person with the need.

Father, help me recognize the opportunities You give me to provide exactly what someone needs, no matter how small it may seem. —GINA BRIDGEMAN

BUT WE PREACH CHRIST CRUCIFIED, UNTO THE JEWS A
STUMBLINGBLOCK, AND UNTO THE GREEKS FOOLISHNESS.
—*I Corinthians 1:23*

Ever since a friend gave me a copy a few years ago, I've been a big fan of Professor Joseph Shipley's book *The Origins of English Words*. Shipley's book is like a huge historical funhouse. Open it looking for information on the origins of one word, and before you know it you will end up someplace completely unexpected, your head full of connections between words and ideas you had no idea existed before.

Take, for example, the word *ascension*. Look it up in Shipley's book, and he will direct you to the Indo-European word root *skand*. Long ago, Shipley explains, these five alien-looking letters had two different definitions: to climb, and to stumble. A strangely opposite pair of meanings for one little word to carry—but as the word changed over history, things got even stranger. For while in its meaning as "climb," the word ultimately gave birth to *ascend* and *ascension*—the words we use to describe Jesus' last act on Earth—in its opposite meaning of "stumble" the word eventually transformed into the Greek *scandalon*. Or in the English of the King James Version: *stumblingblock*. The word Paul uses in First Corinthians to describe Christ's impact on the astonished world He left behind.

Ascension. Stumblingblock. Two words I'd never have guessed had any relationship to each other, but which, thanks to Professor Shipley, will now always be wonderfully and aptly intertwined.

Father, may my witness to Your risen and ascended Son never cause anyone to stumble. —PTOLEMY TOMPKINS

CALL UNTO ME, AND I WILL ANSWER THEE, AND SHEW THEE
GREAT AND MIGHTY THINGS, WHICH THOU KNOWEST NOT.
                                                      —Jeremiah 33:3

I'd just stuck a nickel in the slot of the pay phone when an operator came on the line and said, "That will be another five cents, please."

"But I already put in a nickel," I protested.

"The cost is now ten cents," was her answer.

Well, I didn't have another nickel, so I had to be consoled with having my original five-cent piece *plink* into the metal cup below. At least it was returned.

In our area, the increase came in 1951, when television was still such a brand-new medium we gawkers stopped and stared at the test patterns on TV sets on display in appliance-store windows. I remember the date because I'd just learned I'd been accepted to a school that trained hopefuls for on-camera work, and I couldn't wait to get home to call a friend with my exciting news.

A dime remained the price of a telephone call until 1985. I recall that date because my son had just bought his ten-year-old daughter a pair of "penny loafers," the kind with a slot in its top side, just the right size for inserting a coin. "Here's a dime for each of your new shoes," I said. "Always keep them there so you'll be able to phone someone if you need to."

"Grandma, don't you know it takes a quarter to call anybody?" No, I didn't. I resisted the impulse to reminisce about what I used to be able to buy for a dime and that there were live operators "when I was your age." She might realize I was older than she'd already thought. Certainly I wasn't about to tell her I could even remember a song titled "Hello Central, Give Me Heaven." I'd have to try explaining what Central was.

How grateful I am, heavenly Father, that it costs nothing to talk to You. What's more, Your line is never busy—and You're never too busy to listen. —ISABEL WOLSELEY

BUT AS FOR ME, I WILL LOOK TO THE LORD. . . .
                                          —*Micah* 7:7 (RSV)

On our trip through the Grand Canyon, my husband Keith and
I listened carefully to the lecture on avoiding scorpions. "A bite
from the big black ones hurts pretty badly," the guide said. "The
little gold ones can kill you." He told us to check our sleeping
areas before going to bed and to avoid sticking our hands or
feet into anything without looking inside it first.

"If I get bitten, you'll be the first to know," I warned Keith.
"I couldn't suffer it alone."

In the middle of the night, I felt a sharp pain in the left side
of my neck. I sat upright in my sleeping bag and grabbed the
flashlight out of my shoe. Pain radiated from the spot, past my
eye and into my head. *Lord, be with me,* I prayed. Just as I
flicked on the light, the black scorpion skittered away. *A black
one! Thank You, Lord!*

I yanked open my backpack and pulled out the ointment
we carried for red ant bites. I applied it liberally to my neck,
hoping it would bring some relief. The pain lessened a little,
and I finally thought to wake up Keith.

"You handled all that alone?" Keith asked, surprised.

Not alone at all. Not by a long shot.

Lord, please help me remember that I never suffer alone.
                                          —RHODA BLECKER

AS FOR GOD, HIS WAY IS PERFECT. . . . —II Samuel 22:31

One Sunday morning I was driving along a deserted road between miles of parkland. It was eight o'clock; I had to be at church at 8:30 to teach Sunday school. Suddenly, the car began limping with a sickening *bump, bump, bump.* I pulled over, got out and looked at the tires. *Oh great, I've got a flat! I don't know how to change it, and I don't have a cell phone to call for help.*

I got back in the car, squeezed my eyes tight and reminded myself not to pound the steering wheel. *Lord, I'm buzzing with anxiety. Can You put one thing into my head that might help get this tire changed?* I opened my eyes and saw my shoes—the comfortable walking shoes I'd changed into at the last minute.

A half mile of walking later, a car came along and stopped. "Do you need help?" a young woman asked. "You're welcome to use my cell phone."

Sitting in her front seat, I took care of things at church and called my road service. Then she drove me back to my van and insisted on waiting with me for the service crew.

"I go this way every Sunday on my way to work," she said, "but I'm early today because I have to catch a flight . . ." She began to cry. "You see, my favorite uncle died suddenly last night. I really needed someone to talk to. When I saw you walking . . ."

By the time the road service truck arrived and the tire was changed, she'd finished talking and we'd prayed together. "I feel so much better," she said. So did I.

Lord, only You could get such mileage out of a flat tire. Thank You. —SHARI SMYTH

AND I HEARD A VOICE FROM HEAVEN SAYING UNTO ME,
WRITE, BLESSED ARE THE DEAD WHICH DIE IN THE LORD....
                                            —Revelation 14:13

In our dining room, I have a photo of my father, circa 1942. He's in his Navy uniform, looking all of twenty. He's not wearing his glasses; the Navy would have suspected that perhaps my dad faked his way through their vision test by memorizing the eye exam forward and backward, and that would have been wrong, of course.

I have seen that photo of my father about a thousand times, most recently in newspapers and on television. Sometimes my father is a soldier from Kentucky, killed in Iraq; other times he's an African American from Arkansas, missing in action. Sometimes the photo is of a young woman in the Air National Guard killed in a training mission, but it's still my father. It's still some twenty-year-old from somewhere nearby, someone with promise and a family and a nice smile—a smile you can only see in photographs hanging on the wall like icons.

I'm happy to report that my father is alive and well this Memorial Day. He emerged from World War II uninjured, but I cannot say unhurt—memories remain of those who didn't come back.

It reminds me of a cliché we use at funerals: "paying our respects" to the deceased. Abraham Lincoln was right: No words can add to or detract from their sacrifice. We really go to funerals to grieve with the walking wounded—those left behind. Those who fell have already made it home. Not in a box, not in a picture frame, but really themselves. Alive. At home. At peace.

Lord, thank You for the fallen whom we remember today, and for the consolation of Your Word to those they have left behind. And thank You for the comfort of my father's smile as it greets me each day. —MARK COLLINS

*"CAN YOU BRING FORTH THE CONSTELLATIONS IN THEIR
SEASONS OR LEAD OUT THE BEAR WITH ITS CUBS?"*
                                    —*Job 38:32 (NIV)*

Yesterday we took a picnic lunch up to Elizabeth Furnace in
Virginia's George Washington National Forest. I was packing
up the remains when I glanced under the picnic table. There,
and just outside around the table, were thick chunks of dense
black fur.

There are bears in our mountains. Our son John saw one a
couple of years ago on a bluff above where he was fly-fishing,
and in the past year our family had several more encounters:
My husband Bill and I saw one hopping over the guardrail on
Route 211 over Thornton Gap; our son Tom saw a cub shimmy-
ing down a tree in the north Georgia hills; and my brother Nat
saw one on a farm in Pennsylvania.

We are city folk, and bears both intrigue and frighten us.
Most of the time we frighten them too. Our bear, John's bear
and Nat's bear scurried off when they saw us. But what Tom,
alone with his mountain bike, heard scrabbling in the brush
may well have been the mama bear, wanting to protect her
young. Using his bike as a shield, he walked on down the path.
Suddenly, his cell phone, which had been out of service range
for hours, rang. It was his wife Susan calling to see how he was
doing. Since making human noises is a good way to send bears
scurrying, Tom told her of his encounter in a loud, trying-to-
sound-calm voice. He heard no more scuffling in the under-
growth. And he had no cell service until he was back on the
highway headed home.

None of this is enough to deter us from enjoying the mountains and woods. We're cautious, we've learned what to do and
we know how to pray. The rest is in God's hands.

*Lord, teach me to be wise and alert, but to continue on my
daily path trusting in Your love and protection.*
                                    —ROBERTA ROGERS

ALL WERE AMAZED AND PERPLEXED, SAYING TO ONE ANOTHER, "WHAT DOES THIS MEAN?" —Acts 2:12 (RSV)

I was on a roll . . . or so I thought.

Leading a workshop for about fifteen people, I watched heads nodding in assent to what I was saying. That told me I was connecting with these folks in the ways I hope for when I teach.

Except for one person, an older woman, third row, left side of the room. No matter what I said, she didn't nod; she didn't show glimmers of recognition or understanding. She didn't look like she was enjoying the experience at all.

Which is why I was surprised when she approached me after the session, extended her hand and expressed her thanks. "I didn't think you were enjoying this," I responded. "All the others, they were nodding"—I moved my head up and down— "but you . . ."

She smiled. "I used to listen simply for things I agreed with. But I find I learn much more from what surprises me. So I listen hard for what I didn't know before."

That surprised me. And I've never forgotten it. In fact, it's become a part of my own life and learning, especially in areas like my devotions or adult education at church. I don't just listen anymore for someone to confirm what I already believe. I listen for a challenge, to become what I haven't yet understood.

Open my eyes today, God, to a person or idea I have never considered—but one You have placed before me.

—JEFF JAPINGA

UNDERNEATH ARE THE EVERLASTING ARMS. . . .
                                        —Deuteronomy 33:27

It stands with other mementos on a table in the family room, the framed tribute our daughter Liz gave to her dad on his eightieth birthday—six brief paragraphs recalling ways John had been there for her from earliest childhood through school, marriage, work and raising children of her own.

In addition to the typed message, Liz had pasted two small black-and-white photos of herself and John, taken when she was two. They show a favorite game—one that brought me out into the yard with a camera one summer afternoon.

In the picture at the top of the page, John grips Liz's legs and lifts the tiny girl high in the air. The game is to see if Liz will be brave enough not to hang on to him, but to hold herself erect and balanced, hands behind her back. She does it! In her face is the triumph of overcoming fear and hesitation.

In the lower left corner of the framed page is the scene seconds later as Liz collapses, squealing with laughter, into her father's embrace. I looked at those photos this morning, seeing in them the kind of faith I want to have in my heavenly Father. Isn't this what trust in Him does? Lets us stand straight and strong, knowing Whose arms support us . . . lets us fall gratefully into those arms when our own strength fails.

Faithful Lord, let me feel Your everlasting arms beneath me today. —ELIZABETH SHERRILL

WHO CAN UNDERSTAND HIS ERRORS? CLEANSE THOU ME FROM SECRET FAULTS. —Psalm 19:12

Our twenty-fifth reunion. My wife Carol and I were going back to the college we'd attended too many years ago to mention. Except we were mentioning it—advertising it, even. We were given shirts and jackets and belts emblazoned with the school colors and the number twenty-five. "No way will I recognize anybody!" I declared.

That first day I walked tremulously around campus, staring quickly at name tags before I ever said a name. It was a guessing game to find signs of the twenty-year-old self in the aged remains. Feeling more confident, I got better at it, greeting old friends boisterously.

In the afternoon, at the back of the college chapel, I saw Wade—I was sure it was Wade—with his wife and two kids. No name tag, but I could handle this one. "So good to see you!" I burst out, introducing myself to the wife and kids.

But after five minutes, the man wryly observed, "You seem to have mistaken me for some other handsome dude." If I'd been a chapel gargoyle, I would have turned to dust.

The rest of the reunion I kept telling friends, "I can't believe what a stupid thing I did! It was a guy here for his twentieth reunion. He wasn't even in our class!"

My pal Scott finally put the incident in perspective. "Rick, at least you erred on the side of friendliness."

Yes, and I've been given twenty-five years of forgiving friends.

Give me a generous spirit, Lord. Just don't let me use it at the wrong time. —RICK HAMLIN

The Sovereign Lord will wipe away the tears from all faces. . . . —Isaiah 25:8 (niv)

The phone call a parent hopes never to receive came to me at 11:25 P.M. on June 23, 2004. I stumbled out of bed to pick up the phone. "We're looking for the family of Reggie Weary," the lady on the other end said. "I'm his dad," I said. At the hospital about twenty-five minutes later, Rosie and I learned that our oldest son had been killed in an automobile accident.

In the days that followed, our family shed many tears, but we held fast to the promise of Isaiah that God would wipe them away. I wrote a short letter for my son's obituary as if Reggie himself were writing it:

"In January I moved back into my mom and dad's house. We worked on my budget and made plans, and I was able to get out of debt. In fact, I began to look for a house to buy. My aim was to give Mom a little money every week, so she could use her thriftiness to purchase things for my new home. I never knew that I was going to move so quickly—not to a new earthly home, but to my new home in heaven."

Lord, help me to grieve properly while resting on Your great faithfulness in all things. —Dolphus Weary

HE HAS CLOTHED ME WITH GARMENTS OF SALVATION. . . .
                                                    —Isaiah 61:10 (NIV)

What to wear to church? It wasn't any ordinary Sunday. After
the service, we would have our annual picnic on the side
lawn, weather permitting. I'm ordinarily a skirt-to-church tradi-
tionalist, but this morning I selected khaki slacks, a navy turtle-
neck and my sturdy brown loafers. That seemed appropriate,
considering.

In the church narthex, my friend Helen looked me over.
"You forgot to dress for the occasion," she said.

"What do you mean? You're pretty casual in that red sweat-
shirt yourself!"

"I'm talking about Pentecost," she explained.

How could I have forgotten? Our church makes a big deal
of wearing red on this holiday. Betty arrived in her cardinal-
colored blazer. The priest wore a red stole over his robe. The
liturgical color that signifies love and zeal also represents the
tongues of fire that descended on the disciples when they
received the Holy Spirit fifty days after Easter.

"Oh dear," I said. "Obviously I was more aware of the picnic
than of Pentecost."

"At least you're here. Come on, let's go." Into the festive service walked Helen and I, sisters in Christ, appropriately dressed
for the occasion by virtue of our spiritual attire, clothed in the
salvation of our Lord.

*As Catherine of Siena once prayed, "Clothe me, Lord, clothe me
with Yourself."* —EVELYN BENCE

*HOW CAN I REPAY THE LORD FOR ALL HIS GOODNESS
TO ME? —Psalm 116:12 (NIV)*

My wife and I start our mornings with *Daily Guideposts*. Before
we eat our fresh fruit and oatmeal, Kathy opens the book to
the day's devotional and reads it aloud. It amazes us how often
the story, the Scripture or the prayer speaks directly to us.

When we get our copy of a new year's *Daily Guideposts*,
we quickly page through to see the devotionals for significant
dates in our lives and the dates on which my devotionals
appear. Then we put away the book until January 1.

The weekend of June 5, 2004, found us at a beautiful resort
on the west bank of the Hudson River, where our son Ryan
and his bride Jennifer's wedding reception was to be held.
Since both families were coming from great distances, they
wanted us all to have a place to spend some time together and
get acquainted. But in all the excitement, Kathy and I forgot to
bring our *Daily Guideposts*. So it wasn't until we returned
home on Monday morning that we were able to catch up on
the wedding day's devotional.

Guess who wrote it?

Me.

Guess what it was about?

My feelings about the impending marriage of our son Joel
and his precious Alyssa.

Guess what the theme was?

All the changes about to affect our family, the need to follow
the ESB system: Easy, Steady, Balance.

What timing! What an affirmation that God knew all that
was ahead long before we had even dreamed of our oldest
son's wedding, before we would once again need the reminder:
Easy, Steady, Balance for the days ahead.

*For those moments I know could only be orchestrated by You,
O God, I praise Your name.* —TED NACE

BUT GOD HATH REVEALED THEM UNTO US. . . .
                                         —*I Corinthians 2:10*

Parakeets were never at the top of my favorite pet list. But when someone I know needed a new home for her two birds, Hercule Poirot and Miss Jane Marple, I took them, wire cage and all. The birds nuzzled and chirped all day long—until the time I left the cage open and Hercule and Miss Marple made a run (or should I say, fly?) for it.

I tried catching them with my hands; they flew across the room. I tried throwing a light cloth over them; they seemed to be laughing as they flew by it. I put cups of birdseed on the curtain rods. Then I got a broom, taped it to a blue plastic laundry basket, covered the basket with some pink netting torn from a dress I hadn't worn in a decade and thought, *They'll never get away from this!* Well, they did.

My neighbor, to whom I'd never said much more than "hello," knocked at my door. "I heard such a racket through the wall," she said, "that I wondered if everything was all right."

It's hard to say, "Everything's fine" when you're answering the door, holding a blue laundry basket festooned with pink tulle and fastened with duct tape to a broom handle, two parakeets flying feverishly around your head and cups of birdseed falling to the floor. But with my neighbor's help—she somehow got Hercule to land on her finger and Jane followed shortly after—I got the birds back safely to their cages.

What did I learn from my adventure? Well, I don't know very much about parakeets. And never say no to a helping hand—or finger—no matter the embarrassment.

God, thank You for birds that fly as they were meant to and for good-hearted neighbors. —LINDA NEUKRUG

IF I TAKE THE WINGS OF THE MORNING, AND DWELL IN THE UTTERMOST PARTS OF THE SEA; EVEN THERE SHALL THY HAND LEAD ME, AND THY RIGHT HAND SHALL HOLD ME.
—*Psalm 139:9-10*

I was beachcombing with my husband along the Pacific Ocean south of Seattle. We were dismayed to discover a stranded harbor seal pup that had apparently washed in on the tide. We didn't know what to do, except feel sorry for it.

The next day, from the deck of my sister-in-law's home on Gray's Harbor, we noticed a cluster of people carrying a baby seal to a small secluded beach. They released it on the mud flats, where it flopped awkwardly toward the water. Its mewling carried to us on the wind.

My husband left to find out what was going on. The people returning the seal pup to the sea were community animal control volunteers. The mother seal had gone to deep water to feed, depositing her baby on a sandbar. The waves swept it in to shore, leaving it too weak and tired to follow the tide back out. That's when we had stumbled upon it.

Now the rested pup was being returned to the water near its birthing place, plaintively calling for its mother. She could distinguish her pup's cry underwater and would swim to find it. As we watched the little seal disappear in the waves, our dismay of a day earlier became anticipation at the reunion soon to take place.

There are times when, whether carried away on a tide of my own making or pounded by breakers not of my choosing, I feel separated from God. Then, like that seal pup, I'm out of my element, exhausted and floundering. But wherever I am, God hears my cry. He knows I am His and He will find me.

Loving Lord, help me to remember that You are always near me. —CAROL KNAPP

FAITH COMETH BY HEARING, AND HEARING BY THE WORD OF GOD. —*Romans 10:17*

I've been praying a number of prayers lately that don't seem to be availing much, as James 5:16 says they will. So I've been asking God for a fresh breeze of faith and, of course, I've suggested that answering a few of those prayers would fill my sails just fine.

"If you'd heal Aunt Peggy's cancer, Lord, and Rosalie's and Jim's, that would definitely remind me that nothing is too difficult for You.

"Help Mother find some help, so Daddy can get out of the nursing home—back in his own home where he belongs, back to his wife's cooking, back to his brown recliner in front of his own TV set. A provision like that would move my faith right along, Lord.

"How about a new job for my husband? A challenging, fulfilling one (or even some extra grace for the one he has) would assure me that You haven't forsaken us."

God has answered my prayer for more faith, but not in the ways I suggested. A few nights ago, as I got into bed, He slipped this thought into my head: *Faith doesn't come from answered prayers, Lucy. Faith comes from hearing the Word of God.*

I'd been letting my faith float up, down, up, down, on the waves of answered and seemingly unanswered prayers, instead of anchoring it to the unchanging Word of God. That's where He demonstrates His matchless power, His perfect timing and His commitment to unfaithful humanity. That's where a fresh breeze of faith is always blowing.

Thank You, Father, for Your Word, the source of all faith.

—LUCILE ALLEN

YOU WILL BE BLESSED WHEN YOU COME IN AND BLESSED WHEN YOU GO OUT. —*Deuteronomy 28:6 (NIV)*

It was a day for rejoicing. Our son Chris was about to graduate from college. But by the time we claimed seats on the concrete steps on the crowded square at the University of Southern California, I felt stressed out from traffic, crowds and jet lag. Suddenly Chris appeared carrying the uniform he needed to wear at his Army commissioning ceremony right after graduation.

"Mom," he said, "can you sew on some buttons? I didn't realize when I bought it that they weren't already sewn on." The uniform had come with a detached collection of shiny brass buttons sewn onto a short strip of material.

As Chris handed me a piece of thread and a tiny needle from a hotel emergency kit, I panicked. *How am I supposed to do this sitting here on the steps? I don't even have a pair of scissors!*

As Chris hurried off to line up, I looked down at my impossible job feeling like the whole day was careering toward disaster. Then a woman, who had obviously been through graduations before, walked by carrying a small hand-lettered poster. It read, "Too blessed to be stressed."

I took a deep breath, prayed, "Lord, help me" and examined the buttons on the strip of cloth. They were exactly as far apart as the buttonholes! Between graduation and commissioning, I ran over to a nearby drugstore, got a package of safety pins and pinned the strip of buttons to the coat. Chris kept his coat tightly buttoned during commissioning and, thankfully, no one detected my less-than-regulation job.

The woman with the sign understood that even happy occasions bring with them a certain amount of stress. Luckily, the same God Who sends the big blessings is also the One Who gives us the grace to make it through the unexpected challenges of every big day.

Dear Lord, remind me that on the big days I need Your help more than ever. —KAREN BARBER

AND GOD BLESSED THE SEVENTH DAY AND MADE IT HOLY, BECAUSE ON IT HE RESTED FROM ALL THE WORK OF CREATING. . . . —Genesis 2:3 (NIV)

My daughter Maria and I decided to take a weekend getaway to Tucson, Arizona, while the guys in the family were away on a Boy Scout backpacking trip. It's a short drive from our home in Phoenix, so I was soon poolside, watching Maria splash in the water. I'd brought some work with me, figuring those two days would be the perfect time to catch up. My bag was stuffed with blank thank-you notes, school forms and friends' letters to answer.

But once relaxed in my chaise, I put off any work beyond slathering on sun block and reading a magazine. Usually I have trouble doing nothing, but not that Saturday afternoon. The entire day passed, and I didn't do one constructive thing. I started to feel guilty; I *had* to do more than just relax for a whole weekend. I laid my head back and looked up at the tall, rugged mountains that give this part of the Sonoran Desert its beauty. *God created those mountains and everything else*, I thought, *and then . . . He rested.* God worked hard for six days and then took the time simply to rest.

The Bible seems to say that while work is a gift from God so is time off from it. Relaxation brings rejuvenation and the energy to get back to work. And that's exactly what I did on Monday morning. But Saturday and Sunday were days to do nothing with my daughter, and I enjoyed every minute of it.

Lord, help me keep the balance between work and play that You've created for my life, so I may stay energized for the work You've given me. —GINA BRIDGEMAN

THE LORD IS FAITHFUL TO ALL HIS PROMISES AND LOVING TOWARD ALL HE HAS MADE. —*Psalm 145:13 (NIV)*

"Get out and step away from the vehicle!"

The border guard's words were harsh. My friend and I moved uneasily to a spot about fifteen feet from our van. We had been stopped as we were leaving Yugoslavia to enter Romania back when communism ruled eastern Europe. Inside was a load of Bibles for the Romanian underground church.

In those days I was traveling for Brother Andrew, a man known as "God's Smuggler." On this trip, as on every such mission, we had sought God's guidance and were led to this passage: "The Lord watches over you—the Lord is your shade at your right hand" (Psalm 121:5, NIV).

At the border, when we opened our doors, a handle came loose and clattered to the concrete. Immediately the guards became suspicious. They swarmed over the van, removing door panels, pulling out seats, examining everything from the engine compartment to the undercarriage, which they probed with a mirror on a long pole. They even rapped along the sides of the van, checking whether anything might be stuffed inside.

But they didn't find a single Bible. You see, before the trip, my friend and I had prayed the "smuggler's prayer" Brother Andrew had taught us: "Lord, when You were on earth, You made blind eyes to see, but we are taking Bibles to Your children. Please make seeing eyes blind so that the guards won't see what You don't want them to see." Minutes after the guards' fruitless search, we drove off toward our rendezvous with the underground Christians, rejoicing that our cargo of seven hundred Bibles was intact.

Father, continue to remind us that Your promises never fail so that we'll trust in You, no matter what challenges we face each day. —HAROLD HOSTETLER

*LIE NOT ONE TO ANOTHER, SEEING THAT YE HAVE PUT OFF
THE OLD MAN WITH HIS DEEDS; AND HAVE PUT ON THE
NEW MAN, WHICH IS RENEWED IN KNOWLEDGE AFTER THE
IMAGE OF HIM THAT CREATED HIM.* —Colossians 3:9-10

My granddad was Irish, born and raised poor as a stone. He
spent his adolescence and young manhood fishing for a living,
and then with a surge and a leap he immigrated to America and
donned a white collar and happily spent the rest of his days in
an office. No man was ever so delighted to have graduated
from mud and blood and rain and pain as my granddad. But the
lessons of his labor stayed with him, and he taught them to his
grandson in gentle and oblique ways.

One day we were out fishing on the ocean, and I hauled in
a striped bass. As my gramp had taught me, I apologized to the
fish for taking its life, killed it and took it apart, so that its meat
could nurture our family, its life enter our lives. I was young and
there was a lot of blood and I paused to shudder, but the old
fisherman said quietly, "That's God's juice, son. We all share the
stuff. You want to be careful with it, and don't spill it easily, and
don't lie about spilling it. That's why wars are sins, because
people lie and blood gets wasted. You with me here?"

"I'm with you, Gramp," I said, and I'm still with him, all these
years later.

*Dear Lord, keep my tongue from twisting, please. Let lies die
in my mouth before they emerge to draw blood.*

—BRIAN DOYLE

BELIEVE IN THE LIGHT.... —*John 12:36*

Ray Charles was one of the most influential soul singers of all time. His music, often upbeat, sometimes plaintive, could set my feet to tapping and rock my soul with emotion. Shortly after his death I saw the movie *Ray*. It showed how he began to go blind when he was seven years old and how his mother, a poor sharecropper in Florida, did all she could to help him overcome his disability. One scene in particular stood out in my mind.

Imagine this boy, now totally blind, walking into his cabin and falling to the floor. The audience sees him there, screaming out for his mother. She stands nearby, perfectly still; she knows instinctively that her son must overcome the darkness on his own.

Thinking he is alone, the boy slowly picks himself up off the floor. He moves toward the fireplace and feels the heat. From the open window he hears a horse and buggy passing by. He realizes he is going to be okay. His mother, hovering all the while, weeps and finally embraces her boy.

That scene reminded me of a night when I felt completely alone. I had thought that if I tried hard, God would make everything okay for me, but it hadn't worked out that way. I sat in my backyard in anguish, feeling totally abandoned. But now this memory took on a new dimension. I realized how God had been hovering near, feeling my pain, ready to embrace me with a hug. All I had to do was pay attention. All I needed to do was listen. And with Him by my side, I could pick myself up and feel my way to the light.

Father, in the dark times, keep me believing in the light.

—BROCK KIDD

THOU HAST GIVEN A BANNER TO THEM THAT FEAR THEE. . . .
—*Psalm 60:4*

In 2001, New Yorkers celebrated the 225th anniversary of the Revolutionary War battles of 1776 with a series of reenactments. I took my then-five-year-old son John to several of them. John loved the colorful uniforms, the lively fife-and-drum music, and the demonstrations of musket firing and infantry tactics. And like most little boys, he was especially excited by the profusion of souvenirs offered in tents full of craftspeople and vendors.

The things that appealed to John didn't always fit our budget, but one that particularly fascinated him did: a set of miniature flags of the Revolutionary period. There was the First Navy Jack, showing a rattle-snake on a field of red and white stripes with the legend "Don't Tread on Me"; the Grand Union flag, with thirteen stripes and the British Union Jack in the upper left-hand corner; and the "Betsy Ross" flag, with a circle of thirteen stars in place of the Union Jack. But the flag that caught my attention was the Pine Tree flag that had flown over the floating batteries in Boston Harbor: a green pine tree on a field of white, bearing the legend "An Appeal to Heaven."

I think those Massachusetts patriots had a point: To be at our best as a nation, we have to be aware that our existence as a country is dependent on the One Who rules all the nations. No matter how tall the building or how high the mountain from which our flag flies, heaven is higher still.

Father, as we honor Old Glory on this Flag Day, remind us that in our national life as in our personal life, You are always our Lord. —ANDREW ATTAWAY

*THOU ART A GOD READY TO PARDON, GRACIOUS AND
MERCIFUL. . . . —Nehemiah 9:17*

Don has been my husband David's mentor for years. He was a
professor at Vanderbilt's Divinity School and is the minister
who married us. As I write these words, Don, at age seventy-
three, is also an inmate of a federal prison, serving a six-month
term for civil disobedience.

I wasn't looking forward to visiting him in prison, but here
we were, signing the forms, being searched, then walking
through the door into the visitors' area.

Soon Don was walking toward us, face aglow. He was full of
stories about the other prisoners, the friendships he'd made,
the great opportunities for exercise he was afforded. He had,
however, gotten into a bit of trouble: He'd left a book on his
bed during inspection and had been moved out into the hall
for a time.

"In the hall, I had no space to write, so I devised this little
desk in the laundry room," he told David and me. "Then I got
into even more trouble when I didn't hear the roll call." Missing
roll call in a federal prison is not an especially good idea.

"The warden found me. He wasn't happy. He said, 'Be in my
office at noon.' The men around me were saying I'd probably
have to go to the hole for twenty-four hours."

"What's the hole?" I asked.

"I'm not sure, except that it's dark and solitary," Don
answered, "and those who go once never want to go again.

"I went to the office and stood before the warden. He
looked at me and said simply, 'This time, it's on me. The second
time, it will be on you.'"

A tear slid out of the corner of Don's eye. "A moment of
grace," he said softly.

*Father, You have pardoned me. Now let me be one who par-
dons graciously.* —PAM KIDD

OPEN HIS EYES, THAT HE MAY SEE. . . . —II Kings 6:17

For hours I'd watched eight-year-old Alanzo wait patiently outside our makeshift clinic, an abandoned church with its interior divided by brightly colored sheets. Every day that week, he had made the two-mile trek across the Belize countryside in hopes of finding relief from his headaches. Every day, he sat quietly while the doctors explained that the eyeglasses they had ordered for him had been delayed at customs and might not arrive until the next day.

On the final day of our two-week clinic the glasses arrived. Alanzo, always at the front of the line, eagerly waited as I fished out his prescription and quickly fitted him with a pair of too-large frames that he would eventually grow into. He looked up at me through the lenses, his dark eyes magnified by the prescription. His face lit up and he began pointing. "I see you!" he shouted. Running around the churchyard, he exclaimed, "I see you, rock! I see you, tree!" He turned, pointing to me, "I see you, lady!"

Laughing, I called him back over, holding up a mirror so he could examine himself. Looking into the glass, he drew in a slow breath and whispered, "I see me." That day he went home happy, calling out the names of sticks, buildings and friends as he passed.

I'm a long way from Belize now, but Alanzo's message has remained in my heart. There's a world of beauty all around me, if only I have eyes to see.

Lord, open my eyes to see Your glory in every flower and every face. —ASHLEY JOHNSON

"THE SWIFT OF FOOT SHALL NOT . . . DELIVER HIMSELF."
—*Amos 2:15 (NKJV)*

Whenever I'm in a hurry, people go out of their way to get in my way.

I have nine minutes to get to the dentist, four miles through residential and commercial zones. If I don't make this appointment, I'll have to reschedule, and that means more days of toothache.

One block into my trip I come upon children standing in the street with a sign, urging me to buy lemonade. They scatter when I don't slow down.

I turn a corner, and now an eighteen-wheeler is blocking the street, unloading its cargo. I cut through an alley and try another route. This time I find myself behind a slow driver, a little old man straining to see over the steering wheel of his ancient Crown Victoria. He hangs on to the wheel like he's holding on to a cliff by his fingertips. I honk, then roar around him.

The dentist's office looms in the distance, but now some knucklehead is blissfully driving his power mower down the road and cars are backed up behind him.

It's a conspiracy! These people are out here just to make me miserable!

Suddenly a clearing. I floor it, and soon I am sitting in the dentist's office, breathing hard.

On my way home I stop to buy some lemonade from the children. As I sip it, I think about the old man, who is, in fact, holding on by his fingertips to his freedom to drive. Maybe it's the lemonade, but I'm thinking more clearly now, and the truth is, when people seem to be in my way, it's not them, it's Dan.

Thank You, Lord, for the people who get in my way when I'm impatient. —DANIEL SCHANTZ

I THANK MY GOD EVERY TIME I REMEMBER YOU.
—*Philippians 1:3 (NIV)*

When I arrived at my desk at work that third Friday in June, there was a large envelope addressed to me in bold calligraphy. *It's not my birthday and I'm not sick*, I thought.

I opened the envelope to find a periwinkle blue card with a picture of a bouquet of forget-me-nots tied with a dainty blue ribbon. The front of the card read: "Father's Day is now a day for remembering. A day for smiles and tears. A day to honor what can never be forgotten." *Of course! Father's Day is this coming Sunday.*

The inside of the card continued: "May this Father's Day be special to you for the memories you hold dear in your heart. Thinking of you, Joyce."

It was my first Father's Day without my dad, and someone had remembered. Joyce Boggs, a secretary in the department across the hall, had made the card especially for me on her home computer. A card that communicated some of the most powerful words of friendship: "When you hurt, I notice."

We are most like You, Father, when we stand with people in their pain. Help me to feel others' hurt in my heart and take action. —ROBERTA MESSNER

"YOU ARE MY SON; TODAY I HAVE BECOME YOUR FATHER."
                                                    —*Hebrews 1:5 (NIV)*

My wife's parents decided to celebrate their sixtieth wedding anniversary on a cruise, and they wanted their children and grandchildren to join them. Dianne and I didn't worry about our oldest son Patrick taking the trip. He has traveled extensively and already has a passport.

Ted, our youngest son, was another matter. He's always been another matter. Would he even want to go on a cruise? Yes, as it turned out, but at the last minute he let us know that he didn't have a passport and he couldn't find his birth certificate. We brought a stack of documents to the boarding area, but it was really our begging and pleading that finally got him aboard ship.

We also worried about Ted during the cruise. With his tattoos and waist-length hair, he just doesn't look like any of the young men in the cruise brochures. People we met during the week asked me what my son did for a living. "He makes armor," I said. I didn't say it with shame, but I admit I didn't say it with pride either. How can a parent be proud of a son who drops out of high school and makes armor?

Our last evening aboard ship, Dianne and I saw a stand-up comic. During his performance, he began to talk about the most interesting person he had met on the ship. "This young man caught my attention because he has a huge half-finished tattoo of a butterfly on his back. He makes armor for a living. I asked him what his most complicated project was, and he proceeded to tell me about an ancient Japanese leather helmet he was replicating. I have three PhDs, but I gotta tell you, this young man made me feel ignorant."

"He's my son!" I shouted. Several hundred people turned to stare at me.

"You must be quite proud," the comedian said to me.

"I am," I said. "I am."

Dear God, thank You for the strangers in our lives who allow us to see our sons in a new light. —TIM WILLIAMS

THOU HAS PUT GLADNESS IN MY HEART. . . . —*Psalm 4:7*

June was family time in our vacation cabin at Mammoth Lakes in California. For two glorious weeks, we became part of the history of the rustic log cabin built by settlers in 1908. All the furniture, beds included, was made of massive logs. We put our feet up on the iron rail that fronted a huge rock fireplace and sipped hot chocolate to the rhythmic creak of rough-hewn rockers. No phone, no television, just us and the children, and then just us. Now that my husband John was gone, it would be just me.

"It won't be 'just you,'" my son Ian insisted. "Let's all go. You can fish with the kids, Mom, and I'll teach them to tie hooks at the very same table where Dad taught me."

Apprehensive and sad, I went.

Driving up the highway into the Inyo National Forest was like entering a warm embrace. The snow-capped mountains and dancing aspen were still home away from home. As we stepped into the cabin and my son gave me a teary-eyed hug, I once again felt the comfort of John's arms around me.

We pulled out the photo album. The grandchildren giggled over stories—the dog falling through the iced-over lake, a lightning storm that zapped our power, the bear we met on the climb to the top of the falls. We cozied up in the same rockers and hiked the same trails, absorbed in the nostalgia of *then*. But it was *now*. Time to move on to new adventures.

Traditions kept. Traditions created. Then and now, both better than good.

For tears and sadness turned to joy and gladness, thank You, Lord. —FAY ANGUS

*FOR WITH THEE IS THE FOUNTAIN OF LIFE: IN THY LIGHT
SHALL WE SEE LIGHT.* —*Psalm 36:9*

"This is my favorite time of night," my mother said. "Dark
enough so you can see the fireflies, light enough so you can
catch them. Do you know what lightning bugs are, Solomon?"

My two-year-old looked confused. "I don't think he does,"
I said.

Outside, the moon showed through the clouds in a dim yellow haze. Crickets chirped. Stray sparks glistened in the field
next door. I held Solomon's hand and pointed to the sparks.
"Those are lightning bugs!"

"Look at them all!" Mom said.

The sparks of light twinkled above the tall grass. There must
have been a hundred of them.

"Well," Mom said, "what are you waiting for? Go catch
them!"

Barefoot, I crept over the dew-covered lawn to the field.
Arms outstretched, I reached for flashes, grasping at the air.
Years disappeared, and I felt the same excitement I'd felt nearly
thirty years earlier. The same yard, the same glorious feeling,
being with my mom beneath the stars chasing sparks of light.
In the darkness, I followed the flashes and then I had one, a
tiny little lightning bug safely caught in my hands.

"Look, your mom's got one!" my mother said.

Solomon cheered. "Yeah! Mama's got a light! Mama's got a
light!" Bright yellow twinkled from the creases of my hands.

"That is a firefly, Solomon," my mother said.

"Mommy lights up," he said.

Beneath the stars, we *oohed* and *ahhed* as our hands lit up,
catching fireflies until it got too dark to see.

Later that night, as I lay in bed, my eyes tired from the cool
night air, I felt as if I'd completed a circle: I'd recaptured a
favorite childhood memory and made it stronger and brighter
by sharing it with my son.

*Dear God, thank You for letting me see Your light through the
eyes of my son.* —SABRA CIANCANELLI

So we, being many, are one body in Christ, and every one members one of another. —Romans 12:5

The gym I go to in the morning is situated on the fringes of Manhattan's Koreatown, a bustling center of commerce and entertainment. After my workout, if I have the time, I repair to the pool area to baste in the sauna and percolate in the whirlpool. That's where I see them: a half dozen or so middle-aged Korean ladies who keep up a constant stream of banter in their native tongue. I usually mind my own business and stay out of their way, but it makes me happy to know that they're there.

The other morning when I slipped into the sauna, the Koreans burst into laughter. I spread my towel on the bench as usual. *Were they laughing at me?* I tried to give them a smile back, but I'm sure it came out more like a grimace. I sat down and the giggles subsided.

Later, showered and dressed for work, I ran into a couple of the ladies in the elevator, likewise prepared for the day. One of them told me, "We laughed because we had just been discussing whether or not you would appear, then you showed up. You are like one of the club."

For a while I'd watched them interact. I'd seen them massage each other's tired shoulders, share lotion and give each other hugs. One morning when the terror alert in New York City had been elevated, I watched them form a prayer circle. I don't understand a word of Korean, yet I know that these women share a profound bond of friendship. I know that they care deeply about each other.

And now I am a member of their club.

*Father, thank You for the blessing of friends and community, and for the Korean Ladies Club, of which, I recently learned, I am an official member. —*EDWARD GRINNAN

*"WHO HAS GATHERED UP THE WIND IN THE HOLLOW OF
HIS HANDS? . . ."* —*Proverbs 30:4 (NIV)*

I watched the strong winds move across the water on my backyard pond. A storm was approaching and the wind gusts were
close to twenty miles an hour.

"It's so easy to see the wind on the water now," I mused.
Not so when I was a teenager vacationing in Florida. I spent the
summer sunning, water-skiing and learning how to sail from a
tanned blond instructor named Robby. I remember sitting in his
small two-person Sunfish when he said, "You've got to maneu-
ver the boat into the wind. Look for the breeze on the water
and tack toward it." He pointed ahead to a darkening rippled
area. "The wind on the water looks a bit like fish feeding below
the surface."

I squinted into the sun, looking out across the water for
some sign that the wind was approaching. I shook my head,
frustrated. "I don't see it."

A few minutes later the wind filled our sails. Robby trimmed
them and turned toward me. "We can't see the wind, but we
can see its effect on the water," he said. "It's a little like noticing
God in our life. We can't really see Him, but we can see His
effect."

Looking out into my backyard now, I watched my grown
children and young grandchildren attempt to fly a kite in the
breeze. I watched the wind race across the pond, reach the
kite and lift it high. My grandbabies, their soft, wispy hair blowing in all directions, ran after the kite. My children and their
spouses cheered, and Misty, my oldest daughter, video camera
in hand, documented it all. I joined along in the cheers, not
just for the kite high in the air, but for the ability to see the
effect of God's gracious love on my family and me.

Powerful Creator, may I always see Your presence in my life.
                                                    —MELODY BONNETTE

AND WHAT IS THE EXCEEDING GREATNESS OF HIS POWER TO US-WARD WHO BELIEVE, ACCORDING TO THE WORKING OF HIS MIGHTY POWER. —*Ephesians 1:19*

It was something I had intended to do for ages. Finally, at age eighty-one, I figured it was time. I took a train for the hour-and-a-half ride to Smithtown, Long Island, where Sue Nunziata, historian of the First Presbyterian Church, met me. I had written ahead saying that all I wanted was to see inside the centuries-old church where my grand-Uncle Edward Abbey had been the pastor. Sue had other ideas.

"Liz and Bill Ewing are waiting to meet you," she said, "and Brewster Lawrence, an old-timer, is taking us all to lunch."

I was happy to think of Mom—could it have been a century ago?—traveling by train from Indiana for all the good times she told me about. I remembered well the tall, bewhiskered Edward Abbey at the time that Mom, my two brothers and I were his guests in 1934. He died the following year, but he was quite alive when I again saw his church. It was built in 1826: white clapboard, Federal style, with a steeple reaching up in three balustraded stages to a weather vane. I saw him as the dignified shepherd standing at his pulpit, high up on a white rostrum, looking over his seated flock, the doors to their pews securely closed.

Liz Ewing had a surprise for me: the record of church christenings. There I was, a year old, with Dad's and Mom's names as double proof. They had brought me from Kentucky for the event.

"I was around at the time," Brewster Lawrence said, "but, sorry, I don't remember your christening."

"That's okay," I said, "but it's good to know that it happened."

The living memory of my christening is gone, Father, but the records, like the effects, are still there. —VAN VARNER

TAKE YE FROM AMONG YOU AN OFFERING UNTO THE LORD:
WHOSOEVER IS OF A WILLING HEART, LET HIM BRING IT. . . .
                                                    —Exodus 35:5

When I was a boy, my dad loved to take me to church, and I
loved walking with him through the city streets. It was our
time together, just the two of us.

One summer evening, a few blocks from church, I turned to
my dad and said, "I need money for the offering."

He stopped, put his hand in his pocket, pulled out a nickel
and gave it to me.

"Five cents! Is that all?" I said. I wanted to give a quarter; the
larger the offering, I thought, the more it meant to God.

Dad looked into my eyes and said, "God looks at the heart
more than the gift. God understands that we don't have a lot of
money to give to the church." My father earned very little to
support his family of five and he, too, had only a small offering
to give that night. "You don't need to be ashamed of your offering. God will bless what you give. Remember, give what you
can from what you have."

At church, I couldn't wait for the collection. When I heard
the minister say, "Bring your offering unto the Lord," I stood
up as tall as I could, put my hand in my pocket, took out my
five cents and placed it in the offering plate.

Now that I'm grown up, I try to give to God out of my talents, my time and my treasure. Often that seems little enough.
But whenever I'm in doubt about the value of what I've given,
I remember my father's words: "God looks at the heart more
than the gift."

Lord, whatever I put in the offering today, let me give it with
a grateful heart. —PABLO DIAZ

WHEN THE LORD RESTORES THE FORTUNES OF HIS PEOPLE,
JACOB SHALL REJOICE, ISRAEL SHALL BE GLAD.
—Psalm 14:7 (RSV)

Carrying my new outfit, I strode out of Macy's with a feeling of mission accomplished. Then I reached for my subway pass. No pass. No pocketbook. Somehow, somewhere I had set it down and failed to pick it up again.

Anyone who has lost a wallet knows that sinking feeling. The mind races around in circles hoping it isn't true and thinks of the credit cards, the driver's license, the Social Security card, and the black hole of time and energy required to re-create life's tools. I bought a new pocketbook, replaced all the cards and vowed that this would never happen to me again.

But one thing I couldn't replace: a small silver pillbox with my name engraved on it. It had been a gift from one of my dearest friends. She knew without my telling her that I hated to accept my need for medication and found the discipline of remembering to take it a constant irritation. I had come to treasure this small, useful object that daily reminded me of our friendship.

Three weeks passed. We were having dinner when the doorman called up to say someone was asking for me. His tone of voice was disapproving, so my husband and I went down to the lobby together.

A very bedraggled elderly man was waiting under the watchful eye of the doorman. He took two steps toward me and put my very own pocketbook into my hands. As I stuttered something about a reward, he looked at me, smiled and walked back into the night. Everything was still there.

I'll never know what kind of journey that little bag made during those three weeks. But I do know that I bless the stranger, thanks to whom I'm back taking a daily grain of friendship with my medicine.

Thank You, Lord, for the kindness of strangers and the caring of friends. —BRIGITTE WEEKS

A FRIEND LOVES AT ALL TIMES. . . . —Proverbs 17:17 (NIV)

One of the things I love about our Maggie is her facial expressions. Even if you could press a mute button on her (a concept I definitely contemplate from time to time), you'd still know what she was saying.

This afternoon she came up to me breathlessly excited. I knew instantly that big news was coming. "Mommy!" she exploded. "Mommy! I figured out that God is my friend!"

Happy to reinforce such a splendid thought, I replied, "Wow, Maggie! That's great! And you're right—God *is* your friend!"

Maggie beamed. She paused for a moment, then leaned forward confidentially. "Peter's still my *best* friend, Mom. But God's my friend too."

As my almost-three-year-old trotted off to discover other wonders, I allowed myself a giggle. She's a funny kid, that Maggie. How is it that she can turn my thinking upside down so fast? In less than a minute, she's got me wondering: *Is Jesus just one of my friends, or is He my best friend?* To be perfectly honest, I'm not sure. I don't always talk to Him as much as I talk to others I trust. Nor is He always the one I turn to first for advice and companionship. Would I gladly lay down my life for Him if I had to? I hope so. But if I would, then why is it so hard to simply hand over today?

Dearest Friend Jesus, teach me to be even half the friend to You that You are to me. —JULIA ATTAWAY

*YOUR BEAUTY SHOULD NOT COME FROM OUTWARD
ADORNMENT. . . . INSTEAD, IT SHOULD BE THAT OF YOUR
INNER SELF, THE UNFADING BEAUTY OF A GENTLE AND
QUIET SPIRIT. . . .* —I Peter 3:3-4 (NIV)

When Daniel, the youngest of our four children, was a little boy, we collected seashells together on a Florida beach that has become a part of our family history. Early morning beachcombing is always an adventure—you never know what the sea will have cast up overnight—and there was always a competition between the kids to see who could find the neatest shell. Each was looking for a sparkler—a conch or olive unmarred, unbroken and undulled by countless tumblings in the tide.

All, that is, except Daniel. A broken piece of pen shell, iridescent in the just-blooming sun, was as special to him as a shiny turkey wing or vivid pink bay scallop. In his eyes a shell didn't have to be in perfect condition to be a keeper, admired and treasured.

Too often, it seems to me, we reject—sometimes subconsciously—people and things because of their imperfections, forgetting that we ourselves have many blemishes. I once saw these words inscribed on a pulpit for the benefit of the preacher: WE WOULD SEE JESUS. With effort and practice, some people have learned to look beneath the surface and find Jesus in everything and everyone. We may not be able to see the hearts of others as He can, but we can try.

> *Sharpen my eyes and ears, God, sensitize my soul,*
> *So I hear unspoken words, see the doughnut, not*
> *the hole.*

—FRED BAUER

"HE GOES ON AHEAD OF THEM, AND HIS SHEEP FOLLOW HIM BECAUSE THEY KNOW HIS VOICE." —John 10:4 (NIV)

When I volunteered to help at a Guiding Eyes for the Blind convention, I was required to experience fifteen minutes of sightlessness while being led around a strange building.

Along with about thirty-five other volunteers, I was handed a soft, black mask. After I slipped it on, I was disoriented, my hands groping in front of me for something solid. I stood helpless in a sea of babbling voices, afraid to take a step.

Then I heard a gentle voice coming from directly in front of me. "Take my arm. I'll walk a little ahead of you." It was Bob, my designated guide. For the next fifteen minutes, his voice was more important to me than anything else.

"We're coming to a stairway. Stop. Tap your foot. I'll put your hand on the railing." We went down hallways, through doorways, into a kitchen. "Careful now, we're on an incline." I heard other voices, music, tinkling glasses, scraping chairs. When the exercise was over, and the mask was removed, I went on my own way again, and Bob's voice was soon lost in the crowd.

But when I needed help, I was able to tune out the other noise, listening to the one voice that could get me safely to my destination.

Lord, when my way is dark, keep me from stumbling. And when the world's noise and glitter threaten to distract me, help me to listen for Your guiding voice. —SHARI SMYTH

A MAN'S PRIDE WILL BRING HIM LOW, BUT A HUMBLE SPIRIT WILL OBTAIN HONOR. —*Proverbs 29:23* (NAS)

My husband Rick is a man of many hobbies. Recently, he picked up a new one that made no sense to me. In fact, it embarrassed me: raising chickens in our suburban backyard.

Every week he'd come home with brochures on the various breeds of chickens and how to raise them. He set up an incubator in the basement and sent away for eggs. Then he built a big box surrounded with heat lamps to keep the chicks warm until they were big enough to survive in wire cages.

"Don't you want to go outside with me and watch the chickens?" Rick asked one night as I washed the supper dishes, a folding chair under his arm and a glass of iced tea in his hand. "I'll get you a chair."

"Watch chickens? Watch them do what?" I scrubbed at the stubborn scum stuck in the bottom of a pan. *Why can't you just play tennis,* I thought. *Or maybe get into gardening.*

"They do all kinds of neat things. Chickens are fun to watch—sort of like watching people."

"I don't think so."

The dishes done, I straightened up the kitchen. *I guess I could just tiptoe out for a second and stand there.*

I walked down the deck steps. Rick was squatting on the ground in front of the cage, talking softly to the chickens. "How are my little girls today?" he said. The chickens blinked and cocked their heads as though they understood. "Brenda Sue, you're looking mighty fine." Rick opened the cage and slowly smoothed her feathers.

"Looks like they recognize you," I said.

"Of course. What'd you think?"

I knelt in the dirt beside him feeling an unexpected admiration for this man, secure enough to talk to chickens, no matter what anyone thinks.

Father, forgive me for my pride. And thank You for my husband—and his chickens. —JULIE GARMON

WHEN THEY WALK THROUGH THE VALLEY OF WEEPING IT WILL BECOME A PLACE OF SPRINGS WHERE POOLS OF BLESSING AND REFRESHMENT COLLECT AFTER RAINS!
—*Psalm 84:6 (TLB)*

He was the famous "singing cowboy," hero to a generation of small boys, our son Scott among them. At the end of each TV episode, toy guitar in hand, Scott would sing along, "Happy trails to you, until we meet again. . . ."

I had gone to interview Roy Rogers, not about his screen life but his personal faith. We sat in the family room of his unpretentious California ranch house while I listed just a few of the charities he and his wife Dale Evans supported: orphanages, shelters for abused women, programs for troubled teens, aid for the handicapped and chronically ill—

"Dale and I just try to give back a little of what God's given us," he said, cutting short the recitation.

Someone else, I suggested, might focus instead on what God had taken away. Roy's first wife, I knew, had died of an embolism soon after the birth of their son Roy, Jr. The Down syndrome baby born to him and Dale died before the little girl's second birthday. Their twelve-year-old adopted daughter Debbie was killed in a church bus accident. That same year their adopted son Sandy died during peacetime Army service. Hadn't there been times, I asked, when his faith was shaken?

"Never!" he said. "God's become more real to us with every sorrow."

If there were no valleys along the trail, he explained, there would be no mountains either. "The valleys are where I learn how small I am, the mountaintops where I see how great He is."

Happy trails indeed, I thought, *when both pain and joy lead to God.*

Faithful Lord, be with me wherever today's trail leads.
—ELIZABETH SHERRILL

MAKE EVERY EFFORT TO ADD TO YOUR FAITH GOODNESS;
AND TO GOODNESS, KNOWLEDGE; AND TO KNOWLEDGE,
SELF-CONTROL; AND TO SELF-CONTROL, PERSEVERANCE;
AND TO PERSEVERANCE, GODLINESS; AND TO GODLINESS,
BROTHERLY KINDNESS; AND TO BROTHERLY KINDNESS, LOVE.
                                                    —II Peter 1:5–7 (NIV)

When I raise my blind in the morning, I see velvet-red roses at
my window, given to me by my mother. Sometimes the large
blossoms are slightly bowed with raindrops glistening on the
leaves, beautiful works of art. But it was not always so.

The plant was struggling to survive when I moved it from
my old home where, truth to tell, I had neglected it. After trans-
planting it and myself, I read up on roses and watered the plant
faithfully. I fed it and sometimes buried cut banana peelings in
the soil (gives needed phosphorus, one book said). I checked
the leaves for aphids and black spots, and used the appropriate
sprays. With all this attention, the plant came alive.

I'm not so unlike my roses. When Jesus came to live in my
heart, I received His divine nature. But I must cultivate the love
and faithfulness that were planted then, or I won't grow to my
full potential. What God has worked in, I am to work out with
diligence.

Dear Father, help me make every effort to nurture the fruit of
the Spirit in my life. —HELEN GRACE LESCHEID

TEACH ME WISDOM IN MY SECRET HEART. —*Psalm 51:6 (RSV)*

We were whitewater rafting in Utah's isolated Cataract Canyon. "Here comes the biggest rapid of the trip," the guide said. "If you get dumped, hold on to your paddle. It will help keep you afloat."

With that, the rubber boat folded in half and squirted me out into the turbulent water. Roiling waves broke over my head and into my face. I kicked wildly, fighting the rocks below. The river carried me in my life jacket as if I were light as a feather, then tore the paddle from my hands. *I'll drown!* A rush of adrenaline made it hard to breathe. Panicking was the worst thing to do in a life-threatening situation. I knew that. Yet I couldn't stop myself. *Lord, help me!*

My left tennis shoe slipped off my heel. One thought took over: *I need my shoes!* I plunged my hand down into the violent waters. Here, there, I felt around, searching blindly. But the churning river was no match for my determination. *Got it!*

Shoe in hand, I arrived at calmer water and the guide hauled me into the boat. "I lost my paddle," I said, "but I've got my shoe!" He looked at me strangely because he didn't understand. God had given me a distraction I could handle so that I would forget the fear that threatened to do me in.

Thank You, Lord, for knowing me and what I need in a jam.
                                                    —RHODA BLECKER

*HOW GOOD AND PLEASANT IT IS WHEN BROTHERS LIVE
TOGETHER IN UNITY! Psalm 133:1 (NIV)*

As the airborne school graduation ceremony began at Fort
Benning, Georgia, patriotic music blared over the loudspeaker
and a camouflage-clad column of three hundred men and
women from all branches of the armed forces began marching
past. I strained my eyes trying to pick out our son Chris somewhere within the ranks, about to be presented with the wings
that signified he was qualified to parachute. Unfortunately, as I
peered intently under the brims of hundreds of hats pulled
squarely down on sweaty foreheads, I failed to find Chris.

When the time came for family members to participate in
the presentation of the insignia, we left the stands still not
knowing where Chris was. It was only when we heard a familiar voice call our name that we finally found him.

As I stood in the sea of identically dressed men and women,
I found I could easily distinguish them by their accents, their
faces and the names printed on their nameplates. Suddenly,
I felt as if I were standing in the middle of a living map of
America. *Of course,* I thought, *that's why the word United is
the first word in the name of our country. When we look at
each other up close, we see individuals of different ethnic
groups, denominations and ages. But when we step back and
see the larger picture, all we see are our fellow Americans.*

*Dear Lord, today we pray that we will see beyond our coun-
try's many differences and be united by bonds of faith, love
and brotherhood.* —KAREN BARBER

*HOW GREAT ARE HIS SIGNS! AND HOW MIGHTY ARE HIS
WONDERS!... —Daniel 4:3*

I learned something about myself this summer: I really like fireworks. When we visited San Diego in July, we saw fireworks
almost every night, either at the ballpark, the symphony concerts by the bay or a nearby amusement park, all from our
condo's living room window. I'd hear the *boom, boom* of a
fireworks show and run to the window to watch. After a few
nights my family lost interest, but I never missed a show. I was
enthralled watching the white bursts change to blue, then red,
or seeing hundreds of gold shooting stars fall together from
high in the sky. "Mom, you have more kid in you than we do,"
my son Ross said.

Then late one night, as I was closing the front window,
I glanced out at the ocean. I had started to turn away when I
realized that the bright silvery path shimmering on the water
was moonlight. The waves sparkled as if strewn with dia-
monds. *How did I not notice this before?* The following night
I made sure to catch God's late-night light show, and I wasn't
disappointed.

Fireworks are fun. But even better are the shows God puts
on almost every day in the huge, puffy white clouds that hang
over the mountains near my home in Arizona, and in nearly
every sunset. Now I find myself running to the window a lot
more often; the show is spectacular.

Every bit of Your creation reflects Your awesome power, Lord.
                                                   —GINA BRIDGEMAN

ANGELS CAME AND MINISTERED UNTO HIM. —*Matthew 4:11*

I was rushing to the airport on a business trip, afraid I'd miss my plane. You never know how long the line at security is going to be. I hurried through the terminal but was hungry. No food on this flight. I passed a stand. "Frozen yogurt," it advertised. The perfect thing. "One chocolate," I said. "In a cup."

I ate and walked, sat down to eat some more, got up to keep hurrying. To my relief, the line at security was short. I took my laptop out of its case, took the change out of my pocket, took off my belt. My shoes would be okay. But what was I going to do with my melting yogurt?

"Here," said the security guard, "let me take your yogurt." She put it in a plastic carton with the napkins so nothing would spill in the X-ray machine.

At the other end of security, I put on my belt, placed the laptop in its case, pocketed my change, picked up the yogurt, sticky in my hands, and turned to go.

"You forgot your napkins," the guard said.

I looked at her. She didn't look a whole lot like my wife Carol. The hair was the wrong color and the age wasn't right, but there was a certain similarity.

"You know, that's just the kind of thing my wife would remind me of," I said, picking up the napkins.

She smiled. "We wives are all alike."

"At least someone is looking out for me."

I'm glad to say that I arrived home without a spot of melted yogurt on my shirt, pants or shoes. Business trips have their own angels, you know.

Dear Lord, thank You for those who remember what I forget.
—RICK HAMLIN

*DAY TO DAY POURS FORTH SPEECH, AND NIGHT TO NIGHT
REVEALS KNOWLEDGE.* —Psalm 19:2 (NAS)

My night-loving husband Bill has made me a night owl. I grew
up a city girl and then became a wooded-lot suburbia woman,
so only here in the Shenandoah Valley have I discovered the joy
of the ever-changing night sky.

On many nights from May to September, a cool breeze from
West Virginia dips softly into the valley, and when I'm ready
for bed, I take the chair cushion and a soft blanket and pile into
the Adirondack chair. My clear star view is to the northeast,
over our rooftop. I settle in and wait.

As my eyes adjust to the dark, I see an occasional aircraft
bound for Washington or Baltimore, threading its way, blink-
ing, through the dark. Sometimes a star-white satellite sails
silently far above. Then the stars wink on, one . . . two . . . ten
million. On the clearest nights I can stare in awe at the densest
parts of the Milky Way. Bill and I thought they were clouds the
first time we saw them, until we dug out the binoculars and
discovered myriads upon myriads of stars crammed together
millions of light years away.

I know the Big Dipper; I find it and follow the bowl's line
out to the star that's always stuck between my chimney and
the roofline: Polaris, the pole star. Even if I doze off and the universe turns, when I awake Polaris is still there. I call it my "Jesus
star," the one true constant.

I sit in silent praise, thanking God for His immensity and for
His closeness. Slowly my eyes shut, gently I sink down and soon
I am asleep—safe in the Father's love under the dome of His
universe.

*Father, let me remember that above me always, day or night,
city or country, lie the uncountable stars that show forth Your
lavish love and the Pole Star that reminds me of Your steadfast presence.* —ROBERTA ROGERS

THERE IS A TIME FOR EVERYTHING . . . A TIME TO BE BORN AND A TIME TO DIE. . . . —Ecclesiastes 3:1-2 (NIV)

I watch out the car window as the scenery zips by: fields of corn and beans, freshly painted red barns and herds of grazing Holsteins. I've made this trip to the small town where I grew up hundreds of times. But I realize, as I look at my son-in-law driving and my daughter sitting beside him, I've never before made it sitting in the backseat. Always I was the one driving— each mile bringing me closer to my mother and my sister, closer to the warm familiarity of going home. But now my sister has retired to Florida and Mother is buried in the small cemetery down the road from where she lived.

Small feet kick against the car seat and the sound of a rattle breaks into my thoughts. I turn to look at my six-month-old grandson Drake. He smiles and bangs the rattle against his leg. I reach for his hand and begin singing silly rhymes.

Later, I stand at Mother's grave, shaded by the branches of a giant tree. The only sounds are the calls of birds high overhead. With Drake in my arms, I kneel to place a bouquet of purple roses (Mother's favorite color) at the base of her headstone. "She would have loved you so very much," I whisper into the soft baby neck. Suddenly, Drake leans forward and his tiny hand pats the warm granite.

And maybe, just maybe, somewhere in the halls of heaven, Mother smiles at the touch of her great-grandson's hand on her shoulder.

Comfort us, Father, with the continuing blessing of Your love— in this life and in the one beyond. Let us teach it to our children and our children's children. —MARY LOU CARNEY

PETER OPENED HIS MOUTH AND SAID: "TRULY I PERCEIVE
THAT GOD SHOWS NO PARTIALITY, BUT IN EVERY NATION
ANY ONE WHO FEARS HIM AND DOES WHAT IS RIGHT IS
ACCEPTABLE TO HIM." —Acts 10:34-35 (RSV)

The story I heard that night was both harrowing and
mesmerizing.

In the very church building in which I was sitting, in an
impoverished township of South Africa, hundreds of church
members had spent nights lying beneath their church pews—
no lights, no food, no conversation, quietly shushing their children and hoping they'd fall asleep. Why? Because they had
black skin. And in South Africa in the early 1990s, that was a
crime too often punished with beatings from marauding bands
of thugs, sometimes even to death.

That congregation survived those terrifying nights and
helped their society overcome a system called apartheid. When
I asked them how they had changed such a brutal and oppressive system, the answer I received surprised me: "We talked."

"We don't have to let go of what we believe," one said, "but
we do need to be curious about what others believe—that
indeed, their way of seeing the world might be essential to our
survival."

Those words have stuck with me. In my work, in my family
life, in my relationships with my neighbors, I'm often in the
midst of disagreement. What helps me then? The wisdom of
my South African friends, from a situation far more precarious
than mine: "We talked. . . . For their way of seeing the world
might be essential to our survival."

*Grant me, God, ears to hear Your leading in the voices of
others.* —JEFF JAPINGA

DO NOT LET ANY UNWHOLESOME TALK COME OUT OF YOUR
MOUTHS, BUT ONLY WHAT IS HELPFUL FOR BUILDING
OTHERS UP ACCORDING TO THEIR NEEDS, THAT IT MAY
BENEFIT THOSE WHO LISTEN. —*Ephesians 4:29 (NIV)*

"You look fat! You're pathetic. How could you be so stupid?

Wouldn't you cringe if you heard someone talking like that? Well, guess what? That's how lots of us talk to ourselves, and after a while we believe it. I should know. I've been at this bad habit for a long time.

Here's an example: I walk into my closet in the morning and go at it: *Those pants are too tight. Your arms look like sausages in that sweater. Why can't you lose weight? You shouldn't eat ice cream! Where's your self-control?* By the time I'm dressed, I don't like myself.

My friend Kathy understands, because we often commiserate over our weaknesses. But Kathy's a counselor, so she's one step ahead of me. "When you catch yourself talking like that, stop!" she said. "Then talk to yourself like you'd talk to a friend in the same situation. Me, for instance."

Okay, so I'm back in the closet. *Not that skirt! You can't even zip it up. You'll never fit in that again. . . .*

Stop! If Kathy were standing here in my shoes, how would I help her decide what to wear? "What would be fun—and make you feel good today? You look good in this. . . ."

Get the picture?

Father, help me believe what You believe about me.

                                                    —CAROL KUYKENDALL

*THE LORD IS MY SHEPHERD; I SHALL NOT WANT. . . . HE
LEADETH ME BESIDE THE STILL WATERS. . . . I WILL FEAR
NO EVIL; FOR THOU ART WITH ME. . . . —Psalm 23:1-2, 4*

My wife Beth, our son Jodie and I were on vacation in the
mountains near Lake Lure, North Carolina. One day while we
were hiking along the banks of the Broad River, we stopped to
gaze at a series of small rapids cascading down to the lake.
Suddenly I looked upstream and saw a mother mallard duck
and five ducklings approaching the swirling rapids. The ducklings seemed like puffs of fluff, too fragile to negotiate the dangerous waters.

    As they approached the rapids, the mother duck scooted
in front of the ducklings and they swung behind her in single
file. With determination, she led them over the first drop,
watched each of them disappear underwater and bob to the
surface, and then herded them to the shoreline and calm water.
After a few minutes rest, she led the ducklings back into the
swift current, down the next rapid and back to the safety of the
still water. Slowly they made their way downstream, one challenging descent at a time.

    That mother duck and her obedient ducklings have become
a spiritual symbol for me. They remind me of the way God
leads me through turbulent waters. When I'm anxious or afraid,
I'd like to remember that God is in the river with me, guiding
me over the rapids, one challenge at a time, and on to still
water.

*Lord, when the currents become treacherous, remind me that
You are with me, guiding me toward safety and rest. Amen.*
                                                      —SCOTT WALKER

*YOU ARE A LETTER FROM CHRIST DELIVERED BY US,
WRITTEN NOT WITH INK BUT WITH THE SPIRIT OF THE
LIVING GOD. . . .* —II Corinthians 3:3 (RSV)

It was nearly midnight when I climbed into bed, exhausted. As my eyelids closed in preparation for blissful oblivion, my hand touched something hidden under my pillow. A piece of paper, folded up. I pried my eyes open and turned on the light. It was a letter—typed—from Mary, age five.

"I HOP WE KAN GIT TOO GETR AGIN SUNE. MARY JULIA"

I smiled. Mrs. Julia is Mary's persona when we have tea parties. From time to time I buy a box of fresh cookies at the bakery around the corner, get out the good china and invite my kids to tea. They pretend to be adults, and we sit and chitchat about their children and the challenges of parenting. The kids love it. I do, too, especially when they share their insights on what causes children to misbehave or feel loved.

It was kind of silly how loved *I* felt at that moment, sitting in bed in the middle of the night. We'd had a tea party that afternoon. It was fun, but almost lost to memory after bulldozing the kids through evening chores, keeping night prayers on track, and making sure teeth were brushed, stories told and monsters banished.

It was awfully nice to have a love note. I'd like to have more of them. For that matter, I ought to write a few myself.

Jesus, let's get together again soon. I love You.

—JULIA ATTAWAY

***THEY WILL BE A SIGN AND A WONDER TO YOU AND YOUR
DESCENDANTS FOREVER.*** *—Deuteronomy 28:46 (NIV)*

I went fishing recently with my doctor friend Jim. Jim fishes in
saltwater on Chesapeake Bay, and the techniques he uses are
often different from the ones I used on the freshwater lakes of
Minnesota where I learned to fish.

One day, we were cruising in the middle of the bay when
Jim cut the motor and said, "Cast over to the starboard. The fish
are right there." I couldn't see any difference between that
stretch of water and all the miles of bay around us, but I did as
I was told and caught a fish right away. Jim caught a couple,
then I caught another one and then they stopped biting. Jim
started the motor and moved on, then stopped again, and again
we caught more fish.

Puzzled by Jim's mysterious success, I asked, "How in the
world do you know where the fish are?"

Pointing to the sky, he said, "I'm just following the birds.
Whenever they begin to circle, I know they're seeing a school
of fish just beneath the surface. Works every time."

It struck me that Jim's method is good for a lot more than
fishing. Often the signs of what's going on below the surface
are right in front of us if we just take time to learn them: Which
cry means the baby is hungry and which means he's stubborn?
Which call from your mother is nosiness and which is loneliness? When is your wife really sick of football, and when does
she just want you to turn off the sound and talk to her for a
while?

From the birds, I made up a lesson for myself for all of this:
If you can't figure out something at first, look up, down, left,
right and listen. Somewhere there's a sign that will make it all
easier.

*Lord, give me eyes to see and ears to hear the signs You put in
my life today.* —ERIC FELLMAN

"MAN LOOKS AT THE OUTWARD APPEARANCE, BUT THE LORD LOOKS AT THE HEART." —I Samuel 16:7 (NIV)

I was browsing through the magazine rack at the grocery store when one particular cover caught my eye. It featured a bouquet of sunflowers in an old-fashioned white graniteware pitcher. The pale blue background looked like the sky on a perfect summer day.

After I put away my groceries, I took the magazine and a glass of lemonade and settled into my porch swing. But as I leafed through its pages, the photographs looked strangely familiar. There was a picture of chairs circling a primitive farm table that I was certain I'd already clipped for the folder where I keep ideas for future decorating projects. The editor's page explained everything. As part of a special marketing test, the publisher had printed the same issue with two different covers to see which one attracted the most readers.

I felt cheated. And then it hit me: How often does my outward appearance misrepresent what's really inside me? Just this week I'd covered an irritable mood with a smile when I attended a church banquet. Yet when I returned home to find that my dog had strewn garbage all over the kitchen floor, the smile was gone and my irritation showed through.

I kept both magazines to remind me that although people may judge a book by its cover, the One Who really matters looks deeper.

Lord, keep my heart and motives pure for Your glory.
                                        —ROBERTA MESSNER

*FOR WE ARE HIS WORKMANSHIP, CREATED IN CHRIST
JESUS FOR GOOD WORKS, WHICH GOD PREPARED
BEFOREHAND, THAT WE SHOULD WALK IN THEM.*
                                                    —*Ephesians 2:10* (RSV)

My stepdaughter Mara had decided to go to college in
Washington, D.C. There was an orientation weekend in July, so
my wife Rebecca and I decided to drive her down for it. I'd
grown up just outside D.C. in McLean, Virginia, but hadn't been
back in years. Saturday morning, I dropped Rebecca off at
campus—where Mara had spent the night—with a promise to
meet the two of them in an hour and a half. Then I zipped
over Chain Bridge and into the past.

I drove through the town of McLean, then out to the street
where I grew up. Finally, as a last-minute inspiration, I headed
over to my old elementary school.

I was wandering around the playground when I noticed,
on the steps of the main building, a woman staring at me. The
more she stared, the more uncomfortable I felt. *What on earth
am I doing here anyhow?* I thought to myself. *Always snoop-
ing around in the world of the past . . . she probably thinks
I'm nuts.*

Finally, she walked over. "You aren't from the taxi service,
are you?" she asked.

"No," I said. "I used to go to school here. Are you a teacher?"

"Not exactly. My husband and I are visiting from Colombia
for a teacher's conference. The cab was supposed to be here
forty-five minutes ago. I'm so worried we're going to miss our
flight."

I packed their bags in my trunk, and we headed off to
National Airport—another landmark from my childhood I
hadn't seen for years.

*Lord, thank You for putting me where I'm needed, even when
I least expect it.* —PTOLEMY TOMPKINS

"BE STRONG AND COURAGEOUS, DO NOT FEAR OR BE DISMAYED. . . ." —II *Chronicles 32:7* (NAS)

My husband Gene and I were ready for bed when the doorbell rang. As Gene unlocked the door, I recognized my thirty-six-year-old son's voice. We hadn't seen or heard from Jon in months. We knew he was homeless—back into drugs after almost a year in a rehab center in Florida.

Oh, Lord, he's hungry. He's got nowhere to sleep. I don't think I'm strong enough to turn him away—to show tough love. I'm weak and afraid.

Jon's beautiful booming voice once again filled our home—and my heart. "Hi, Gene. How 'ya doin', buddy?"

"Jon!" Gene answered. "How are you? Come on in." I heard them in the kitchen: Gene warming up homemade soup, making a sandwich, pouring soda, cutting chocolate cake. I remained frozen on the sofa, grateful that Jon had food.

I heard Jon putting his dishes in the sink. They came into the living room, and Jon plopped down in the brown recliner like old times. His warm smile touched me like morning sunshine. I glanced at him. *So much thinner.* Stretching, yawning, he said, "Think I'll spend the night, Mom."

God, give me Your strength. "You can't stay here, Jon."

"Mom . . ."

Show tough love, Marion. I picked up the phone and said the unthinkable. "I'm going to call the police if you don't leave now." I desperately longed to add "son."

Calling, "'Night, Mom. 'Night, Gene" over his shoulder, Jon walked out.

My heart is breaking, Father, but Your strength always arrives in the nick of time. —MARION BOND WEST

WHO SINGS SONGS TO A TROUBLED HEART.
                                    —*Proverbs 25:20* (NAS)

My daughter Julie had joined Al-Anon to find out how to do
what was best for her brother Jon. Her advice to me was of the
variety "Let go and let God," "One day at a time" and "If you
love him, don't help him." Her stern words didn't take away
any of the agony of rejecting my son.

   Then Jon's twin brother Jeremy called. "Mom, he keeps
showing up here, begging to stay with me." I heard the pain
in his troubled voice. Jennifer, my middle child, cried on the
phone. "He's our flesh and blood!" Jon phoned occasionally
himself, sometimes in a rage, other times gentle and funny.

   In the midst of the turmoil, I searched for peace. Sitting in
the brown recliner that Jon loved, I closed my eyes, listening
hard for God's silent voice.

   Gene had started leaving the radio on day and night. "It's for
the cat," he explained, "so she doesn't get so lonely when we're
out." Sure enough, we often came home to find Girl Friend
curled up by the radio. My heavy heart seemed to curl up there
too:

> *Morning by morning, new mercies I see.*
> *All I have needed Thy hand hath provided;*
> *Great is Thy faithfulness, Lord, unto me!*
>   —(Thomas O. Chisholm, 1866–1960)

How faithful You remain, dear Lord, no matter how discour-
aged I am. —MARION BOND WEST

"KEEP SILENT, AND I WILL TEACH YOU WISDOM."
                                          —*Job 33:33* (NAS)

"Collect call from Jon West. Will you accept the charges?"

"Yes, operator."

"Mom, I need help. I want to go back to rehab . . ."

Oh, Lord, finally! He wants to return to that city of refuge where You restored him once. He'd called many times before, but we were certain he wasn't desperate yet, and we'd refused to help. I put Gene on the phone and watched as he wrote down directions Jon gave. I had so much to say to my son—suggestions to make, questions to ask. Gene assured him, "We'll be there, Jon. It'll take about two hours."

"He's at a friend's house," Gene explained as we drove to pick him up. "The friend is long gone, and the house has been repossessed. He'd walked a couple of miles to a pay phone."

Jon, Jon! You're finally ready for help. Here we come, son!

Gene pulled up the driveway of an elegant home. Jon stood waiting. He wore a wide-brimmed straw hat and an even wider smile, a T-shirt, knee-length jeans and sandals. "I don't think we should say very much," Gene said softly.

But I had so much to say!

They put his few belongings in the car. The July heat and humidity were overwhelming. I felt instant relief when Jon settled in by Gene and got the full force of the air conditioning. "Nice house," Jon said as though things were normal, "but all the utilities have been cut off for a while."

From the backseat I studied the back of Jon's head. I wanted to lean forward, kiss him, hug him and say so much. But I sat still and quiet, silently praising God.

Lord, I had no idea silence could be so powerful and satisfying.
                                          —MARION BOND WEST

"RETURN TO ME WITH ALL YOUR HEART. . . ."
                                              —*Joel 2:12* (NAS)

"Mom," Jon said, "I'm going make you a garden while we're waiting for rehab to accept me. A flower garden with a rock wall." Gene drove him to the garden center, where they bought rocks and all kinds of flowers and mulch. Jon worked daily in the broiling sun, stopping only to wolf down enormous amounts of food.

It was hot, dirty work, and his strength seemed unbelievable. "Mom, come look!" he called. I ran outside to marvel. The garden was perfect, as if it had come straight from the pages of a magazine—charming, enchanting. There were sunflowers, blue morning glories trailed over our picket fence, yellow and red zinnias, shy purple flowers leaning against the fence, roses, red petunias, gardenias. . . .

He watered it slowly, gently. I tried shooting water from the hose, full force. "No, Mom," he explained. "Easy—like this. Just a trickle."

From time to time Jon phoned the rehab center to make his request. To be admitted to the rehab program, he had to be patient as well as persistent. He was told to call every other day. Callers must be serious—desperate—and desire restoration.

Jon didn't use drugs or smoke at our house for three weeks. His only addiction seemed to be to hard work and food. But I knew his addictions were numerous, dangerous and longstanding.

Gene bought Jon a new Bible, *The Message*. Jon read aloud from it, insisting that we listen. "I'm a new Jonah. Just add an *ah* to my name. I've been running for so long."

Late one evening, Jon and I stood together and admired the garden. I hung a small hand-painted sign, JON'S GARDEN-7/7/04, on the fence.

"It seems like more than a garden, son."

"It is. It's a place to meet God. A place to return to Him and get my heart right."

I'll always be close to You in this garden, Father—and close to Jon. —MARION BOND WEST

HOW CAN I GIVE YOU UP . . . ? HOW CAN I SURRENDER
YOU . . . ? . . . —Hosea 11:8 (NAS)

Finally, on a morning in late July, we left at 5:15. Our destination
was Okeechobee, Florida—Dunklin Memorial Camp. The interview would be mostly a formality, my son Jon thought. He
seemed certain that he was in. After ten hours we pulled up at
the camp and were welcomed by 1940s-style buildings, sandy
roads, old trucks and smiling men of all ages.

Gene and I were asked to sit in on Jon's interview early the
next morning. It got off to a rough start and then got worse.
Jon's answers were way off base. His posture showed indiffer-
ence; he didn't make eye contact. No, he didn't think he'd been
rebellious. He disagreed with some of the Dunklin programs.
He lacked humility. He showed no gratitude for the chance to
be readmitted.

Gene and I stared at each other in silent horror.

"Man, what's going on?" Jon was asked. "You know the
answers—what we expect. You could teach most of these
courses, Jon. You aren't giving us anything to work with."

My eyes locked with those of the man asking the questions,
and I saw open, deep regret in his brown eyes. "We can't
accept you, Jon. Maybe another time, when you're really ready
for help. When you're humble and ready to be restored."

Back in the room we'd been staying in on the Dunklin campus, I slung my things into a suitcase. Jon found me as Gene
packed our station wagon. Casually, he said, "Mom, when we
get back—"

"You can't go back with us, Jon. You're on your own."

How can I give you up, Jon? How can I surrender you? Lord
Jesus, help me—please. —MARION BOND WEST

*THOUGH THE FIG TREE SHOULD NOT BLOSSOM . . . YET I
WILL EXULT IN THE LORD. . . . THE LORD GOD IS MY
STRENGTH. . . . —Habakkuk 3:17-19 (NAS)*

As we prepared to leave Dunklin, Gene volunteered to take
Jon to the bus station. The camp was twenty-five miles from
civilization.

"No, I can't see him again," I said. "I've relinquished him so
many times in the last twenty years—and I have to do it again."

As we pulled away, Jon walked down the hot, sandy road to
ask permission to use the office phone, the only one in camp.
"What am I supposed to do?" he called out to us.

"Whatever," I answered, my voice cracking.

"Well, praise God," he said.

Gene and I drove silently mile after mile. "Do you want me
to go back, honey?" he asked.

"No. Just keep driving."

*This isn't what I had in mind, Lord. Not leaving him prac-
tically on the side of the road.* I knew he had only ten dollars.
*God, You have to help me give him up again. You must be
bigger than this anguish.*

We'd been driving a couple of hours when a sky-blue truck
loomed ahead. *Where is he, Lord? If I just knew. . . . Okay, Lord.
When we reach the front of this eighteen-wheeler from—*I
squinted to read the words—*Omaha, Nebraska, at that exact
moment, I'm relinquishing Jon to You. Regardless of the circumstances, I'm going to trust You.*

As we passed the truck, my cell phone rang. It was Jon. "Hi,
Mom. A friend wired me money and someone from Dunklin
drove me to the bus station."

I'm encouraged, Father, by Your faithfulness, Your timing.

                                        —MARION BOND WEST

"TO THE LORD I CRY ALOUD, AND HE ANSWERS ME FROM HIS HOLY HILL." —Psalm 3:4

We arrived back home from Dunklin at 10:30 P.M. Early the next morning I went out to Jon's garden. I let water trickle over the flowers. Back inside, I opened the refrigerator and stared long and hard at the pimento cheese Jon had made.

I felt like stone—cold, emotionless, tearless. I went into his room. He'd made up his bed almost perfectly. As I stripped off the sheets, an invisible blow knocked me to the bed. I lay there, holding on to the pillows. *Jon. Oh, Jon. Jon!* I squeezed the pillows harder, burying my face in them.

Unexpectedly, pent-up tears erupted—the noisy kind with racking sobs. I wailed freely, loudly. *Why couldn't an addict be all bad? All lying? All manipulative? All selfish? Why does he have to have deep rivers of sweetness?*

Julie had been right when we talked earlier that morning: "You let yourself fall in love with him again."

The phone rang. "Hello?" I tried to sound okay.

"Mom, I'm in Macon. I had a five-hour wait in Jacksonville. I don't know what to do when I get to Atlanta."

Like a litter of puppies clinging to me, my mother-emotions begged to be acknowledged, but I answered coldly. "You had lots of answers at the interview." The curt words tasted nasty, bitter.

Despite his repeated calls, no one went to the bus station to pick him up. Our family stayed on the phone most of the day, trying to comfort each other. Around midnight he arrived at his twin brother's apartment. He'd walked about fifteen miles. Reluctantly, Jeremy had let him in.

Now the story of our beloved addict would start over. I had nothing left to give him but my prayers.

Because of Your great faithfulness, Father, my prayers for Jon remain steadfast. —MARION BOND WEST

*AND EVERY ONE THAT HEARETH THESE SAYINGS OF MINE,
AND DOETH THEM NOT, SHALL BE LIKENED UNTO A FOOLISH
MAN, WHICH BUILT HIS HOUSE UPON THE SAND: AND THE
RAIN DESCENDED, AND THE FLOODS CAME, AND THE WINDS
BLEW, AND BEAT UPON THAT HOUSE; AND IT FELL: AND
GREAT WAS THE FALL OF IT.   —Matthew 7:26-27*

The children's sermon quiz was "What is the shortest verse in
the Bible?" "God is love" was my first thought. The answer:
"Jesus wept," in the passage that describes Lazarus being raised
from the dead (John 11:35). That got me to wondering how
short a devotional I could write. Here's my attempt.

Last year we decided to remodel our Indiana lake cottage
that has been in the family since 1910. I wanted to save as
much of the original building as possible, but the carpenter
balked. "Putting up new walls over an old foundation won't
work," he advised.

When I hesitated, he asked if I knew what happened to the
guy who built his house upon sand. His point made—we both
knew the parable told by another carpenter, or maybe more
correctly, a carpenter's son—a new footing was poured.

If you build your house (your life) upon rock (God's Word)
and not upon sand (temporal things), Jesus told His listeners,
you will be safe and saved from all winds and floods (forces
that would separate you from God's love)—now and forever.
That's the short version of a very long truth.

> *Help us, Lord, to see the big picture,*
> *Eternity's part in this life's mixture.*
>   —FRED BAUER

"HE WILL REJOICE OVER YOU IN GREAT GLADNESS; HE WILL LOVE YOU AND NOT ACCUSE YOU." —Zephaniah 3:17 (TLB)

It's interesting how a human being can help you feel closer to God. When I was a boy, it was my Uncle Tom, who lived in a lakeside cabin in Minnesota, surrounded by white birch and fir trees.

Uncle Tom was like his cabin: rugged, strong, but charming too. A generous man, Uncle Tom waited hand and foot on Aunt Mart, who was as beautiful as the roses she raised. Most of all, I was enchanted by Uncle Tom's humor. Anyone who can make me laugh has my heart. Uncle Tom was a storyteller, a Minnesota Bill Cosby.

But Uncle Tom was not perfect. In his younger years, he didn't go to church, he smoked, and he teased the girls constantly. And I didn't like the way he shot porcupines, just because they chewed on his axe handles, looking for salt.

Yet my sweetest memories center around Uncle Tom's place by the lake: swimming in crystal waters, seining for minnows, trolling for walleye and then butter-frying them over a campfire. We collected arrowheads and made toy birch-bark canoes. Not even the mosquitoes and snakes dampened our joy.

Uncle Tom was "perfect" because I loved him. He loved me, but it was not because I was an angel. Once I disobeyed him and went wading in a stagnant pond. I returned with my legs covered with leeches, but he never scolded me.

Because of people like Uncle Tom, it's easy for me to think of God in a good light. I feel safe with Him because I know what it's like to be loved. When I go to church, it's like going to a quiet cabin in the woods to visit a wonderful man who loves me. Now that I'm an uncle and grandfather, I'm trying to pass along to my little followers the love that I received from Uncle Tom. I know that how they see God may depend on how I treat them, and I want to be a good reflection.

Help me not to be afraid of You, God, but to see You as my nearest and dearest friend. —DANIEL SCHANTZ

HE THAT WATERETH SHALL BE WATERED ALSO HIMSELF.
—*Proverbs 11:25*

I had driven the fifteen miles from our house to the International Market in downtown Nashville to buy vanilla beans. At my local grocery, when I gasped at the $6.99 price tag on a single bean, a fellow shopper had given me a tip: "They're half that much at the International Market." So here I was, in a store where no one seemed to speak English, asking ever so slowly for vanilla beans.

"Ah," the proprietor answered. He scooped a small cellophane bag from a drawer and handed it to me. "Three dollars each" was written across it.

"I'll take three," I said, holding up three fingers. Then, distracted by the chores that waited, I wrote a check, grabbed my package and headed home.

Back in my kitchen, pleased with my bargain, I dipped my hand into the bag. *Oh no!* There, along with my three beans, was the cellophane bag as well—the store's entire stash of vanilla beans. I counted them: thirty beans. *Why, that's ninety dollars' worth!* I thought. *If they trace my check back to me, I'll get in trouble.*

I drove back to the store, went up to the counter and pulled the beans out of the bag. *I have no time for this*, I thought. *It's their fault, not mine!* But then the proprietor's eyes looked into mine, and I saw the shimmer of grace reflected there. Even though my heart wasn't in it and I hadn't felt it, I had done the right thing.

The man followed me as I left the store, trying to give me gifts from the shelves. I finally agreed to take a bottle of cold water for the drive home. The water was pure and sweet. I'll remember the taste for a long time to come.

Father, even when I stumble into Your grace, kicking and screaming, You find ways to amaze me. —PAM KIDD

FOR IT IS GOD WHO WORKS IN YOU TO WILL AND TO ACT
ACCORDING TO HIS GOOD PURPOSE. —*Philippians 2:13 (NIV)*

My dad and I walked into a dirt-floor bedroom that had no light other than a tiny black-and-white TV flickering on top of a table. Across from the table sat a twenty-year-old man named Luis, wheelchair-bound because of a rare bone disease that had weakened his skeletal structure. I was in Mexico because a local pastor had figured that since I'd lost my left leg to cancer we "had something in common," namely our disabilities.

"We're taking a group of young people to camp, and we'd really like you to come," I said through the interpreter.

Several days later when we were loading the bus, I was surprised to see Luis rolling his wheelchair down the street toward us. Once at camp, however, Luis mostly sat in his wheelchair and watched everyone else have fun. I figured our efforts to encourage him were in vain.

Two years later I returned to Mexico to help out at the same camp. At Luis's request, my dad had given him a pair of forearm crutches like the ones he saw me use to play soccer. I wasn't sure if he had learned to use them, but I was wrong. Luis was out of his wheelchair, walking around on the crutches, talking and laughing with everyone he saw. He even went with the other kids on a two-mile hike up the side of a mountain.

I've tried hard to encourage people with my words. With Luis, I didn't say much of anything. Evidently my example—and a pair of crutches—was all he needed.

Lord, thank You for using me to make a difference in ways I may never know. —JOSHUA SUNDQUIST

*LET US COME BEFORE HIS PRESENCE WITH THANKSGIVING,
AND MAKE A JOYFUL NOISE UNTO HIM WITH PSALMS.*
—*Psalm 95:2*

Years ago, before I retired from Guideposts, I invited you to
look at the objects on my office desk. Now I want you to see
my desk at home where, just a swivel away from my computer,
lies the bric-a-brac of my life. For instance, the brass stand sup-
porting a glass receptacle—that's an inkwell. In my youth, people still dipped pens in ink. The well was Mother's, as were
the two brass sleeves holding the large blotters. I still buy blotters, but I wonder why since there's no ink to blot.

That can of animal crackers reminds me of childhood
moments when I would line up the lions and elephants before,
reluctantly, devouring them. The stuffed toy dog attests to a
lifetime of best friends. Here, too, are mementos of trips I've
taken and of the friends who went with me: the round plate
from Israel; the little blue vase from Petra; the Gentleman's
Relish jar (still unopened) from England; the eggcup from
Xian, China; the glass penguin from Antarctica; the miniature
canopic jar (the jackal's ears are badly damaged) from Egypt.
Even the latest gift from my friend Lola, who brought back
from her native Honduras a horse that rears on its hind legs
and stares me in the eye. "You have writing to do. Get at it," he
seems to say.

Still, the most precious object on my desk is the marble
paperweight that marked Guideposts' fortieth year (Guideposts
is sixty now). "O Lord, support us all the day long," the inscrip-
tion on its face begins, and whenever I turn out the desk light
and head to bed, the prayer is part of me.

Father, for this day, I am grateful. —VAN VARNER

*FOR YOU WERE ONCE DARKNESS, BUT NOW YOU ARE LIGHT
IN THE LORD. LIVE AS CHILDREN OF LIGHT.*
—*Ephesians 5:8 (NIV)*

The underground portions of the "El" transit system in Chicago
are cool even in the summer. They are dark, damp, concrete-and-
metal caverns. People come and go—mostly in silence—to
catch their trains. Though the city is constantly making improve-
ments, they are not great places to hang out.

But sometimes at my stop there's a man singing. Sometimes
he plays an electric guitar, sometimes an electric keyboard. I
wonder what courage it must take to convince himself to
trudge down to the darkness to play. Bundled in a green military fatigue jacket, he sings while people, in keeping with subway etiquette, pretend to ignore him.

His voice is beautiful, clear and strong. As much as people
try not to look at him, it's possible to see that they're listening:
Their shoulders relax; sometimes they smile.

He sings as though he is in a stadium, as though at the end
of his performance there will be a big check coming. His performance gives me chills. I forget where I am, and the wait for
the next train does not seem so long.

*Thank You, God, for the power of one voice to roll away the
darkness.* —SHARON FOSTER

*AS IT IS WRITTEN, "NO EYE HAS SEEN . . . NO MIND HAS
CONCEIVED WHAT GOD HAS PREPARED FOR THOSE WHO
LOVE HIM." —I Corinthians 2:9 (NIV)*

Reading the verse above, I began to wonder, *Will heaven have
sights even more wonderful than what I recall from my growing-
up years?*

Will heaven have libraries where children tiptoe into their
hushed interiors to check out storybooks as exciting as *Billy
Whiskers, The Bobbsey Twins, Nancy Drew, David and Goliath,
Joseph and His Bad Brothers?*

Will there be neighbors gathered to hand-crank homemade ice
cream? Kids sucking on scattered ice chips—compliments of an
icehouse man who slings fifty-pound blocks with black tongs onto
a car's bumper for the ride home? Will there be red-checkered
tablecloths covering plywood tables shaded by the trees lining the
crystal streams?

Will there be stellar circuses with outlandish clowns and tra-
peze stunts and brassy bands and hawkers shouting, "Free peanuts!
Free popcorn!"?

Will we be in the heavenly host congregating on Saturday
nights for sacred concerts in a celestial band shell, parking on
golden streets to people-watch, joining others for sodas beneath
oscillating fans until the hands of a courthouse clock signal curfew?

Will there be treadle-sewing machines transforming cloth into
gossamer wardrobes for us? Rocking chairs to nod in? Yellow
roses and verbenas and hollyhocks thriving under inundations of
environment-safe soapsuds tossed from dishpans off kitchen stoops?

Things I'm sure won't be in heaven: potato bugs and tomato
worms to pick off plants; washboards to scrub laundry; potbellied
coal stoves with teakettles whistling full-speed ahead; outdoor bath-
rooms with crescent windows; wool long johns that itch; glued-on
shoe soles. It wouldn't be heaven, you see, with these things.

But as for what it's like . . . I think I've caught a glimpse of those
sights.

*What an infinite future You must have for us, Father, far
beyond what we can possibly imagine!* —ISABEL WOLSELEY

LET THE WORD OF CHRIST DWELL IN YOU RICHLY. . . .
—*Colossians 3:16* (RSV)

On a high mountain slope above our cabin in Colorado stands a grove of bristlecone pines, kin to the famous bristlecones of California. With their twisted trunks and bearded cones, they are purported to be among the oldest living things on earth, some of them as old as two or three thousand years.

My husband Larry and I hiked up to that grove of pines one day, and I placed my hand against the trunk of the thickest tree. I imagined that tree standing there, solidly rooted through two thousand years of winter storms, spring rains and summer sun, ever since Jesus was born. It gave me a feeling of connection, as though I were reaching back through time to become a part of Jesus' world.

Back at the cabin, I picked up our Bible, sat down on a chair near the fireplace and opened to the middle of Matthew. I read once more the parables, the prophecies, the drama of the Crucifixion and Resurrection. Then came Jesus' last message before He ascended into heaven: "Lo, I am with you always, even unto the end of the world" (Matthew 28:20).

Connected to Jesus? Yes! His words, strong and enduring through two thousand years, stand firmly rooted in the assurance of His love. For me. And for you.

Father, I face this day with confidence, because I know You are with me now and forever. —MADGE HARRAH

FOR THE WORD OF GOD IS LIVING AND ACTIVE....
                                        —Hebrews 4:12 (NIV)

A sea of excited faces looked back at me as I introduced
myself. Today was the first day of my family's medical mission
trip to Antigua. While my parents and more medically minded
brothers would be handling the examinations, my sister Kristi
and I were running the Vacation Bible School, a small setup
underneath a tarp that easily doubled as day care. Having
packed two suitcases full of crayons, colored paper and small
toys, we were prepared to deal with heat and boredom, but
not with enthusiasm.

Kristi and I distributed piles of brightly colored beads and
began our lesson about the feeding of the five thousand. The
kids could hardly sit still; they began crafting fish from the
beads and pipe cleaners as they listened to us.

Imagining we were making an incredible impact, I rounded
out the story, reminding the children that Jesus' miracle of feeding all those people with just a few fish and a couple of loaves
of bread showed God's love for us. Then I asked the kids what
the story meant. One eager boy's hand shot up. "I know!" he
cried. "God loves fish!"

All the children cheered and scurried away to spread the
message they'd just learned. Kristi and I could do nothing but
laugh. We stood and began cleaning up the scattered beads. "I
think they might be missing the point," she said.

We watched the kids gesture and laugh as they explained
the day's "lesson" to their friends. "Maybe it doesn't matter,"
I said.

*God, thanks for the wonder of learning and the pure excite-
ment that Your Word can bring.* —ASHLEY JOHNSON

BRING JOY TO YOUR SERVANT, FOR TO YOU, O LORD, I LIFT UP MY SOUL. —Psalm 86:4 (NIV)

When my husband Joe, our daughter Sarah and I were in Italy a couple of Augusts ago, we took a tour of a vineyard in the Tuscan countryside. On the way our bus passed through the lush green countryside and then began a long, winding climb up a steep hill to a beautiful old manor-turned-winery. As we peered out the windows at the vineyard, we were shocked. The ground was rocky and powdery dry, and the vines appeared thirsty and stressed.

Our bus stopped at the top of the hill where the winery stood. Inside the sprawling building our guide led us downstairs into a cool, musty cellar containing giant wooden casks of aging wine. She explained the lengthy process of making fine wine, and then she revealed why the vineyard looked so dry: The most stressed vines make the best wine.

That started me thinking about the previous summer, when I was struggling to recover from an operation during which I nearly died. In the first difficult days of recovery, I wondered why God had allowed the surgical blunder that left me fighting for my life. I had been thoroughly prayed for before and during the surgery, so what was God doing? I didn't feel Him near; all I could do was cling to His Word.

Now here I was a year later, fully recovered and traveling with a magnified appreciation for everything. My marriage was richer, I'd learned amazing lessons of God's faithfulness, and I was grateful for even the smallest things.

There have been grievous times in the last year, too, such as the loss of several precious friends. But I've learned that hardships can add robustness to the flavor of simple blessings and sweetness to the unchanging goodness of God, even when I don't always understand the way He works.

Faithful Father, when life deals me difficult times, let my harvest be a deeper, richer, more thankful dependence on You.

—MARJORIE PARKER

*LIKE ARROWS IN THE HANDS OF A WARRIOR ARE SONS
BORN IN ONE'S YOUTH. BLESSED IS THE MAN WHOSE
QUIVER IS FULL OF THEM. . . .* —Psalm 127:4-5 *(NIV)*

My husband Wayne and I were blessed with four children in a
five-year span. By the time Dale, our youngest, was born, I hadn't
slept through the night in three long years. The house was in
constant chaos, and in those pre-disposable-diaper days, the
washing machine was going day and night. My hands were
more than full with the demands of our growing family.
Thankfully, I was blessed with wonderful parents who visited
us often. Soon after Dale's arrival, my mother came to help.

Early one morning, when our newborn woke for his feeding, his older sisters and brother came looking for attention.
Jody sat on one knee and Jenny on the other, and Ted shared
space with his infant brother on my lap. All too soon, the older
three started squabbling and whining.

My mother woke up and joined us in the living room. "Oh,
Debbie," she said with a smile, "these are the happiest days of
your life."

Aghast, I looked at her and said, "Mom, you mean it gets
worse?"

Now, in retrospect, I can see how very blessed I was. Mom
had the perspective to see it then; thank God, I can see it now.

*Lord, give all parents the patience, the prayer and the sense of
humor they need to raise their children in Your grace.*
—DEBBIE MACOMBER

I WAS AS A BEAST BEFORE THEE. —*Psalm 73:22*

"How is Charlotte?" I asked my teenage grandson Ryan.

"Still wild," he said, sounding discouraged. "I just can't get her to trust me. It takes Dad and me both to get a halter on her, she won't lead, and she kicks like crazy when anyone walks behind her."

A year earlier, Ryan's black Angus cow Isabel and her sleek calf Charlotte were champion pair at the county fair. Ryan planned to show Charlotte in this year's heifer competition and was sure she'd win a blue ribbon. But to compete, Charlotte had to be gentle enough for Ryan to brush her and lead her around the show ring. She'd have to stand still while the judge ran his hands over her back and down her legs. With only ten days until fair time, Charlotte needed to shape up fast.

But she didn't. She remained wary and stubborn, even butting at Ryan when he fed her. Because a spooky animal is a danger to other exhibitors, Charlotte didn't go to the fair. To complete his heifer project, Ryan took Charlotte's picture, wrote a story about her and "showed" her through the pages of a notebook.

Charlotte's behavior wasn't all that unusual—for a cow. But as I turned the pages of Ryan's notebook, I wondered how often did I miss out on God's best for me because I stubbornly insisted on my own way, chafed under His discipline or refused to trust His leading?

Guiding God, You want the best for Your children. Help me remember that when I follow You, I'm always part of Your main event. —PENNEY SCHWAB

WE DO NOT HAVE A HIGH PRIEST WHO IS UNABLE TO
SYMPATHIZE WITH OUR WEAKNESSES, BUT WE HAVE ONE WHO
HAS BEEN TEMPTED IN EVERY WAY, JUST AS WE ARE. . . .
                                                    —Hebrews 4:15 (NIV)

"Slow down," my doctor said. "You're not superman, you know."

I'd been complaining to him about a nagging summer cold. I hoped he'd whip out his trusty prescription pad or give me a shot of something miraculous. Instead he went into Marcus Welby mode.

"When we get older, it can take more time to recover from a bad cold or infection. We're more vulnerable."

That word *vulnerable*—I'd come across it just recently in another context, something Catherine Marshall had written about "the vulnerable Jesus." Christ, in His years on earth, thirsted, got tired, wept. Presumably He caught colds; perhaps He had sinus problems, bad vision or sore joints—the dreary commonplace ills that dampen folks' spirits everywhere. And when He hung on the Cross, He suffered as any of us would under such torment.

Yet I resist admitting my own vulnerability. I always have. Vulnerability equals weakness, doesn't it? Oh, I don't really *believe* that, or at least I think I know better than to buy into that old masculine stereotype. But stereotypes die hard, and recognizing my inherent human vulnerability is not so easy for me.

Still, this is what Christ's life taught us: that in our weakness we are made strong, that in obedience we find freedom, that in surrender we embrace victory. And what better way to give proof to this than by taking on our humanity and living as we do, with all of our frailty. Jesus showed us not just the nature of God but also our own.

Lord, help me to see that in my search for myself, I will always find You. —EDWARD GRINNAN

*"STAND BY THE ROADS, AND LOOK, AND ASK FOR THE
ANCIENT PATHS, WHERE THE GOOD WAY IS; AND WALK IN
IT, AND FIND REST FOR YOUR SOULS. . . ."*
—*Jeremiah 6:16 (RSV)*

"According to the map," I said, "the return trail should be right
. . . here."

We looked around. No trail. I studied the state park map for
a long time, even enlisting my three daughters' young eyes to
decipher the small print.

"Well," I announced finally, "there's nothing to do but blaze
a new trail, straight up."

"We're *lost!*" seven-year-old Grace said.

"We can't be lost, honey," I said. "We know the car is at the
top of the hill. The map is wrong."

"The map is wrong?" Hope asked. To an eleven-year-old, official instructions—especially those written on glossy paper by
adults—could never be wrong.

"Trust me," I said. "We came down, now we must go up."
With that, my three charges followed me—either on faith or
because they had no other choice. And, as predicted, the car
was there.

Their obedience won't last forever, I know. A few more
years and my girls won't take their dad or maps or any other
authority on face value. They'll question, they'll rebel, they'll
grow up. Eventually they'll write their own maps—a peculiar,
personal cartography full of detours and well-intentioned
wrong turns, just like the journey the rest of us follow. But if
my wife and I have done our job, we can hope that they find
their true path—long and never straight but ever upward—
and always, always, always leading home.

*Lord, by whatever paths my children travel, bring them—
bring all of us—home to You.* —MARK COLLINS

"HE IS NOT FAR FROM EACH ONE OF US." —*Acts 17:27 (RSV)*

I hadn't wanted to go to church that Sunday; it was a long time since I'd felt close to God. Simply out of habit, I dragged myself to the ten o'clock service anyway—only to find myself sitting in front of a crying child.

Crying? Howling was more like it, a din that drowned out the opening prayer, the announcements and the first hymn. At last, the mother took the sobbing child out—a little boy about four years old, I saw as they passed my pew. The damage was done, though; whatever chance I'd had to feel God's presence was thoroughly squashed.

Nor did the sermon help. The regular minister was away and a lay preacher droned through a printed dry-as-dust lecture. I went to the coffee hour (the coffee was lukewarm) in a grumpier mood than when I'd arrived.

The four-year-old was there, a cookie in each hand, screaming fit over. "I'm so sorry for the racket," his mother apologized to the group around the coffee urn.

It had taken her a long time, she went on, to calm him down enough to learn what the trouble was. "He kept saying, 'God's gone!'" Finally his mother realized it was because the minister wasn't there. "We've told him that this is God's house, and he must have thought that the minister in his robe was God."

All of us chuckled at a four-year-old's mistaking a man for God. And yet, I thought as I drove home, wasn't I doing something just as foolish? Mistaking my own absent faith for the absence of God Almighty? My mood—uplifted or downcast, attentive or bored—what did it have to do with the changeless reality in Whom "we live and move and have our being" (Acts 17:28, RSV)?

Faithful Lord, help me seek You in fact and not in feeling.
                                                        —ELIZABETH SHERRILL

HE ALSO SAW A POOR WIDOW PUT IN TWO VERY SMALL
COPPER COINS. "I TELL YOU THE TRUTH," HE SAID, "THIS
POOR WIDOW HAS PUT IN MORE THAN ALL THE OTHERS.
ALL THESE PEOPLE GAVE THEIR GIFTS OUT OF THEIR
WEALTH; BUT SHE OUT OF HER POVERTY PUT IN ALL SHE
HAD TO LIVE ON." —Luke 21:2-4 (NIV)

My husband Charlie and I were in Key West, Florida. A homeless woman, swathed in blankets despite the ninety-degree-plus
heat, was huddled in the dark against a stone wall near where
we'd parked, surrounded by her possessions.

Feeling rather proud of myself, I took a few dollars we had
left from some purchase and walked over to her. Remembering
Jesus' admonition to give alms in secret, I noted with satisfaction that there was no one to see me other than Charlie.

I bent down and handed the woman the money, not meeting her eyes. Suddenly, I felt her thin fingers grasp my wrist. She
pulled me toward her and grabbed a small brown paper bag. "I
have an extra peanut butter and jelly sandwich," she said. "Do
you want it? Homemade jam too!"

Her eyes, when I finally met them, were clear and curious.
Embarrassed, I shook my head and gently pulled away. As I
got back into the car, I realized I still had a lot to learn about
charity.

Father, teach me to give generously . . . and respectfully.
                                            —MARCI ALBORGHETTI

A WISE MAN WILL HEAR, AND WILL INCREASE LEARNING. . . .
                                                    —Proverbs 1:5

The wild country outside of Caribou, Maine, had called my dad and me back for a second year of fly-fishing. My brother-in-law Ben had turned our adventure into a threesome. But the fishing turned out to be terrible, and a succession of dreary days dampened our spirits. When I awoke to the sound of rain pelting the roof of our little cabin, my impulse was to pull the covers over my head and sleep till noon.

"No way am I going out in that slosh," I said.

Dad shook the foot of my bed. "Brock," he said, "sometimes the best fishing is in the worst weather." Begrudgingly I put on my waders, loaded up my fly vest and headed out to the river. I left Ben upstream and crab-walked my way into the current. Soon I was caught up in the calm rhythm of fly-fishing. I enjoyed the feel of the cast as the line rose in graceful loops, then unfolded forward to land on the surface of the water. All at once my fly was enveloped with a slurp, my line tightened, and my reel began to scream. The trout had to be huge, and if I fought too hard too fast, it would snap my line. If I was going to land it, I would have to chase it downstream.

"Ben," I hollered, "bring your net! I need some help!"

I fought that fish for almost fifteen minutes, and with Dad and Ben's assistance I finally got it in. A beautiful eighteen-inch brook trout, the biggest any of us had caught.

But the biggest catch of the day came at dinner when Dad said, "I hope you'll remember that God can use the bleakest day to deliver His gifts." And how!

Father, no matter how dreary the day, You're always ahead of me, waiting. —BROCK KIDD

GRAY HAIR IS A CROWN OF SPLENDOR. . . .
>   —*Proverbs 16:31* (NIV)

I slid into a pew on the side aisle, checked on baby Stephen sleeping in the stroller and looked around. The church wasn't crowded, but a goodly number of people were there for the funeral. Most of them I recognized.

I hadn't been back to the church where Andrew and I met and married since we'd moved away eight years ago. The nineteenth-century building still looked to be in pretty good shape. I was kind of surprised, though, at how much older the people seemed. It actually took me a few moments to identify a couple of them.

Stephen murmured that he was awake, so I unbuckled him and picked him up. When I looked around again a few moments later, I saw that people had noted my presence too. Much to my surprise, I could see mild puzzlement on a few faces. It was almost as if they didn't quite recognize me.

Did I look older too?

I added up the signs of my aging. I have some wisps of gray now. ("Don't complain," Andrew chides me. "At least you have hair!") My skin isn't quite as taut as it used to be. I think I look my age.

Even though the mirror had been hinting at this transformation for some time, it was disconcerting to see my aging confirmed in the eyes of others. I looked down at Stephen as if to ask what he thought. He gurgled and smiled and made a grab for my streak of gray. I smiled back. Stephen couldn't care less how many wrinkles I had, as long as they creased into smiles of love. That seemed to be a good way to look at it.

Lord, help me remember that age is merely a measure of the gifts You have given me. —JULIA ATTAWAY

NOW NO CHASTENING FOR THE PRESENT SEEMETH TO BE
JOYOUS. . . . —Hebrews 12:11

It was to be a busy summer day in Williamstown, Massachusetts, and I was thrilled. The year was 1932, and fifty airplanes would visit the tiny airport between Williamstown and North Adams. In my entire life, I had never seen an airplane on the ground. After breakfast I would walk the two miles to the airport. It seemed like a dream.

There was a reason for the celebration: The pilots were there to greet a famous couple who would be arriving at noon. Once the couple arrived, a limousine would speed them to the Institute of Politics on the campus of Williams College. This was a day to remember in our tiny village.

As I was about to leave, Mother said, "Oscar, you need to mow the lawn."

"But, Mother," I cried, "this is a big day. I need to go to the airport. . . ."

"Your responsibilities come first. There's always time for fun later."

I was so disappointed I couldn't think. Now I would miss everything! I finished the lawn in a huff. Then I walked up Main Street and sat on the cement block in front of the Commons Club on the campus, feeling extra sorry for myself.

Suddenly a black limousine loomed in sight and stopped at the foot of the stairs. A petite, dark-haired lady stepped out, followed by a tall, slender, curly-headed gentleman—Charles and Anne Morrow Lindbergh, the famous people I had hoped to get a glimpse of at the airport. Now they were so close I could reach out and touch them. They smiled and then stepped inside. In a moment, they were gone.

In subsequent years I saw many airplanes close up. I even worked as an engineering technician on the Gemini space program. Sometimes those responsibilities kept me mighty busy. But there were always rewards that came—unexpectedly, delightfully and as personal as God's grace. Good thing I did mow the lawn that day.

Mysterious Master, our plans may not be Your plans, but Your plans are far-reaching. —OSCAR GREENE

"I HAVE BEEN SENT TO SPEAK TO YOU AND TO TELL YOU THIS GOOD NEWS." —Luke 1:19 (NIV)

The gray-haired man sat quietly fishing off the dock at a small Minnesota lake on a cloudy August afternoon. We exchanged greetings. I would have moved on had he not spoken softly, "I come here to think about the Bible, God's Word."

I felt drawn to talk with him, and I learned he had been an officer in the South Vietnamese army during the Vietnam War. Twice he'd been injured by land mines. Fragments of shrapnel in his arm still caused him pain.

At war's end, he was thrown in jail by the North Vietnamese regime. He endured horrendous conditions for ten years. Often there was no food or medicine. Many of his fellow prisoners died.

Upon his release, he returned home to what little family he had left. He felt empty inside and without hope. Then he read two words on a sign displayed outside a church—"Good News." He didn't know what the Good News was, but he knew that he needed it.

He went alone to the church the next Sunday and heard the good news of Jesus Christ. The faith he found that day eventually led him to pastor a Vietnamese congregation in the United States.

I'd walked out on the dock that day feeling alone and discouraged. God used a fisherman to remind me that the Good News is never old news.

Jesus, no matter what other news clutters my day, it's always a Good News day with You. —CAROL KNAPP

LORD . . . YOU HAVE MADE MY LOT SECURE. THE BOUNDARY
LINES HAVE FALLEN FOR ME IN PLEASANT PLACES. . . .
                                                    —*Psalm 16:5-6 (NIV)*

Three-year-old Kyle, my nephew's son, lives on seventy acres
covered with woods and pasture. Within view of his front door
there's a farm pond with quiet fish and noisy bull frogs. Kyle's
never seen my city apartment, shaded by a few maple trees
sheltering noisy mockingbirds.

I visited my sister, Kyle's grandma, last month, and Kyle was
there. He wanted to play a pencil-and-paper letter game with
me. He doesn't know how to write letters, but he's obviously
grasping the concept.

"What's the first letter of your name?" he asked me.

"E," I said. He wrote down some indistinguishable squiggles.

"What's the first letter of your father's name?" J.

"What's the first letter of your mother's name?" F.

"What's the first letter of your frog's name?"

"My what?" I thought I'd misheard.

"You know, your frog—in your pond."

It took me a second to figure . . . "Babe, I don't *have* a
pond." Or a frog. "I'm not as blessed as you."

Since then, when I've needed a smile, I've thought of Kyle's
blind assumption that everyone has a personal pond. That
everyone has the same good fortune as he.

But as I walk my small yard and hear the mockingbird's
songfest, I also know I was too quick in my comeback that
Kyle is more blessed than I. I have my own good fortunes. Some
are in my natural environment: my maples and song birds. Some
are in my natural family: my siblings who eagerly shape joys
and sorrows. Another is three years old with a pond of his very
own. The letter of his name is K.

Lord, my good fortune may not seem to be as expansive as
someone else's. But in Your good grace, help me to see how
very blessed I am. —EVELYN BENCE

*". . . FOR YOUR DAUGHTER-IN-LAW, WHO LOVES YOU AND
WHO IS BETTER TO YOU THAN SEVEN SONS. . . ."*
—*Ruth 4:15 (NIV)*

Last August 13, Joy and I were expecting our first girl. I was excited because I've been waiting to have a girl in the family since 1980, when Jonathan, our youngest, turned out to be a boy.

Now before you can say, "Aren't Joy and Eric a little old for that?" let me tell you that the girl we were waiting for was Jess, a beautiful, black-haired twenty-five-year-old who was nutty enough to marry our middle son Nathan.

During a visit to Jess's family before the wedding, I was looking for some fatherly way to connect with her. While Jess and the two moms looked at wedding dresses, I found out that her car wasn't running very well. Poking around under the import's hood produced the fatherly diagnosis of worn spark plug wires.

Nathan and I headed for the auto parts store where, like all parts for foreign cars, the wire set was outrageously overpriced. I knew the cost would strain Nathan's budget, so like a good dad I paid the bill. Several skinned knuckles later the car was purring, and we proudly showed it off to the girls. Nathan tried to thank me for footing the bill, so I put on my best gruff but lovable voice and said, "It wasn't for you. I can't have Jess driving home alone some dark winter night and stalling out on the side of the road." The high-voltage smile and hug I got from the bride-to-be told me I'd blundered into a great start to my relationship with my first daughter.

Lord, keep love at the center of all the relationships in our family, especially those who will join us through the years.
—ERIC FELLMAN

*EVERY THREE YEARS ONCE CAME THE SHIPS OF TARSHISH
BRINGING GOLD, AND SILVER . . . AND PEACOCKS. AND KING
SOLOMON PASSED ALL THE KINGS OF THE EARTH IN RICHES
AND WISDOM.* —II Chronicles 9:21-22

We have an abundance of Solomon's riches in our community
in the form of peacocks, and they can be an outright nuisance.
Like the time the children called from the driveway, "Mom,
come quick! He's so beautiful." Feathers spread out like an iridescent fan, the peacock was strutting and prancing. Then,
feathers flattened, he fiercely pecked at his reflection shining
from the passenger door of our car. He didn't like the competition of another bird in his territory. I didn't like the damage to
our car. I chased him. He chased me. He won!

On the other hand, the music of Beethoven, Mozart and
Tchaikovsky will never sound the same as when played under
the stars one memorable night in August. The maestro of the
California Philharmonic Orchestra raised his baton, and the
opening of the *Eroica* symphony had us spellbound. That's
when the peacocks joined in. From the trees where they
had perched for the night, they mewed and screeched in rau-
cous disharmony. They continued on during Mozart's Violin
Concerto no. 3. We in the audience loved it when the maestro
raised his baton to the treetops as though to cue them. Too bad
that when darkness fell and we came to *Capriccio Italien*, the
peacock obbligato diminished to a few muted mews.

Oh, the whimsy of creation! A conundrum, that a most
beautiful bird has a screeching awful voice and the modest little meadowlark thrills us with lilting song. How wondrous is
God's curious world.

*For soul-soaring music with peculiar twists, for picnics and
people, and all our fine pleasures, we praise You, O Lord.*
                                              —FAY ANGUS

BE SILENT BEFORE THE LORD GOD! . . .
                                    —*Zephaniah* 1:7 (RSV)

My sister Betsy stayed silent for an entire week when we were young. She was perhaps twenty years old, a student of spirituality. I was thirteen, a student of surliness. She announced that she would be silent for a week and then commenced to do so.

My parents were graceful about it. "Seems like there's more room in the house," said my dad.

"We should applaud this form of prayer," said my mom.

"Is this permanent?" said my brothers.

Eventually my sister spoke again—to yell at me, as I recall—but I never forgot that week. I was reminded of it recently when she emerged from a whole summer's silence at the monastery where she now lives. I asked her what her first words were when she emerged from her silent retreat, and she grinned and said, "Pass the butter," which I did, which made her laugh, because those actually were her first words after retreat.

"Is it hard to be silent?" I asked.

"In the beginning it is," she said. "Then it becomes a prayer."

This morning, thinking of my sister, I rise very early and sit silently over my reading, and men talk to me of silence. "All profound things and emotions of things are preceded and attended by Silence," says Herman Melville. "Silence is the general consecration of the universe." And Thomas Merton: "A man who loves God necessarily loves silence." And Jorge Luis Borges: "Absolute silence is the creative energy and intelligence of eternal being." And prickly, crusty, brave Job, who says to the Creator, "I put my finger to my lips . . . I will not answer again." And again Melville: "Silence is the only Voice of our God."

To which I can only say silently, *Amen.*

Dear Lord, let me sometimes sense and practice the extraordinary eloquence of silence. —BRIAN DOYLE

BUT HE SAID TO ME, "MY GRACE IS SUFFICIENT FOR YOU,
FOR MY POWER IS MADE PERFECT IN WEAKNESS." . . .
—II Corinthians 12:9 (NIV)

My friend Bill had just been diagnosed with a rapidly progressive form of cancer and lay in the hospital dying. "I'm off work tomorrow," I said to his wife Carole. "Could I sit up with you tonight?"

As a nurse, I knew that Bill could very well live for days, weeks even, so I mentally prepared for the long haul. *I'll offer to stay tomorrow night too,* I thought. *That will give Carole a chance to go home and get a good night's sleep and take a shower. And Tuesday, I'll bake some cookies for the grandkids. Thursday, I'll see if Carole will come to my house for a break.*

In all of my fretting, though, I neglected to tell Bill how much I loved him, how handsome he'd always looked in those V-neck sweaters and in that tuxedo at my wedding, and to thank him again for helping me move to my first apartment.

I had just changed into my pajamas that morning when I got a telephone call. Bill had passed away right after I left the hospital. The long haul had never happened. To this day I regret the things I never got to tell him.

Tomorrow, I've learned, always takes care of itself when I place it in God's hands. I don't need to rehearse every possible outcome, just simply rely on His sure and sufficient grace for the moment I'm in.

Thank You, Lord, for using the times when my plans go awry to turn me back to Your grace. —ROBERTA MESSNER

I WILL BE GLAD AND REJOICE IN THEE. . . . —*Psalm 9:2*

We couldn't have been more excited as we boarded the airplane at Boston's Logan Airport. A transatlantic flight, a connection in Paris and we'd be touching down in Italy. My wife Carol had been invited to a conference outside Venice, and the rest of the family had decided to tag along. Visions of cannoli, hot espresso and gondola rides danced in our heads.

We settled into our seats and waited for takeoff. And waited. And waited. Then a voice came over the intercom: "The flight has been delayed due to a mechanical problem. We should be ready for takeoff in half an hour."

Four hours later, we were still waiting. The kids looked ragged, the cabin was boiling hot and the passengers were grumbling, even shouting at the flight attendants. Carol took me aside. "This doesn't look good," she said. "We're not going to make our Paris connection, and that means I'll arrive too late to give my talk." She worried, too, about putting the kids through the ordeal of a long flight after such a delay.

Then the announcement came: The flight was canceled, the plane would be towed back to the departure gate, and passengers would have to rebook their flights the next day. After a brief consultation, we decided to cancel our trip and return home. Bitterly disappointed, we checked into an airport hotel.

The next day, we climbed into our rented car to head for the highway when Carol suggested that we spend the day in Boston; it had been a long while since we'd explored the city. So we visited the science museum, explored shops, even sipped espresso in a downtown café. It wasn't Italy, but it was a wonderful family outing, filled with joy—and the added gladness of knowing that such pleasures can be found close to home.

Thank You, Lord, for reminding me that happiness is a matter of spirit, not of place. —PHILIP ZALESKI

*WHAT MANNER OF MAN IS THIS, THAT EVEN THE WINDS
AND THE SEA OBEY HIM!* —*Matthew 8:27*

It was the middle of August and all week long I'd been complaining about the weather. Not because it was hot, but
because it wasn't. In fact, that very day we had broken a record
for cool temperatures that had been set back in 1903! So when
my sister Libby called from Florida late that night, I was all set
to complain some more.

But before I could she said, "We're having to evacuate. A
tropical storm and a hurricane are headed our way." I could
hear the tension in her voice. My sister had always hated
storms and now, as a full-time resident of Fort Myers, she was
facing these great forces of nature for the first time. "Our
mobile home is only two feet above sea level, so we're not sure
what we'll find when we get back."

"What did you pack to take with you?"

"Tax papers, medicines, Mother's handmade quilts, a few
pictures. It's interesting what you choose to squeeze into the
backseat." She laughed. "And, of course, the dog."

I assured her of our prayers; she promised to call from the
road. Suddenly, the blanket I had to add to our bed for warmth
hardly seemed worthy of notice.

Two days later, Libby and her husband were back in their
home. When she called to tell me that all was well, she asked,
"How's the weather there?"

I didn't even have to think about it. I pulled my sweater a little tighter and said, "Perfect. Just perfect."

*Oh, God, You are Lord of wind and wave—and unseasonable
temperatures. Help us to accept whatever comes our way with
fortitude and good cheer.* —MARY LOU CARNEY

THE RIGHTEOUS SHALL FLOURISH LIKE THE PALM TREE. . . .
THEY SHALL STILL BRING FORTH FRUIT IN OLD AGE. . . .
                                                    —Psalm 92:12, 14

My husband Tony and I bought an abandoned farmhouse about an hour away from where we live. The house needed a lot of work, but the yard was the true challenge. Years of neglect had left knee-high grass and dead trees covered in poison ivy.

For weeks we worked diligently on our weekends, collecting fallen limbs and raking seasons of dead grass. The lawn was just taking shape when our rider mower broke down. The acre of hills was nearly impossible to mow by hand, and we didn't have any money left to fix the mower.

A few weekends later, I drove to the farmhouse with our son Solomon. I was astonished to find that the lawn was completely mowed. *Tony must have gotten the rider mower working,* I thought. But when I looked down the hill, I saw the rider mower still sitting on the spot where it had broken down. Tony was just as puzzled when he arrived a few minutes later.

I spotted our neighbor washing his car and asked if he had seen anyone. "Oh," he said, "I've been meaning to thank you. It means a lot for Pop to mow your lawn."

His father had lost a leg to diabetes, but it didn't seem to have slowed him down. Cruising on his mower, he kept their five acres so beautifully maintained it resembled a golf course.

"Thank you!" I said. "And please thank your father."

"Don't mention it," he said. "Pop loves being able to help out. After watching your lawn fall apart for all those years, he gets such pleasure making it nice."

Our mower is fixed now, but it's sitting under a tarp in our barn. I don't think it'll be getting much use.

Thank You, Lord, for the people who give me a glimpse of Your goodness. —SABRA CIANCANELLI

BLESSED ARE THEY WHICH ARE CALLED UNTO THE
MARRIAGE SUPPER OF THE LAMB. . . . —Revelation 19:9

Beryl was in church today. I was surprised. Pete, our deacon, told me the other day that she was confined to her apartment. She's ninety-nine years old and frail. When he took communion to her, he said she just looked at the bread in her lap, wondering what to do with it. How would she act during communion this morning? She stared around the church as if she were seeing it for the first time, which is certainly not the case.

I hated to think of her getting old. She and her daughter Carmen have been bulwarks in the congregation ever since we joined twenty-five years ago. They were always so warm, welcoming our newborns, monitoring the boys' growth, celebrating their baptisms and confirmations, rejoicing in the milestones of our life. For years they have been the church's unofficial greeters.

Communion came. Beryl rose unsteadily. She was in the second row. The whole congregation was focused on her. Carmen took her hand, and they walked slowly to the front. Beryl paused, confused. Carmen didn't even have to look around. Another woman was right behind. She offered an elbow, and Beryl took it. All at once, Beryl seemed like a bride in a wedding, confident of where she was and what she was doing.

She took the bread and dipped it in the cup. She smiled. She returned ever so slowly to her seat.

"Send us out in the world in peace," we prayed, "and grant us strength and courage to love and serve You." I was glad I wasn't going out into that world alone. In Christ, I would be with Beryl and she would be with me.

We are never lost when we are with You, Lord.

                                                —RICK HAMLIN

*AND TO KNOW THE LOVE OF CHRIST, WHICH PASSETH
KNOWLEDGE, THAT YE MIGHT BE FILLED WITH ALL THE
FULNESS OF GOD.* —*Ephesians 3:19*

When I was a child, we lived down a dusty dirt road from my
paternal grandmother. I loved going to her house to sit with her
under the shady pecan trees as she shelled peas or prepared
fresh corn from her garden. I was always barefoot, and on
scorching summer days I'd hop along on the high spots where
the sand was thinner and the heat less intense. Finally, I'd reach
the shade of Grandmother's big yard and cool my feet on the
green grass.

My grandmother was not a demonstrative person, and at
my young age I sometimes wondered whether she really loved
me. But then Grandmother would produce a dime from some
unseen pocket and my heart would leap. That was my cue to
walk to the neighborhood store to buy a soda for both of us.
The sand was still unforgiving, but the thought of the cold
drink on my parched tongue would have taken me across
hot coals. Grandmother may not have smothered me with
kisses, but that cold soda on a hot summer day showed that
she loved me.

There are times in my life when I feel that God's love is not
so evident either, and I wish He would smother me with kisses.
But then, just as the heat of the situation seems intolerable, I
spot the proverbial dime: It may be a Scripture or a magnificent
sunset or a wise word from a friend. Then I know that all I
have to do is wait on Him and trust in His love. It never fails.
That assurance makes the trip up the hot, dusty road of life
worth every bold step.

*Father, grant that I may recognize Your love for me, especially
in the small things that often go unnoticed.* —LIBBIE ADAMS

THEN THE WATERS HAD OVERWHELMED US. . . .
                                                    —*Psalm 124:4*

I'm in the midst of what I call "convergence," a kind of storm of stressful things all happening at once. "Troubles come in threes," the old-timers used to say, and I'd add, "sometimes in sevens."

My wife and I have been building a new home. Nothing I have done in all my sixty-one years has tried my patience like working with contractors, bad weather, discontinued products and hundreds of on-the-spot decisions. Now the moving-in process has begun, with all its frustration. Meanwhile, I'm trying to meet deadlines and prepare for school, which starts in fourteen days. With a doubled enrollment, it will be more chaotic than ever. And today the phone rang with the worst news of all: my brother calling to tell me that my father has only a few days to live.

I don't think there's any conspiracy about these storms. They happen for the same reason that everyone in the grocery store comes to the checkout stand at the same time—they just do. Perhaps it's best that we just get all the stress over at once.

As painful as these storms are, I think they draw out hidden strengths in us. I heard about a musician who had been bedridden for many years, but when his house caught on fire, he got up, still dressed in his underwear, and managed to drag out the piano and two music cabinets.

No one escapes these storms of convergence, but the Psalmist goes on to remind me that, "Blessed be the Lord, who hath not given us as a prey to their teeth." The Psalmist adds, "Our help is in the name of the Lord, who made heaven and earth" (Psalm 124:6, 8).

I'm counting on that.

I'm sorry, Lord. I'm so distracted I can't pray a sensible prayer; so I turn this chaos over to You. —DANIEL SCHANTZ

Be honest in your estimate of yourselves, measuring your value by how much faith God has given you.
—*Romans 12:3 (NLT)*

"I want that," declared Sophia, my two-year-old granddaughter. She had chosen a pluot, a reddish-colored sweet fruit that is a cross between a plum and an apricot.

We were at French Market Produce, a wonderful open-air seafood and produce market in Mandeville, Louisiana. Tables were piled high with dark green seedless watermelons, pink-skinned nectarines, oversized, sweet Vidalia onions and jars of local honey. Large green ferns hung from the rafters. And wafting throughout the market was the pungent aroma of boiled seafood.

We bought our pluot and walked over to a bench next to the snowball stand. Sophia took a bite, the sweet juice running down her chin. Minutes later an elderly gentleman sipping a spearmint snowball sat down beside us.

"Whew," he said. "Shopping with my daughter and her boys gets a bit hectic. Those boys go a mile a minute."

"I know what you mean."

"I was going to buy them snowballs. It's something I remember my pop and me doing every Sunday afternoon in the summertime." He shook his head. "But those boys have better things to do."

"Don't sell yourself short," I said. "We're important to our grandchildren, even if they're too young or too busy to know it. Some of my fondest memories are of my grandmother. I remember her helping me get dressed on chilly winter mornings in front of our fireplace. One Christmas she ate all my homemade cookies that my brother and sisters wouldn't eat." I pulled Sophia onto my lap and kissed her forehead.

The gentleman stood up to leave.

"Time to go?" I asked.

He winked at us. "I'll be right back. I know a couple of boys who might just love a snowball."

Lord of the young and old, help me to see the value in my relationships with others, especially my grandchildren.
—Melody Bonnette

*"IN EVERY WAY AND EVERYWHERE WE ACCEPT THIS WITH
ALL GRATITUDE."* —Acts 24:3 (RSV)

Last summer, Shirley and I took our clan—kids and mates and
grandkids, nine of us all told—on a weeklong excursion to
England. For the young'uns, it was their first trip there, so we
made all the important stops: Buckingham Palace, the British
Museum, the Tower of London, Stonehenge and Shakespeare's
birthplace, Stratford-upon-Avon, where we saw a powerful performance of *King Lear*. The play lasted nearly four hours, so it
was an endurance test for some of us, but its message about
ungratefulness came through loud and clear.

In the play the aging Lear divides his kingdom among his
three daughters, two of whom prove to be less than devoted:
"How sharper than a serpent's tooth it is to have a thankless
child," he says. It's Shakespearean tragedy par excellence. By
final curtain the bad guys and gals have all gotten their come-
uppance, and there are bodies lying everywhere.

Ungratefulness is always ungracious and reprehensible. In
the story of Jesus healing ten lepers, only one of those healed
returned to thank Him for the miracle. I wonder, *Would I have
been one of the nine who failed to acknowledge His gift?* In
our daily lives we can never express our thanks too often to
those who help us, befriend us, love us, or to the One Who has
given us life and sustains it.

> *God, prompt me when I become distracted and
>   forget
> That giving thanks is more than proper etiquette.*
>   —FRED BAUER

DO GOOD . . . HOPING FOR NOTHING. . . . —Luke 6:35

Just home from the office, my husband walked into the kitchen with a big smile on his face.

"What's up?" I asked.

"The funniest thing happened to Barb today," David answered. "She stopped for a quick lunch at a fast-food restaurant, and while she was in the drive-through waiting for her turn to pay, the girl at the window said, 'The lady in front of you just paid for your lunch. She said to tell you to have a good day!' You can't imagine how happy that made Barb."

The more I thought of Barb's adventure, the more it reminded me of God's grace: a gift utterly undeserved, joy undeserved, blessings undeserved. An idea ripened in my mind.

"I've got a great idea," I told David after dinner, my face brimming with mischief. "Why don't we go out for a quick ice cream?" His eyes lit up.

In the drive-through, David explained our mission to the cashier. "We want to pay for the people behind us," he said.

"Are you sure? It's fourteen dollars and two cents."

"I'm sure," David answered, handing her a twenty.

We felt like pulling into a parking place and enjoying the surprise, but we knew instinctively that watching would somehow break the spell. Grace is best when you aren't expecting anything back. But as we pulled out of the parking lot and onto the street, we started to laugh. We laughed all the way home.

Oh, Father, the sheer joy of sharing Your grace is all I need. Thank You. —PAM KIDD

SO HE WENT DOWN AND DIPPED HIMSELF SEVEN TIMES IN
THE JORDAN . . . AND HIS FLESH WAS RESTORED LIKE THE
FLESH OF A LITTLE CHILD, AND HE WAS CLEAN.
　　　　　　　　　　　　　　　—*II Kings 5:14 (NAS)*

A few years ago I experienced clinical depression. Before then
I'd been strong and dependable, the kind of person people
turned to for help. I'd prided myself on my self-sufficiency. That
horrible year my mother visited almost daily to check on me. I
hated her coming and I hated her leaving.

Today I found a notation she made in my Bible. She wrote,
"For Julie, August 26, 1994." Mom prayed for my immediate
healing and noted her prayer right next to God's command to
Naaman the leper to be dipped in the Jordan River seven times.

I desperately wanted my healing to happen on the very day
she prayed. That way I'd never have to tell anyone. I could
maintain my image: Julie, the strong one. I just knew God
would fix me instantly, like Naaman. But that wasn't God's plan
at all. The opposite happened: I got worse, much worse. I
stopped sleeping and eating, and cried most days.

On November 11, 1994, I finally saw a doctor. The doctor
prescribed an antidepressant, and I saw a counselor. I wasn't
healed my way, in secret or quickly. Very slowly, God directed
me to seek help from others. In His perfect way, He dipped
me in the Jordan River seven times and healed me.

Oh, Father, thank You for Your healing! You restored me from
my point of complete brokenness at just the right time and
not one day sooner. —JULIE GARMON

*"UNLESS YOU CHANGE AND BECOME LIKE LITTLE CHILDREN,
YOU WILL NEVER ENTER THE KINGDOM OF HEAVEN."*
—*Matthew 18:3 (NIV)*

Donna and Dan are caretakers of a cabin in La Plata Canyon, a steep-sided sliver of forested land that winds between two high Colorado mountain ridges. Recently they invited my wife and me and a few other friends to the cabin for supper. We left our hot desert home in the late afternoon and arrived in the blessedly cool canyon less than an hour later. Donna brought one of her "kids," whose name is Barbara. Donna's kids are developmentally disabled adults whom no one else seems to have time for.

The sun set behind the west ridge, and it was dark by the time we finished eating. The stars shining through the partially open canopy of aspen trees cast the only light around the cabin. I wish I could tell you that it's impossible to gossip in such a natural cathedral, but our conversation proved otherwise.

We talked about a family most of us felt had wronged us. While I was waiting for an opening in the conversation for some disparaging remarks of my own, I heard Barbara mumbling to herself. "I'm having a wonderful time," she said. "I just love it here. Thank You, God. I'm having a wonderful time. I just love it here." She said this prayer over and over, until it was all I could hear. One by one, everyone turned to listen to her.

I think we were all grateful for the darkness at that moment; shame is better shared in darkness. We'd been talking to one another out of spitefulness. Barbara had been talking with love to her God.

Dear God, may my words to others always be prayers to You.
                                                              —TIM WILLIAMS

"IT WAS NOT YOU WHO SENT ME HERE, BUT GOD. . . ."
                                        —*Genesis 45:8* (NAS)

"I'd been picking the wild grapes from those vines along the veranda, but before I made jelly from them I thought I'd stretch out on the sofa for a short nap," my elderly mother explained as she recalled the details of that day on the phone. I could just see her on the old maroon sofa, slippers kicked off, glasses folded on the paper stand, purple grape juice staining her bib apron.

"I don't know how long I slept," she went on, "but when I really woke up I was already halfway across the street on my way to Helen's house." Helen was another senior who lived kitty-corner to Mom in the little village. Helen had lived alone since her husband was hospitalized. "I felt so foolish," Mom continued. "I was wearing my slippers and apron, and I didn't even have my glasses on. I thought for a minute I should go back home and change, but something told me I was needed."

Helen invited her in. Just as they were about to enjoy a cup of tea together, Helen's phone rang. "Hello? Yes, this is Helen speaking. No, I'm not alone. A neighbor just dropped by unexpectedly."

As Mom watched, Helen suddenly sat down, her face ashen. Replacing the receiver with trembling hands, she looked at Mom with tear-filled eyes. "That was the hospital calling. My husband just passed away."

Suddenly Mom knew why she had come and Who had urged her on.

Lord, help me to follow through faithfully on Your nudges.
                                        —ALMA BARKMAN

I HAVE CALLED DAILY UPON THEE, I HAVE STRETCHED OUT MY HANDS UNTO THEE. —*Psalm 88:9*

Stark terror. That's what I felt on this sunshiny morning as I tramped on the North Carolina beach. I shaded my eyes and looked out at what long-ago sailors had dubbed Cape Fear. Its ferocious currents had made it a graveyard of ships.

Battling my own private shipwreck, I walked to a spit of land by the swirling ocean. I sat in the shade of a dune and pulled a sandy, soggy, year-old note from my jeans pocket. "Keep your chin up. We're praying for you," it said. A few weeks before that note arrived, my husband and I had separated. After thirty-one years, I was on my own, with no job, no career, no confidence. The note, signed by several friends, had been a lifeline. Many readings had left it creased and coffee-stained.

I hadn't sunk: I'd gotten a job, and I was paying my bills. Best of all, Whitney and I had gone into counseling, and our marriage was mending. Soon I would move back home. But on this morning, on Cape Fear, the good news was washed away by terror. I stared, trembling, at the ocean crashing on rocks. My toes curled into the sand as if looking for something solid to grip. "Life is so uncertain," I whispered. "Who knows what our future will be?"

A gust of sea air rattled the paper in my hand. I read it again and again, until its truth stilled my fear. *The real lifeline is not in the note,* I thought. *It's tied around me in unbreakable cords of prayer.* I reached for that lifeline and felt a tug from the One Whose hold on me is as certain as the ocean's on the sand. The fear left.

Lord, thank You for the lifeline of prayer. Help me use it to reach out to others. —SHARI SMYTH

*LET EACH ONE DO JUST AS HE HAS PURPOSED IN HIS
HEART; NOT GRUDGINGLY OR UNDER COMPULSION; FOR
GOD LOVES A CHEERFUL GIVER. —II Corinthians 9:7 (NAS)*

A few days ago I attended a Bible study taught by my friend
Todd Still, a New Testament scholar as fluent in Greek as he is
in English. As we read from Paul's letters to the church in
Corinth, we focused on the familiar phrase "God loves a cheerful giver."

"The most literal translation," Todd said, "is 'God loves a
hilarious giver.' *Cheerful* is the most common translation. But
that word is mild. The most literal interpretation of the Greek
adjective is *hilarious*. And that word is extreme."

I jotted down this bit of knowledge in my notebook and
quickly forgot about it. A few weeks later I received a letter
reminding me that the pledge I'd made to a worthy cause was
due. The day before I had paid my son's college fees and
expenses, and when I consulted my checkbook, I discovered
that I was almost broke.

Suddenly I recalled Todd saying, "God loves a hilarious
giver." Sitting down at my desk, I wrote the check. And then I
began to laugh. I laughed at myself, old grouch and tightwad
that I am. I laughed at the smallness of the check amidst the
immensity of God's love and provision. I laughed from a joy
that can only come from giving "not grudgingly or under compulsion," but out of a hilarious and ridiculous freedom.

*God, bless me with the laughter that only comes from giving.
Amen.* —SCOTT WALKER

"I HAVE SET MY RAINBOW IN THE CLOUDS, AND IT WILL BE
THE SIGN OF THE COVENANT BETWEEN ME AND THE EARTH."
                                                    —*Genesis 9:13 (NIV)*

This past summer we moved our family to a small central
Florida town. Although my husband and I grew up in south
Florida, we felt it was time to get away from the city and live a
simpler, quieter life in the country.

One month after moving into our lovely new home,
Hurricane Charley arrived with eighty-mile-per-hour winds.
When we went outside to survey the damage, we saw not one
but two rainbows in the sky. They were so lovely that I took a
photograph of them to put in my daily journal, under which I
wrote, "God sends extra reassurance today." Of course, we had
no idea that Charley was only the first of three hurricanes that
would strike us over the next four weeks.

A terrible month followed, during which our home sustained more damage, and we lived for weeks without electricity or running water. Whenever I felt as if I couldn't endure
another minute, I'd look at the photo of those two rainbows.
They reminded me of the presence of God in my life, and
knowing I was not alone gave me the strength I needed to
keep going.

Heavenly Father, thank You for comforting me and guiding
me through every storm. —REBECCA KELLY

FOR THY STEADFAST LOVE IS BEFORE MY EYES. . . .
                                            —*Psalm 26:3* (RSV)

The morning news was filled with tragedies, arthritis pain had
kept me awake all night, and I was feeling that the universe
was a pretty unfriendly place. That's when God reminded me
of an eleven-year-old girl who had felt the same way.

I was that girl, and I didn't have a single friend in ballet
class. When we did a *pas de deux*, everyone seemed to have
chosen a partner already and I'd have to do the routine alone.
Between lessons we were supposed to get together in smaller
groups to practice, but every group was full when I tried to
join. After the Christmas show, I dropped out.

It was nearly two years later that I became friends with one
of the girls from that class. "We all used to think you were so
stuck up," Ann said as we walked home from school one day.
"You'd never wave or smile back."

"What do you mean?" I said.

"I mean you'd be all friendly with me one day and the next
you'd walk right by as though you didn't see me."

As though you didn't see . . .

It was a light going on in the dark place where I'd kept the
hurt and rejection. I was twelve when my poor eyesight had at
last been detected, glasses had been prescribed and a bright
sharp world had come into focus.

Before, people had smiled at me and I hadn't seen!

The memory of that walk with Ann leapt across the years.
Do I seem uncaring? God said. *Come closer and look again.*

*Faithful Lord, remind me that when I cannot see Your smile,
it is my sight and not Your love that is limited.*
                                            —ELIZABETH SHERRILL

OBSERVE THE COMMANDS OF THE LORD YOUR GOD,
WALKING IN HIS WAYS AND REVERING HIM.
—*Deuteronomy 8:6 (NIV)*

Last Saturday my brother Nat walked twenty miles. Last Saturday I walked one mile. While he's conquering the Appalachian Trail section by section, I'm conquering my own mountains and valleys, one step at a time.

I used to walk every day until a few years ago, when my weight caught up with my lower back and sent me limping home after a quarter of a mile. My walks became fewer and further between. I prayed for the Lord's way out of both the weight and the pain. This spring I learned of an exercise program just for women, downloaded its calorie/exercise counting program from the Internet and finally gathered up my courage to start the training, signing up for a year in advance to enhance my determination. The first month I gained a pound and a half. "Muscle!" they said.

Now I'm five months and maybe one-fifth of the way to my goal. Last Saturday, for the first time, I went up to our community park cinder track, took a deep breath and stepped out. In twenty-five minutes I had walked a mile—yes, there were aches, but the back held up. Now it's been seven miles, one step, one day, one mile, one "praise You, Lord!" at a time. As my brother strides north through New England, I plod diligently around the track, each of us walking in the Lord's place for us.

Today, Lord, I ask You to show me Your pathway to or out of _____. —ROBERTA ROGERS
    (FILL IN THE BLANK)

LISTEN, MY BELOVED BRETHREN. HAS NOT GOD CHOSEN THOSE WHO ARE POOR IN THE WORLD TO BE RICH IN FAITH AND HEIRS OF THE KINGDOM WHICH HE HAS PROMISED TO THOSE WHO LOVE HIM? —James 2:5 (RSV)

Each year my husband Larry and I drive a thousand miles to attend the Orr family reunion, which is held at the Ozark Prairie Presbyterian Church outside Mt. Vernon, Missouri. This small brick church was built by Larry's impoverished but stalwart Scots-Irish ancestors after they immigrated to America from northern Ireland in the early 1870s. The church is a replica of the one the family left behind in Aghadowey and has been in use ever since it was built.

Each reunion begins the same way. Everybody stands and sings, "Faith of our fathers, living still in spite of dungeon, fire and sword. Oh, how our hearts beat high with joy whene'er we hear that glorious word!"

My heart beats stronger, too, as I share those words with the family members who carried their faith across the ocean to America so long ago and have now passed it down through six generations.

Faith. What an inheritance to give one's family!

Father, today I will share my faith with someone who may not know the promises of Your Word. —MADGE HARRAH

REMEMBERING WITHOUT CEASING YOUR WORK OF FAITH, AND LABOUR OF LOVE. . . . —I Thessalonians 1:3

It was fall 1999. I was a few weeks into my brand-new job at Guideposts when Celeste, the editor in the office next to mine, motioned me to follow her into the big meeting room where Prayer Fellowship happens every Monday morning. "It's a surprise party for Sidney," Celeste explained as we stepped into the meeting room, which turned out to be packed with the rest of the staff.

I didn't know much about Sidney Fields, but I'd heard in passing that he was Guideposts' oldest editor, both in terms of years at the magazine and years on earth. In fact, it turned out that this party was to celebrate two events: Sidney's fiftieth year at Guideposts and his ninetieth birthday.

A moment later, Sidney came through the door and was greeted with a rousing "Surprise!" Watching as he received hugs and congratulations from one person after another, I tried to fathom what it must be like to enjoy the place you work at so much that you stay there for half a century. Up to that time, I'd never worked in one place for more than a year or two.

Later, when the party was over and everyone was back at work, I happened to find myself standing next to Sidney at the sink in the men's room.

"This must be a pretty good place to work," I said.

Sidney turned, looked me up and down, and gave me a smile. "Stick around," he said, "you'll find out."

I did, and I have.

Thank You, Lord, for the work You've given me to do, and for the people who've helped me to do it. —PTOLEMY TOMPKINS

"AS THE BRANCH CANNOT BEAR FRUIT BY ITSELF, UNLESS IT ABIDES IN THE VINE, NEITHER CAN YOU, UNLESS YOU ABIDE IN ME." —John 15:4 (RSV)

My daughter Lindsay is into the minimalist look, especially when it comes to decorating. Her home in San Diego has a clean, spacious look. In the living room with its large comfy couch and two chairs, I'm able to appreciate the few pictures and accents in sight.

I have too much stuff everywhere. My closet is full of clothes I rarely wear. My office area is filled with knickknacks that distract me when I work. Even my computer screen shows I have seventy-three e-mail messages to delete. Lindsay looks at my cluttered countertops and bookshelves, and suggests I put at least half of it away. "Less is more," she keeps telling me.

My soul has been overstuffed too. In the morning I skim random Scriptures in my Bible. At night I gulp down short sections from the stack of inspirational books by my bed. So I'm trying the minimalist look, starting from the inside out. I focus on a single Scripture, marinating in its meaning and application until it tenderizes me at a deeper place. For the last couple of weeks my verse has been about "abiding in the vine" from John 15, a word-picture that becomes more powerful the more I repeat it and walk around inside it. Less is more, so this is my prayer:

Lord, as I take in a bit less, please deepen me more.
                                                    —CAROL KUYKENDALL

I PRAYED FOR THIS CHILD. . . . —I Samuel 1:27

When my sister teased me on the phone the other day that I was always our mother's favorite, I was prepared to deny it, as usual. Yes, I was the baby of the family. And, yes, I came along late in my mother's life. Her "surprise," she liked to say. Still, I always thought my siblings made too big a deal of it. And after so much time, I would think they'd be tired of teasing me. I mean, we're all adults now.

Besides, parents may love their children differently but never one more than another. "Oh no," my sister always says, "you were the apple of her eye!"

Was that really true? My sister and I have talked about it a lot, and when we get serious, she always says that without me my mother would never have survived the death of my brother Bobby, the second youngest child, four years my senior. "You know, when Bobby died, if Mom hadn't had another little boy to love, I don't know what she would have done. You were her godsend."

My sister is right: My mother probably gave me enough love for two kids. In fact, maybe that's just what she was trying to do.

Father, You make a gift of us to others. Thank You for letting me be the little boy my mother needed to love twice as much.
                                                        —EDWARD GRINNAN

THE LORD HEAR THEE IN THE DAY OF TROUBLE . . . SEND
THEE HELP FROM THE SANCTUARY, AND STRENGTHEN THEE
OUT OF ZION. —Psalm 20:1-2

In the early 1970s, my husband Norman and I were visiting friends when we saw a household item that interested us. Our friends told us the name of the store where they'd bought it. "And by the way," they said, "ask for Mr. Benton, the young man who sold it to us. He was very helpful."

A day or two later, Norman and I stopped by the store. Mr. Benton was out to lunch, and Norman told the salesperson that we'd come back later. When he asked us why, Norman said that Mr. Benton had been recommended to us. "Besides, I feel I should see *him* for some reason."

Later in the afternoon, we went back to the little shop. Mr. Benton was at the warehouse. Again, Norman decided we'd come back later.

Two days later, Norman went back again. This time he found Mr. Benton in his office. Norman introduced himself and told him that some friends had sent him.

"I know who you are, Dr. Peale, but your friends didn't send you here," he said.

"They didn't?"

"No," said Mr. Benton. "God sent you. I planned to kill myself last weekend. Then I decided to wait one more week—this week—and ask God one more time to send me help. And here you are."

Norman got up and closed the office door. "Tell me about it," he said to the young man.

Mr. Benton poured out a tragic story about his involvement with his best friend's wife, who had committed suicide.

Norman was able to offer a measure of peace to the troubled young man and eventually helped him start to rebuild his shattered life.

Was it just a coincidence? Mr. Benton didn't think so. I didn't either.

Thank You, Lord, that when I call to You for help, You answer by sending it. —RUTH STAFFORD PEALE

*THERE IS NEITHER JEW NOR GREEK, THERE IS NEITHER
SLAVE NOR FREE, THERE IS NEITHER MALE NOR FEMALE;
FOR YOU ARE ALL ONE IN CHRIST JESUS.*
—*Galatians 3:28 (RSV)*

Our oldest son turned eighteen and voted for the first time last fall. Moreover, he's named political science as his college major and has set his sights on Washington, D.C.

I have some very mixed feelings about sending my only son into the rough-and-tumble world of American politics. Republicans, Democrats: to me, the climate of politics seems increasingly hostile. And yet I'm reassured by the memory that one of my most important political insights came courtesy of that same young man, back in second grade.

Mark's school class was typical of many public schools today: widely diverse in ethnicity, economic status and academic ability. Children of doctors studied at desks adjacent to children of migrant farm workers. Some were reading at a fifth-grade level, others barely at all. Nearly half the class came or went that year. And the behavior of some of the kids created racial tensions in our community.

I asked Mark about all of it the day he reported that one of his classmates wouldn't be in school anymore because the boy's mother had been arrested for selling drugs. Mark's response: Not everyone has had the same opportunities. But everyone should have the same respect because God created each one of us.

Mark won't change the climate of American politics—at least, not overnight. But his understanding is a good lesson for all of us.

Is it true, God, that what we hold in common—Your image within us—is stronger than our differences? Thanks be to You.
—JEFF JAPINGA

BEAR WITH EACH OTHER AND FORGIVE WHATEVER
GRIEVANCES YOU MAY HAVE AGAINST ONE ANOTHER.
FORGIVE AS THE LORD FORGAVE YOU.
                                        —*Colossians 3:13* (NIV)

One of my favorite fall events is the annual used-book fair
hosted by our local museum on the weekend after Labor Day.
This past year, when my stack of treasures grew too tall to
carry and shop at the same time, I took the books outside to the
checkout counter. "They should be safe over here," one of
the volunteers suggested as she motioned to a spot behind the
long table where she was working.

But when I returned twenty minutes later, my books
were nowhere to be found. A country decorating tome by
Mary Emmerling—gone. Another decorating guide by Lynette
Jennings—also gone. Also missing was the sequel to a novel
I'd just finished reading as well as Guideposts classics I'd long
looked forward to adding to my collection.

It was then that my scowl turned into a smile. *Just wait
until those people discover the books by Catherine Marshall
and Marjorie Holmes and those old* Daily Guideposts, I
thought wryly. *Why, they just might change their lives!* And
right then and there I prayed: "Bless the people who have my
books, Lord. Draw them close to You and help them to apply
the concepts in those books to their lives.

"And yes, Lord, could we make this praying-for-the-people-
I'm-angry-with thing a lifelong habit?"

*You knew long before me, Lord, that when I pray for someone
I'm angry with, two of us receive a blessing*
                                        —ROBERTA MESSNER

FOR NOW WE SEE THROUGH A GLASS, DARKLY; BUT THEN FACE TO FACE: NOW I KNOW IN PART; BUT THEN SHALL I KNOW EVEN AS ALSO I AM KNOWN. —I Corinthians 13:12

Grandma Johnson was a tiny, energetic woman with a truck-load of determination. Every member of the Johnson clan has stories to tell of her feistiness. My father talks about how his mother came to New York City, alone, in the early 1920s to earn a Master of Fine Arts degree. My mother saw Grandma's single-minded drive when she came home one day to find Grandma intently painting the inside of some dresser drawers, oblivious to the three young children she was supposed to be looking after. My own memories of Grandma's visits include the time she took over my high school swim team's annual dinner, unperturbed by the fact that she was a complete stranger and that others had already planned the event. Strong-willed, determined, controlling—whatever you wanted to call her— Grandma Johnson was a force to be reckoned with.

Then while I was in college, Grandma became quite sick. She needed full-time care, so my parents moved her halfway across the country to live with them. She was in her eighties, and no one expected a full recovery. But her health slowly returned, and as it did, Grandma's arresting eyes mellowed into a softer, warmer blue. Her commanding arm now reached out primarily to clasp a hand gently in her own. She was gentler, sweeter, a pleasure to be with. It was as if her illness had released her from her need to be in charge, and the effect was transforming.

Surely there had been love there all along, yet something had obscured it. Perhaps our own prickly reactions to her had made us incapable of seeing it.

Dear Lord, thank You for grandparents, in all their wonderful, human and sometimes frustrating complexity.

—JULIA ATTAWAY

AND FEAR NOT THEM WHICH KILL THE BODY, BUT ARE NOT
ABLE TO KILL THE SOUL. . . . —Matthew 10:28

I am visiting a high-school class, and they want to talk about
September 11, as every class of students I've ever visited wants
eventually to talk about September 11, no matter what else
we've talked about or are supposed to talk about.

After a while I tell them of the men I knew who died that
day in the South Tower, their bodies sent aloft as white ash to
be breathed in all over New York City: Farrell Lynch and Sean
Lynch and Tommy Crotty.

Suddenly I'm weeping and shouting, "They murdered my
friend Tommy Crotty, and his wife is a widow and his daughters
are unfathered! They murdered my friend Tommy, but they cannot kill the hymn of him, they cannot kill who he is! They cannot kill his smile and verve and spirit and soul, the Tommy
Crottyness of that man! There was only the one ever before
and only the one ever to be, just like you, just like every one of
you! There is only the one you, and your body will eventually
fail and dissolve and melt, but you will not! No one can kill
the you of you, do you see?

"Do you see the miracle here? Do you see how your birth
utterly defeats your death? Tell me you do, tell me your hope
and faith and love will defeat the murderers, tell me you will
sculpt a better world for my children after I am dust and ash!"

Dear Lord, give me strength to fight for grace under duress.
Please. I beg You. And then bring me home to Your stunning
brilliant towers. But not yet. —BRIAN DOYLE

HE WHO HAS EARS TO HEAR, LET HIM HEAR.
—Matthew 11:15 (RSV)

Of the five senses God gave us, His gift of being able to hear seems to trigger most of my memories. I think of things like:

The distinctive shrill whistle of the Rock Island train—headlight urgently flashing—as it roared past our place in a symphony of sound. The swaying cars *clatter-clattering* on metal rails, the smokestack making a staccato *phuff-phuffing*, the mammoth engine plaintively *chuch-chuch-chuching* into the distance.

The *whump whump* of a carpet beater when my mother dangled and then whacked rugs over a clothesline to dislodge dirt during her twice-a-year house cleanings.

The *pawk-pawk-puh-dock* from the chicken house when a hen was bragging about having deposited a fresh egg—a day's work for her.

The hypnotic *ticktock tick* of the parlor's dignified mantel clock. Counting its sonorous *bong. . . . bong*, I could tell the time without looking.

The rhythmic *squeak-squeak* of the porch swing. It was nearly drowned out by the nightly drone of the locusts' *zoo-ree, zoo-rees* or the chatter of passers-by who simply dropped by on hot summer evenings without calling ahead.

And then there are sounds I can still hear today, but only in near silence: faint *rustles* of cottonwoods startled by a breeze, *plips* of surfacing fish, contented *eep eeps* of baby birds nestled for the night.

It makes me wonder if one of the reasons Jesus spent time alone was so that He could rest surrounded by the solacing sounds He couldn't detect in the midst of a noisy crowd.

It's hard to hear still small voices—including Yours, precious Lord—when bedlam abounds. Show me a corner where I can bask in luxurious quietness. —ISABEL WOLSELEY

I UNDERSTAND MORE THAN THE ANCIENTS, BECAUSE I KEEP YOUR PRECEPTS. —*Psalm 119:100 (NKJV)*

The label on my chainsaw says, "Do not attempt to stop chain with hands." Just one more silly product-warning label. Like the one on an iron: "Do not iron clothes while they are being worn." Or the sleeping pills that warn, "May cause drowsiness." Then there's the sunshield for the car that says, "Do not drive with sunshield in place." And the warning on a wheelbarrow: "Not for highway use."

Doubtless these warnings are there to protect their makers from lawsuits, but I suspect many of them are based on long experience with lunatic customers. Someone probably did try to finger-brake a chainsaw or push someone down the highway in a wheelbarrow. Impatient drivers probably have left the sunshield in place and peeked over it. And I have no doubt that some "Odd Couple" bachelor has tried to iron his shirt while wearing it.

To modern ears many of the laws of God probably sound just as silly as those warning labels. "Do not swear," "Do not steal" and "Do not commit adultery" seem like sensible requests to me, but not to everyone. Not anymore.

But I'm grateful to a heavenly Father Who anticipated what lunatics people can be and gave certain behaviors a strong warning label.

Thank You, Lord, for the warnings along the way.
                                        —DANIEL SCHANTZ

*"BECAUSE YOU ARE PRECIOUS IN MY EYES, AND HONORED,
AND I LOVE YOU. . . ."* —Isaiah 43:4 (RSV)

It was time to say good-bye to my little granddaughter Hannah.
Our far-flung family had gathered for a rare reunion. Now
Hannah was continuing on to visit her other set of grandparents. As she waited in her car seat in the rented van, I leaned in
and said, "You have lots of fun with Grandma Patti."

Hannah was quiet for a moment. I could tell she was thinking hard about something; perhaps she was visualizing the special things she and her other grandmother would do. Then she
looked at me intently, and in her no-frills four-year-old style she
said, "But I will still love you." Hannah's heart held a space for
me no matter who else was there.

I've thought about Hannah's words a lot since then. They
remind me of the way God loves me. He has billions of people
to attend to, but He still loves me. He sees all my failures and
mistakes, but He still loves me. He knows my every thought and
doubt, but He still loves me. And I have the sure sign of His love
for me in the shape of the Cross on which His Son died.

*Lord, in all the times and places of my life, Your love never
leaves me.* —CAROL KNAPP

YE SHALL BE COMFORTED. . . . —Ezekiel 14:22

I am a lackadaisical knitter. I enjoy knitting, but I don't follow through. A search of my craft basket would show four half-finished scarves, one sleeve for a sweater, and two booties that would be a pair if they weren't different colors and sizes. When my nephews were born, I began knitting a soft woolen blanket for each of them. They're starting school next week and I still haven't finished their blankets.

Over iced tea one day, I told all this to my friend Nina. "And to make matters worse," I said, "everyone around me seems to be knitting and crocheting all the time."

Nina shrugged. "So? Everyone has different talents. Maybe knitting isn't yours."

"But it seems so easy! I read about a woman who donates over a hundred hand-knitted sweaters to charity every year!"

"Linda," she persisted, "I once read a saying I like: 'To compare is to despair.'"

It was true. I was always comparing myself to others and always coming up short. Maybe my slow knitting wasn't the problem.

"Besides, if you must compare yourself, compare yourself to me! By the time I finished my nephew's baby quilt, he was in school."

"Oh really?" I asked, feeling somewhat better.

"Really," she said. "And, Linda, the school was Brooklyn College!"

We burst out laughing, and I vowed to stop looking at everything in life as a race or a test. Have I been successful at this? Yes—in my own way, at my own time, at my own pace.

Thank You, God, for the comforting and healing power of laughter. —LINDA NEUKRUG

GOD SETTETH THE SOLITARY IN FAMILIES. . . . —Psalm 68:6

Socks, shorts, T-shirts, jeans, khakis.

A lot of T-shirts in Tim's pile. Twice as many as usual. I guess that means soccer season has started. All those practices after school mean one more dirty shirt a day. He loves soccer, but he's been worried about doing well on the team. The stakes are getting higher now that he's in high school. I want him still to enjoy playing. I pray that competitiveness doesn't get rid of the fun.

Will's socks. I can never match the socks right. Will's grown so tall and his feet are so long they look like flippers. He used to be able to wear my shoes, but he's outgrown my size. So why can't I tell his socks apart from mine? I have a pile of socks, and I'm just going to have to put them in pairs and hope they find the right drawers. He's almost an adult, but when I look at his socks I remember the tiny booties he once wore. God willing, he won't lose his childlike wonder as he grows into manhood.

Carol's bandanas. I think my wife uses them at the gym. Funny, I've never asked. I usually fold them into quarters so they can fit into a pocket like a handkerchief. They come in beautiful colors: turquoise, lemon, raspberry. And there's the one that has the map of nearby hiking trails on it. Reminds me of the spring day that we took one of those trails and hiked to the top of a mountain. We need to do that again.

Eventually everything's sorted and folded. Laundry is done. Sure, it's a chore, but when I do it, I'm reminded of what I love about the ones I love.

Lord, within this chore there's something to be thankful for.
—RICK HAMLIN

SING AND MAKE MUSIC IN YOUR HEART TO THE LORD,
ALWAYS GIVING THANKS TO GOD THE FATHER FOR
EVERYTHING. . . . —Ephesians 5:19-20 (NIV)

I love the old hymns, and I'd looked forward to singing them in church on Sunday morning—or at least part of them, usually the first, third and last verses. But recently a new worship leader took over the music part of our services. And now when we sing a hymn, we sing it all. Even if it has five verses! And you know what? I've found a wealth of sound theology and lyrical language in those formerly unsung verses.

I think of those slighted stanzas whenever I'm tempted to shortcut other things in my life. To skim those professional journals I promised my boss I'd read. To "only stay a minute" when I visit my neighbor in the hospital. To *always* pick up the store-bought apple pie instead of baking one using Mother's recipe. "Anything worth doing is worth doing well," she used to say, often with flour on her hands. She was right: worth doing well—and completely.

Father, help me sing with enthusiasm all the verses of this life You've chosen for me. —MARY LOU CARNEY

FOR THE LORD IS A SUN AND SHIELD. . . .
—Psalm 84:11 (NAS)

My husband Rick and I are building a log house in the woods. It's been a long time coming. We started thinking about it twenty-five years ago, even before we were married.

As soon as we put the FOR SALE sign in the front yard of our current house, I started writing daily lists for Rick. I had a plan, the best plan, the logical way things should happen.

Last night, we visited our home-in-progress. I like to go every few days, so I'll be surprised with the changes. Normally, I use these visits to keep Rick on task. But last night a different line of thought nagged at me. *Why don't you try not to ask any questions this time? Don't ask him if he scheduled a framing inspection. Don't ask how soon he can plant grass. Don't ask if he's ordered the wood-burning stove. Trust. Be quiet.* As we walked around, I let go just a little and didn't prod.

We drove off in the September sunset. Without talking, I reached over and laced my fingers through Rick's as we looked at the orange-pink glow of the disappearing sun.

"God did a pretty good job of the sunset tonight, didn't he?" I said. And the thought came: *Even without my help.*

Father, You created the sun and the entire universe. Surely, You can orchestrate the details of my life too.

—JULIE GARMON

BE KINDLY AFFECTIONED ONE TO ANOTHER. . . .
                                      —Romans 12:10

As a college freshman it was clear to me and everyone else that I wasn't cool. I had nothing in common with the blonde Redskin Beauties or the trim, polished girls in Angel Flight. I was too tall, and my hair was ironing-board straight. I snorted when I laughed, tripped over curbs and looked like a giraffe when I tried to squeeze into an MG. On rainy days I actually wore red overshoes.

Maybe that's why my cousin Tuffy took me aside to give me tips on the social graces. Tuffy was smooth, and he exuded a genuine charm that made him popular with people of all ages. Four of his lessons have served me well the past forty years. They are:

1. How to allow a gentleman to help with my coat. *(Don't struggle, don't try to twist yourself into it, keep your arms low.)*
2. How to walk downstairs without looking at my feet. *(Put your heel against the back of each stair. You'll look elegant and you won't fall.)*
3. How to dance without heavy breathing. *(Take small, shallow breaths through your nose, not your mouth.)*
4. How to be kind to the people I meet. *(Smile, listen, help if you can, and remember that Jesus loves them just as He loves you.)*

If you're a clumsy kid, a not-so-cool teenager or a slightly unpolished adult, take heart—and take some advice from a grandma who still wears red overshoes. Don't neglect the social graces, but make lesson number four your top priority. It's the ultimate secret to deep-down, genuine charm.

Thank You, Lord, for cousins and other people who've taught me essential life lessons. —PENNEY SCHWAB

STRAIT IS THE GATE, AND NARROW IS THE WAY, WHICH LEADETH UNTO LIFE. . . . —Matthew 7:14

I hurried across the plaza at Rockefeller Center. I was late, late enough not to notice the beautiful weather. As I ran up the steps at the side of the famous skating rink, I stopped dead in my tracks.

Above me was a slender silver column reaching up to the sky at a seventy-five-degree angle to the earth. It glittered in the sunlight. And walking up the steep silver slope were seven life-size figures.

For a minute I was confused. The figures weren't a troupe of acrobats; they were part of a daring and eye-catching sculpture. *Who are they?* I wondered. *Where are they going? Who created this amazing sight?*

"Excuse me," I said to a security guard leaning against the wall, "but could you tell me what that is?" I pointed to the sculpture.

"Yes, lady," he said. "That's 'Walking to the Sky.' Put up just the other day."

"What is it doing there?" I asked.

"I dunno. Sometimes they put things up here," he replied.

What "they" had put up there was a hundred-foot-tall sculpture, the work of Jonathan Borofsky, an artist from Maine, on temporary display in the plaza as part of a public arts program.

One of the life-sized figures was a woman wearing a red skirt that looked as if it were blowing in the wind. She and her six companions seemed to be climbing that mysterious path upward to heaven itself. The sun was shining and I wanted to be climbing with them.

Lord, we are all making life's climb together. Help us to keep our feet on the narrow beam. —BRIGITTE WEEKS

"The Lord himself goes before you and will be with you. . . . Do not be afraid. . . ."
—*Deuteronomy 31:8 (NIV)*

Late in the baseball season a couple of years ago, I ran across the story of Jackie Mitchell, "the girl who struck out Babe Ruth." Jackie was seventeen years old in 1931 when, signed to a minor-league baseball contract with the Chattanooga Lookouts, she struck out Ruth and Lou Gehrig in an exhibition game. Prior to the game, many fans said Jackie couldn't possibly handle such legendary hitters. But that didn't stop her. Determined to use the physical gifts God had given her, Mitchell faced her fears and succeeded, continuing to play exhibition games in an all-male sport for several years.

That story inspires me now because I'm facing something I'm not sure I can do. I was asked to teach Sunday school at the Spanish-speaking mission church begun by our congregation. I agreed to assist another teacher in a class of fourth- through sixth-graders, but then the leader called, desperate—she had no one to teach the two- to four-year-olds. *By myself, with the youngest kids? That's not exactly my strength. And they don't speak English.*

I wanted to say no. What was I getting into? Then I remembered feeling the same fear years before when my daughter had asked me to teach her Sunday school class. Yet God had given me the tools to succeed. Now, as then, I feel Him saying, "Trust Me. I will be faithful to you." So, like Jackie Mitchell, I'm ignoring all the reasons why I can't do it, stepping on the mound and giving it a shot. I'll let you know how it goes.

Give me what I need, Lord, to do this job right for You.

—Gina Bridgeman

BLESSED ARE THEY THAT DO HIS COMMANDMENTS, THAT THEY MAY HAVE RIGHT TO THE TREE OF LIFE, AND MAY ENTER IN THROUGH THE GATES INTO THE CITY.
—*Revelation 22:14*

I was in a small Botswana island camp called Jacana in the water plain of Okavango. It was September, early spring in southern Africa, and the waters had yet to recede; about two feet remained among the reeds, papyrus and lilies that grew everywhere. Travel was by *mokoro*, a canoe-like boat with a flat bottom. It held only two people and a native guide who stood and propelled it, gondola-style, with a long pole forked at one end.

One morning five of us and three guides set out, our binoculars ready as ever for anything that luck would bring. Godfrey, my guide, glided the mokoro through the water soundlessly. We pulled ashore on an island. "You will like this especially," he said, "for its Three Sisters."

I was unaware of what he meant until I trudged up through the sandy footing. "What a strange sight," I said. The Three Sisters had merged into one enormous tree, a baobab, not very high, but hugely fat. Its bark was gray and smooth, and its leafless branches were disproportionately spindly, as if they did not belong to the same tree. It was, I thought, ugly.

"This tree is four thousand years old," Godfrey said.

"And it's still alive," I marveled. I was standing before something that was already old in the time of Jesus. I wanted to touch it, to feel its texture, but I wasn't able to do so, for suddenly an elephant came laggardly through the brush and we hastily retreated to our boats.

But, Father, I was, and am, closer to You because of that baobab tree. —Van Varner

MAKE A JOYFUL NOISE UNTO THE LORD. . . . —*Psalm 98:4*

At services, my *havurah*—a kind of extended family—always tries to sit together. We are six couples who have shared holidays, life-cycle events and just plain fun for years now. We enjoy sharing the services, too, though not everyone can attend every time.

One Shabbat (the Jewish sabbath), most of my *havurah* was not in attendance. Only two other wives sat with me, one on either side. When the singing started, I raised my voice high. I love singing in the synagogue. Somehow the prayers seem richer to me when I can lift my voice in praise. But this particular Shabbat it was quickly obvious that neither of my two companions could carry a tune. Their off-key singing drowned me out.

I looked at my friend on the left. She smiled. My friend on the right gave my hand a squeeze. I love these women dearly. To pray between two people I cared for so much was a gift. Joy overwhelmed me, and I forgot how we sounded, for our prayers were rich. Deep friendship and companionship have a harmony all their own.

Thank You, God, for showing me that making a joyful noise to You means more than just singing on key.

—RHODA BLECKER

AS ONE WHOM HIS MOTHER COMFORTETH, SO WILL I COMFORT YOU. . . . —Isaiah 66:13

"Mom, this is Paul. Cheryl is in intensive care in critical condition!" My son's voice broke. Paul's wife, mother of their eight children, had been ill only a short time. She was forty-five years old. Just last Monday, she had been put on the liver transplant list. It was now Thursday. Barely able to get the words out, Paul sobbed, "Mom, I don't know what I'd do without Cheryl!"

My husband Robert and I threw a few necessities into a suitcase, cancelled some appointments, and began the four hundred-mile trip to Kearney, Nebraska. By the time we arrived, Cheryl had died.

Family members were gathering at the home of their oldest son Matt and his wife Brian. With tears in my eyes, I hugged Paul and each of the children and then sat down by my son. As he told me of the events of the night before, Paul shared with me something I'll hold in my heart always. While he was in the intensive care room with Cheryl, the nurse shined a light into her eyes as Paul held her hand and said, "There's no response and all of her vital signs have stopped. I'm sorry. She's gone." In the next moment, Paul felt Cheryl squeeze his hand. The doctor came in, checked her and confirmed the nurse's conclusion.

I can't explain what happened. Perhaps the nurse was wrong, but Paul and I choose to believe Cheryl was saying good-bye and letting him know that *all is well*. It was her last gift to her husband, one that will comfort him through his great loss.

O Holy Spirit, thank You for comforting us in our grief.
—MARILYN MORGAN KING

AND A LITTLE CHILD SHALL LEAD THEM. —Isaiah 11:6

Everyone was stunned by my daughter-in-law Cheryl's death. How could this happen? How could her husband Paul and their eight children bear such wrenching grief? How would Paul manage, with four children still at home, ages fourteen, nine, seven and five? He was working long hours, and the four grown children were living on their own, with full-time jobs. There were no easy answers and so many hard decisions that no one had ever expected to make.

Robert and I went with Paul, Cheryl's brother Steve, and Amy (age fourteen) to the mortuary to help make arrangements. Together, we chose a casket and time and place for the funeral. We talked with the minister, chose Scriptures, music and a poem, and arranged for Cheryl to be buried next to her mother.

In the afternoon, my daughter Karen and the older children went to buy a new dress for Cheryl and picked out a pretty cross pendant with lavender stones to match.

While they were gone, five-year-old Kayla sat down by me and started telling me about the school supplies her mother had bought for her. My heart ached for my granddaughter, who was starting kindergarten next week without her mother. And I thought, *Kayla doesn't fully realize the terrible thing that has happened.*

Then her soft blue eyes looked up into mine and she said, "You know, Grandma, I won't see Mommy anymore because she died. But she still loves me, and she can see me from heaven." In that moment, some tight place in me was released, and I hugged Kayla and affirmed that what she had said was true. By the grace of God and with the help of a child's pure faith, I trust that Paul's family will make it through this tragedy.

O Holy Spirit, grant us faith to bear our grief.

—MARILYN MORGAN KING

*AND YOU, THAT WERE SOMETIME ALIENATED . . . IN YOUR
MIND . . . YET NOW HATH HE RECONCILED.* —Colossians 1:21

Twenty-one years ago, my two sons Paul and John had a falling
out that has kept them at odds ever since, despite the efforts of
family members and professional counseling. This has been the
greatest sadness of my life. At family get-togethers my sons
were civil to each other, but the deep brotherly closeness they
had once shared was lost.

When Paul's wife Cheryl died, John called me and said, "Do
you think it would be all right if I came to the funeral? I'd really
like to be there for Paul." I was touched, though a bit uneasy for
fear Paul might not accept John's desire to reconcile. But I said
he should come nevertheless.

Now, Paul and Cheryl's brother Steve had suggested five
friends for pallbearers and wondered who might be the sixth.
When I told Paul about John's call, he responded enthusiasti-
cally, "I'd love to see John! Can he be a pallbearer?"

John arrived, and Paul thanked him for coming. Then a miracle happened. Each apologized to the other for the events that
had caused their long-standing alienation. They accepted each
other's forgiveness and hugged and wiped the tears from their
eyes. I cried too—tears of joy and thanksgiving. My sons were
brothers again!

*Thank You, God of love, for Your healing grace, even in the
midst of tragedy.* —MARILYN MORGAN KING

*BEHOLD, I SEND AN ANGEL BEFORE THEE, TO KEEP THEE
IN THE WAY. . . . —Exodus 23:20*

Two days after my daughter-in-law Cheryl's funeral, my daughter Karen and I went with my son Paul and the children to their school open houses to meet their teachers and help them get oriented. After that, the family sat down together and each of the older ones offered to take over some special responsibility of their mother.

Dawn, the older sister, offered to take the younger children to school each morning. Karen would pick them up and take them to Dawn, who would take care of them until Paul got off work. Matt (the oldest of the eight) and his wife Briean offered to keep the children while Paul worked on weekends to make enough income to cover the family's expenses. Others volunteered for household jobs, and in this way, arrangements were made for the family. Karen, my son John and his wife Tasha went shopping for some new school clothes for the younger children.

By the time my husband Robert and I were on the road back to Colorado, the ache in my heart was beginning to lift. I could see that Paul and his family would manage.

But a couple of weeks later, Karen called and told me she was worried about fourteen-year-old Amy, who was depressed, refused to eat and wouldn't talk about her feelings at all. But when my daughter went over to Paul's house the next evening, Amy gave her a picture she had made in school. It showed a girl reaching upward through an open window. In the sky outside was an angel reaching toward the girl. In the angel's hand was the cross pendant with the lavender stones that Karen and the children had chosen for Cheryl. Then Amy pointed to the angel and said, "That's my mom."

I know it will be hard for Amy, but I pray that when a teenager can express her feelings in her own way, she has a head start on healing her heart.

My trust is in You, Holy One, to watch over all children, especially those who are grieving. —MARILYN MORGAN KING

"LO, I AM WITH YOU ALWAYS. . . ." —*Matthew 28:20* (RSV)

Today is my daughter-in-law Cheryl's birthday. She would have been forty-six. I'm sitting in my home office trying to focus on my writing, but I can't help worrying about my son Paul and the children. It will be a hard day for them.

I called my daughter Karen. I suggested that she get helium balloons for Paul and all the children and let them release them at the cemetery, wishing their mother a happy birthday.

The next day I received an e-mail from Karen, who had done that and much more. She had brought magic markers, and each child wrote something or drew a picture for Cheryl on one of the balloons and then they released them all together. Next they opened the presents Karen had brought for them. She had looked through all of her pictures and found one of Paul with Cheryl and one of each child alone with Cheryl, enlarged and framed them, and gift-wrapped them. For each of the seven households, she also framed a five-by-seven enlargement of Cheryl and printed in calligraphy the words *I am with you always*. In addition, Briean had brought everyone pinwheels that lit up in the dark, and they placed them all around the grave. Then Joe, nine, gathered white rocks and formed the letters MOM. The other children arranged stones into hearts.

What a healing way to celebrate the life of this young mother who dearly loved them all.

Lord, You know my tears and my joys. Help me to celebrate the lives of my loved ones who have come home to You.

—MARILYN MORGAN KING

COMFORT YE, COMFORT YE MY PEOPLE, SAITH YOUR GOD.
—*Isaiah 40:1*

Recently, on the evening news, my husband Robert and I watched mothers outside a school, crying for their children who had been held hostage by terrorists. I wept for those mothers and for what we humans have become.

But just this morning, I received some heartwarming news in an e-mail from my daughter Karen. A caring family "adopted" my son Paul and his now-motherless family as part of the program Adopt-a-Family. They bought new clothes and shoes for the four children who are still at home, three boxes of groceries for the family, and an envelope full of fast-food gift certificates. They also paid for the children to attend an after-school enrichment program.

I cried as I read Karen's e-mail, but these tears were not like those I shed when I watched the news. No, these were the tears of a mother's heart deeply moved by the generosity and caring and deep-down goodness of human beings. Though the adopting family chose to remain anonymous, the children wrote thank-you notes and Karen enclosed pictures of them opening these much-needed gifts. Those who manage Adopt-a-Family will forward the notes.

You were right, little Kayla. Your mother still loves you and watches over you. And to your "second family": Whoever you are, wherever you live, I pray that you'll know this. Tonight there is a grandmother in a small village in Colorado whose faith in the goodness of human nature has been restored by your caring hearts.

Creator of us all, thank You for creating the golden-hearted people. —MARILYN MORGAN KING

O LORD OUR LORD, HOW EXCELLENT IS THY NAME IN ALL THE EARTH! . . . —Psalm 8:1

During my seventy-three years, I've experienced the deaths of many loved ones. Every time that has happened, I've noticed that, along with the grieving, I receive a precious gift—a renewed appreciation of life. I begin to notice things that I would normally take for granted. Many ordinary moments catch my attention, like the first yellow crocus breaking through the snow to say hello to spring.

Last week a friend and I had a creekside lunch at a nearby restaurant. As we were having dessert, we noticed a tiny ladybug crawling across the table. Suddenly, we were immersed in a moment of great wonder as we watched her whimsical little body stop and carefully examine the crumb of chocolate cake I had placed in front of her. After opening and closing her little wings a couple of times as if preparing for takeoff, she tucked them back in again. She had decided to stay awhile. We continued to watch as she made her way across the table, not knowing where she was going, not needing to know. When we left the restaurant, I felt a deep gladness and gratitude for this moment of great wonder and for life itself. And I wondered why I often tend to neglect the jewels of this very life, exactly as it is with all of its grief and ordinariness and enchantment.

I want to look for one thing each day that gives me a sense of childlike wonder, and when evening comes, I'll write it in my journal in memory of my daughter-in-law Cheryl and give thanks to our Maker for this amazing gift of creation—and for the even greater glory that awaits.

O Great Creator, may I see Your hand today in something ordinary and amazing. —MARILYN MORGAN KING

*BE YE THEREFORE MERCIFUL, AS YOUR FATHER ALSO IS
MERCIFUL.* —Luke 6:36

First Communion was a big deal to me. For years I'd coveted
the lovely little glasses of grape juice and the bites of bread that
passed by each time the Lord's Supper was observed. But in my
old home church Communion was forbidden to children until
they became official members, baptized and blessed. Now,
at twelve, I'd finally met all the requirements and my big day
had come.

The anticipation almost took my breath away as the tray
drew nearer to the pew I shared with my father. Then, at
long last, I was reaching into the shimmering honeycomb of
Communion glasses, my hand searching for the fullest one.
Sitting there, waiting for the minister to give the go-ahead, I
gazed down into the glass . . . and promptly spilled the grape
juice down the front of my Sunday dress.

I was horrified at the mess I'd made, embarrassed, humili-
ated. Then I felt my daddy's big hand fold over mine. When he
lifted his hand, I found myself holding his glass. I brought it to
my lips and drank.

Daddy might have raised his eyebrows in rebuke or
given me a whispered scolding. Instead, he made my First
Communion a shining moment of grace.

*Heavenly Father, let me be mindful of the precious gift of Your
grace and alive to the possibility of sharing it with others.*

—PAM KIDD

WHAT TIME I AM AFRAID, I WILL TRUST IN THEE.
                                                              —Psalm 56:3

What were the chances of our friend Dan's phoning the very day we learned that our son had to undergo surgery? We'd had a warm but brief relationship with Dan Montgomery years earlier; it had been a decade and more since there'd been any communication at all between us.

But here was his voice, cheerful and caring, and because I know that Dan is a psychologist with long experience counseling people in crisis, I poured out my anxiety. We lived so far away from our son, we had so few details, I could get no answer either on his home phone or at the office—

"Walk right now to the wall nearest your phone," Dan broke into this outburst.

Surprised and puzzled, I took a couple of steps to the wall next to my desk.

"Stand a foot or so out from the wall," the instructions continued. "Now lean against it. Be far enough away that if the wall weren't there you'd fall."

I moved out from the wall, then let my weight rest against it.

"Now," Dan said, "relax your muscles. Let the feeling of trusting the wall spread all through you. Feel how effortlessly the wall upholds you. See how you can rest, even while you yourself are off balance."

It was true. Leaning on the wall, I gradually released the tension in my shoulders . . . my arms . . . my stomach. . . .

"In a time of crisis," Dan said, "we can learn to lean on God the way you're leaning on that wall. It's when we learn the difference between believing in God and trusting Him."

Two good gifts came with that phone call: a reminder to lean on God through the anxious days of our son's surgery and slow recovery and, for any time, a faith-builder that's as close as the nearest wall.

Faithful Lord, let me notice walls today—and remember that the walls of Your city stand forever. —ELIZABETH SHERRILL

BLESSED ARE YE THAT WEEP NOW: FOR YE SHALL LAUGH.
                                        —*Luke 6:21*

My wife Carol was almost in tears when she came in from the garage, where our washer and dryer are.

"What is it, honey?" I asked.

"Look," she said, holding out our cell phone. "It must have fallen into the laundry basket. It went through the wash!"

There was another reason that she felt so upset. Six months earlier she had taken our previous cell phone along to her women's Bible study. When she returned home, she ran into the house. "Something's sizzling in my tote bag!" she said.

It was our cell phone. Carol's water bottle had somehow leaked, frying the cell phone's circuitry. I wasn't too upset because I'd hoped to upgrade to one of the newer flip phones.

But this time was different. We had both enjoyed the new phone.

"You've drowned another phone!" I exclaimed.

"Can you ever forgive me?" she asked.

Before I could say anything more, I began to laugh. Soon Carol was laughing too.

"Honey, don't worry. Of course I forgive you," I said. "I'll just go down to the store in the morning and see if I can get another one like it."

Not only did I replace the phone the next day, I got one that was even better.

Father, thank You for the gift of laughter that helps me put things in their proper perspective. —HAROLD HOSTETLER

THE END OF A MATTER IS BETTER THAN ITS BEGINNING,
AND PATIENCE IS BETTER THAN PRIDE.

—*Ecclesiastes 7:8* (NIV)

The barking woke me. I rolled over and tried to go back to sleep, but the open window made it impossible. Pulling the curtain, I looked down. Our neighbor Patty struggled on the sidewalk with two dogs, leashes taut in her hands.

"I might as well get up," I said to myself, shaking my head at our luck. Our neighbor seemed to have adopted two large, loud mutts. *Maybe she's just babysitting*, I hoped. *Maybe it's just for the weekend.*

When I went outside later to get the mail, I noticed Patty filling her bird feeders.

"Those sure are some dogs," I said, crossing the street.

Patty rolled her eyes. "It's going to take a few months before they're settled."

"Months?" I tried to hide my displeasure. "So they're yours?"

"The brown one spent eighteen months at the shelter. He got a home, but then the people took him back, so he spent another twelve months there. The other one was brought to the shelter with all kinds of problems. I asked for the worst cases, the ones no one would take."

"No one but you," I said.

She nodded and sighed.

For the rest of the summer, when the barking woke me, I reminded myself that patience was the least I could give to the cause. Eventually I learned to ignore it.

Just as the leaves were beginning to turn shades of maroon, I happened to look out the window and saw Patty and her dogs. It was the first time I'd seen them without hearing them first, and I couldn't get over the transformation. No longer tense and scared, the dogs pranced quietly, proudly, their heads high and straight as if they were escorting a queen.

Lord, help me to put up with little annoyances for the sake of a greater good. —SABRA CIANCANELLI

IN HIS HEART A MAN PLANS HIS COURSE, BUT THE LORD DETERMINES HIS STEPS. —*Proverbs 16:9 (NIV)*

This was a bet I was going to win. My brother and I, both teenagers who had never had a steady girlfriend, made an agreement: Whichever of us had a steady girlfriend first would get to watch the other perform one hundred push-ups all in a row without stopping.

Since I was away at college when we made the pact, my brother wasn't aware that there was a girl at school with whom I'd been spending a lot of time. I figured that when I went home for the summer, my brother would be in for a tough workout. My plan fell apart when this girl told me she was in love with a two-hundred-pound varsity football player. Needless to say, I was back to square one in the competition with my brother.

A few weeks later he called. "Guess what?" he said.

I didn't really need to guess. I could tell from the tone of his voice.

"What?"

"I have a girlfriend."

"Bummer. Er, well . . . I mean congratulations."

I should have known better than to make a bet with my brother, but I'm the kind of person who likes to think that he has the future mapped out. Unfortunately, something always changes, and then I'm upset that my plans were not God's plans.

So these days I try to hold loosely to my goals and accept God's timing for my future. When something unexpected happens, I try to trust Him.

As for as the push-ups, I'm still in training. Yesterday I did eighty.

Lord, let me trust You. —JOSHUA SUNDQUIST

WHATEVER IS TRUE, WHATEVER IS NOBLE, WHATEVER IS RIGHT, WHATEVER IS PURE, WHATEVER IS LOVELY, WHATEVER IS ADMIRABLE—IF ANYTHING IS EXCELLENT OR PRAISEWORTHY—THINK ABOUT SUCH THINGS.

—Philippians 4:8 (NIV)

My day was overbooked and hours ahead of me before it began. Company was coming: Rooms had to be decluttered and cleaned; menus had to be planned; grocery shopping done. Then I remembered, *Oh no! I have to take Mom out today for a picnic. I promised. That's a minimum three-hour project, and there's no other day this week to do it. But I've got to get the piles off the dining area table, and I've got to get to the grocery store, and I've got to. . . .*

Tension was building, energy was draining, and I was headed for the rocks. "Whoa!" I said. (I talk to myself sometimes.) "Girl, stop a minute. Look around you. Think. You have friends coming. Wonderful friends. You love this house that's big enough to handle company easily, and you love how it looks when it's cleaned up. You like to provide food and fellowship for people, and you can do it without straining your budget.

"Moreover, you prayed for years for a chance to make a friend of your mother. And getting out of the assisted-care place makes her so happy. Girl, your life isn't full of *got-to*'s, it's full of *get-to*'s!"

Lord, I hear You! I get to clean and cook and take out my mom still! I get to practice joyful hospitality! I get to be changed! Thank You! —ROBERTA ROGERS

*"I WILL SETTLE THEM IN THEIR HOMES," DECLARES THE
LORD. —Hosea 11:11 (NIV)*

My wife Rosie and I attended a house dedication outside of
Mendenhall, Mississippi. A lady called Mama Buckley had built
a new house after a fire had burned down her old one. I wondered why she'd gone to all the trouble at her age when she
could easily have moved in with one of her children.

Mama Buckley greeted us with a big hug, her eyes filled
with excitement. She insisted on giving us the grand tour. She
showed off her bedroom closet; this was the first time in her
life that she'd had one to hang her clothes in. Now she had
closet space for towels, too, and carpet on the floor, and a room
where she could wash and iron. Insurance money had covered
the materials and, with the help of her children and their
friends as well as volunteers from church, she was able to have
the house built without going into debt.

At age eighty-seven, Mama Buckley still believes that God is
faithful. She'll live in her new earthly home with joy until God
takes her to her eternal home in heaven. What a great way to
enjoy the blessings of God!

*Lord, help me understand that no matter how old I am, I can
still trust in Your faithfulness.* —DOLPHUS WEARY

HE WHO TENDS A FIG TREE WILL EAT ITS FRUIT. . . .
—*Proverbs 27:18 (NIV)*

The last time Dad had been to church he had driven his car and walked into the service on his own. This time we pushed him in a wheelchair after a difficult recovery from stomach surgery.

We headed straight for Dad's customary place in the sanctuary —a special bench in a small alcove near one of the side doors. Dad had helped put the bench there seven years earlier when my mother needed a wheelchair after a stroke. Now Mom was gone, and it was Dad in the wheelchair and me beside him on the bench.

When I picked up the hymnal, I worried that Dad might not be able to read it. But as I handed him the book, I was surprised to discover that it was a large-print edition. As Dad's voice joined with mine in song, thankfulness came over me for the unknown person who had put it there.

I felt the solid bench underneath me. Dad's years of faithfulness to Mom during her disability had become the means through which God, in turn, showed His faithfulness to Dad. Dad had been there Sunday after Sunday, making the bench a comfortable place for the disabled to worship with their families, never guessing that someday he would need it himself.

I suppose that's the way it is with those who faithfully serve and give. They never guess the ways in which their acts of kindness will be returned to them in their own time of need.

Dear Father, thank You that our small acts of faithfulness have a way of returning to us. —KAREN BARBER

"'FOR I KNOW THE PLANS THAT I HAVE FOR YOU,'
DECLARES THE LORD. . . ." —*Jeremiah 29:11* (NAS)

My husband Gene and I had to stay over for two nights after a
conference in Montrose, Pennsylvania, in order to get reason-
ably priced flights home. "What will we do?" I wailed. "Everybody's gone now."

"Maybe God has special plans just for us," Gene said.

"Like what?" I asked, arms folded. "We don't even have
a car."

"Want to walk uptown?"

When I was growing up in Elberton, Georgia, my friends
and I walked "uptown" to the square almost every day. But I
hadn't done such a thing in almost fifty years.

As we approached the tiny town nestled in the hills, I felt as
though we had walked into a Grandma Moses painting. The
two-story Victorian houses we strolled by had beautifully manicured lawns, huge ancient trees and neat picket fences. At the
Montrose Country Store, Gene rocked in a chair by the door
while I browsed inside. Across the street at a pet store, four little kittens followed us around. We enjoyed lunch at a sidewalk
café and ordered double-scoop ice cream cones, finishing them
off while walking around the square. As we walked back to
the conference ground, Gene reached for my hand.

That night we were the only people in camp. A soft rain
became a lullaby; after it stopped, we listened to the crickets
and frogs. There was no television, not even a radio. We weren't
expecting any phone calls. "Why don't I read to you?" Gene
asked.

"Okay."

Gene picked up his Bible and read several Psalms. The gentle rain started again and I drifted off to sleep anticipating
tomorrow.

*Oh, Father, when will I learn to trust Your lovely plans for
me?* —MARION BOND WEST

LEAD ME IN THY TRUTH, AND TEACH ME. . . . —Psalm 25:5

"Will you do the devotional at tomorrow's staff meeting?" my boss asked me nonchalantly one morning.

"Sure," I answered, trying to sound equally nonchalant. But, actually, I dreaded the responsibility of doing a devotional. I work in the main office of MOPS International, which is a ministry to mothers of pre-schoolers around the world. At least twenty-two people attend our regular staff meetings, and many know the Bible better than I do. How would they respond?

I went home that afternoon and prepared a devotional using the word *kairos*, which I'd stumbled upon in the last week. It's a Greek word that means "a decisive point in time when something eternal happens." It is used in the New Testament to mark those *Aha!* moments when God breaks into the mundane and does something that sparks deeper faith in the person experiencing that moment—like the moment in church the last week when I was singing "Amazing Grace" and suddenly the familiar words struck me in a whole new way.

The next morning as I took my place at the table in the staff meeting, I felt the twinge of dread descending again. "Do you know the meaning of *kairos*?" I quietly asked one of the seminary graduates sitting next to me.

"It's one of the toughest words in the whole Greek language to define," she said.

"Oh, swell," I said. Somehow I got through the devotional, feeling inadequate and self-conscious. But for the rest of the day, in the halls and lunch area, I heard people talking about their *kairos* moments. Obviously, I shouldn't have worried so much about the responsibility of doing a devotional. Sure, I was responsible for the preparation, but as far as the listeners' ability to respond, that's God's responsibility.

Aha! A *kairos* moment for me.

Father, when I have the opportunity to do a devotional or talk to others about You, help me to know the difference between Your responsibility and mine. —CAROL KUYKENDALL

JERUSALEM REMEMBERS IN THE DAYS OF HER AFFLICTION . . .
ALL THE PRECIOUS THINGS THAT WERE HERS FROM DAYS OF
OLD. . . . —Lamentations 1:7 (RSV)

Note to my daughter's social studies teacher:

Dear Ms. Hoffman,

Please excuse Hope's essay on the Whiskey Rebellion, which did not happen in 1066. Sorry. I told her it did. Age has gnawed away the meat of my memory, leaving tiny crumbs that are ferried about by even tinier ants that struggle to carry things ten times their weight. Anyway, it was the Norman Conquest that happened in 1066. I also remember Norman Lear, Norman Bates and Norm Cash, who once batted .361 for the Detroit Tigers, in case you're curious.

My brain is now a rucksack of randomness. I remember phone numbers that begin with letters, the engine size of my first car, German nouns in the dative case.

Then again, some of the arbitrary things I do remember seem worthwhile: my mother reading *Wynken, Blynken and Nod*, wetting her finger as she turned each page. I remember the smell of a ginkgo seed I stepped on during my first day of college. I can almost feel the weight of the three-legged cat that slept on my chest. I remember Hope's first steps—she had footed pajamas and a toothless grin, arms like Frankenstein, falling forward into Sandee's lap. I remember as if it were yesterday.

So, Ms. Hoffman, I admit I can't remember why those crazy folks in my hometown of western Pennsylvania rebelled. But it doesn't mean my memory is faulty, just selective. If I miss a date or two, so be it—as long as it's not a date with my daughter, so I can tell her all about ginkgoes, Frankenstein and Norm Cash.

Sincerely, Mr. Collins

Lord, thank You for the memories that weave my life together.
—MARK COLLINS

JESUS OFTEN WITHDREW TO LONELY PLACES AND PRAYED.
—Luke 5:16 (NIV)

Little Stephen has a bad cold. His nose is stuffed, he coughs himself awake when he finally gets to sleep, and from the way he swallows, I'm guessing he has a sore throat. The poor little guy is miserable.

I'm miserable, too, of course. Not just because I'm an empathetic mommy, but because when Stephen doesn't sleep, I don't either. When he's sick, Stephen wants to be held constantly. He cries a lot. He can't entertain himself. He won't eat. After forty-eight hours of nonstop fussiness, I'm worn to a frazzle. I'm desperate to escape and have a little time to myself.

Perhaps this is why I feel a particular kinship with Jesus when He goes off to a lonely place to pray. I know that desire for solitude. After a hard day's work I want quiet in which to recover and draw strength from God. Often I don't get it. The crowd tracks me down, just as it did with Jesus.

I've sometimes wished that Christ at least grumbled when the crowd showed up, so I'd be justified in grumbling when Stephen clings to me, crying, while I'm trying to get supper in the oven. But after ten years tending to the needs of my little ones, I think I'm beginning to get an inkling of how Jesus kept going. It wasn't that He ignored His need for quiet time. It was that He knew the healing loneliness of self-sacrifice. When He had to, He was able to find spiritual refreshment in *that* lonely place too.

When I think I've reached my limits, Lord, show me how I've limited the ways Your love can nourish and sustain me.
—JULIA ATTAWAY

CEASE FROM ANGER, AND FORSAKE WRATH. . . .
—Psalm 37:8

Although he's usually the sweetest, most affable guy on earth, my husband Charlie does have a temper. You don't want to be around when his BlackBerry wireless handset is on the fritz. And he can't bear certain noises—barking dogs, large beeping vehicles and pounding music.

Last fall we rented the bottom half of a two-story cottage on the bay near San Francisco. Everything was perfect. The cottage was charming, the water was sparkling, the seals were playful. And then the upstairs tenant came home.

Within moments, the whole place was shaking with a series of tuneless, booming vibrations. First came the muttering. Next came the pacing. Then before I could say a word, Charlie shot out the door and raced up the steps to the second floor. I wondered how long it would take me to pack up everything again.

Five minutes later Charlie was back downstairs. "The guy upstairs mixes movie tracks," he said, smiling happily. "He's got a whole studio up there! And he invited us to a *Lord of the Rings* party he's having for a bunch of friends. They're going to screen all three movies!" Humming to himself, he went to enter the date into his BlackBerry.

I shook my head in astonishment. When I get angry, I can simmer for hours, ready to boil at the least provocation. When Charlie boils over, he really steams! But it's over in an instant and he doesn't hold a grudge. *I could learn a lot about anger management from my husband*, I thought. And, suddenly, the pounding music didn't seem so bad.

Father, cleanse my heart of anger and help me to find peace in all situations. —MARCI ALBORGHETTI

THERE ARE VARIETIES OF WORKING, BUT IT IS THE SAME
GOD WHO INSPIRES THEM ALL IN EVERY ONE.
                       —I Corinthians 12:6 (RSV)

On Saturday morning I teach a high-energy indoor aerobic
cycling class called spinning. Most of my students are serious
outdoor cyclists who are looking for some conditioning
between rides. They like long, grueling simulated hill climbs—
essentially running hard uphill on a bike—punctuated by vigorous sprints. I put a lot of thought into my classes, combining
music and exertion to achieve the most effective and beneficial
aerobic experience. I expect riders to stick to the program and
climb the hill together. And, all in all, my students are pretty
good at following my lead.

Except for Beth. Every Saturday she sits up front, just a few
feet away from me, and invariably does her own thing: pedaling
like mad when the rest of us are working slowly; sitting when
we're standing and vice versa. No matter how clearly and forcefully I give instructions, she ignores them. The other morning it
was so bad that I vowed to talk to her after class.

"I have about a seventy percent hearing deficit," Beth
explained. "I'm usually fine, but with the music blasting and
everything, it's hard for me to decipher what you're saying. So
I just tune everything out and do what feels best. It's a great
workout. Thank you for teaching."

I set the music a little lower these days, but half the time
Beth still does her own thing. That's all right, though. Perhaps
I was being a little too rigid about everyone following my routine exactly. People get what they need in different ways, and
maybe I'm a better teacher since Beth taught me to lighten up
a little on the bike. Yes, there are many different ways to get to
the top of a hill.

Lord, help me to see that my way is not always the only way.
                       —EDWARD GRINNAN

*HE GIVES FOOD TO EVERY LIVING THING, FOR HIS
LOVINGKINDNESS CONTINUES FOREVER. —Psalm 136:25 (TLB)*

It was hearty fare, thick leek-and-potato soup, with cheese
served on a slab of bread fresh from the oven.

More than a hundred of us had come to the historic
California mission for spiritual refreshing. The tranquil hills and
simple accommodations encouraged meditation and prayer.
The *padre*, dressed in a flowing brown habit, welcomed us and
explained the bells that would signal our meals and get us up
in the morning. Several of us, he grinned, would have the
opportunity to get up before six o'clock to be the ringers!
Others would know the joy of serving one another by clearing
tables. A chosen few would bless the meals.

One of these lucky ones, a bright-eyed girl at our table,
pulled a card from her pocket: "Heavenly Father, out of love You
have created us. That merciful love keeps us from day to day.
Bless the food we are about to take. Bless us and these Your
gifts." Then she surprised us. "Before you leave the hall," she
said, "please wait. I have a prayer for after meals too."

I wasn't used to praying after meals. "What if we don't like
the food?" I said with a chuckle. But her prayer was much more
than thanksgiving for the food, so much more that I've been
giving thanks with it ever since.

*"Father of mercy, we thank You for Your kindness. Gifts with-
out measure flow from Your goodness, and the meal we have
just partaken will renew our strength to continue serving You
in our life's journey until we reach the joy You have prepared
for us. Amen."* —FAY ANGUS

LOVE NEVER FAILS. . . . —I Corinthians 13:8 (NIV)

In the years after my mother died, my father's health deterio-
rated to the point where it appeared that it was no longer safe
for him to remain in his home. Yet as his health care surrogate,
one question haunted me: When does a person's ability to
make decisions truly end? Competency, it seemed to me, was
something that fluctuated from day to day, and I didn't want to
make choices for Dad if he still had the right and capacity to do
so for himself.

Finally, I made an appointment to talk with my father's
general practitioner. "Ah, my good friend James's daughter,"
Dr. Narayan said as he reached out his hand. We discussed my
father's lingering illness, how Dad was never the same after
the stroke he had the afternoon my mother died. We talked
about how Dad loved his living room recliner, playing his fiddle
at two in the morning, eating cereal for dinner if the mood
struck him. Dr. Narayan smiled as I recounted how Dad always
looked forward to his appointments with his "wonderful Indian
doctor."

But as I stood up to leave his office, I was as perplexed as
when I arrived. I asked one final question: "How will I know
when it's time?"

Dr. Narayan's response was startling in its simplicity, yet it
proved to be precisely the answer I needed: "Let love be your
guide."

Today, as always, Lord, when all else fails, love is the answer.
                                             —ROBERTA MESSNER

*HE RESTED ON THE SEVENTH DAY FROM ALL HIS WORK
WHICH HE HAD MADE.* —*Genesis 2:2*

One of the things I learned from Leonard LeSourd, who was editor when I came to Guideposts, was to take afternoon naps. Len was a young man, and I couldn't figure out why anyone his age would need an after-lunch siesta. But, Len proclaimed it was a rejuvenator and that I should try it. I did, and now, decades later, I'm still at it. Fifteen or twenty minutes on the couch gives me a new lease on life, or at least a little rent.

While touting afternoon naps to a friend the other day, I was reminded of a lesson in animal husbandry I received many years ago. For about eight weeks one summer, Shirley and I took our four kids hiking on the Appalachian Trail. (Daniel was one and a half and rode in a carrier on my back.) We were accompanied by our schnauzer Heidi and two Sardinian donkeys, Pinocchio and Figaro, who carried our gear. The donkeys were hard workers, until they felt fatigued. At that point Pinocchio would slump to the ground and lie on his side, and Figaro, the copycat, would do likewise. No amount of prodding would get them to their feet. Only when they were rested would they continue.

Donkeys have a reputation for being stubborn, but after that summer I considered them wise. When it comes to work, we might do well to follow their lead. Instead of working beyond our capacity, burning the candle at both ends, maybe we need to take breaks more often, catch our breath, make an inventory of our chores and continue on a measured pace. Even God took time out.

And what about afternoon naps? I consider them holy too. Just ask Shirley if she wakes me before I'm finished.

> *Thank You, Father, for the blessing of sleep,*
> *And the healing of body and soul we reap.*
> —FRED BAUER

FOR IF THEY FALL, THE ONE WILL LIFT UP HIS FELLOW. . . .
—Ecclesiastes 4:10

Ron was the first client I spoke to when I made the decision to change brokerage firms. I had no idea if any of my clients would want to transfer their accounts, but I knew I needed to talk to them. "Come over to the house, Brock," Ron said when I called him.

Ron was a widower, and in the course of handling his investments I'd come to think of him as a friend. But I was pretty stressed when I dropped by. "Changing companies was a tough call, and now I have to ask my clients to trust my decision and follow me," I said. I went on, telling him my reasoning and what the new company could do.

"Brock," he said, "of course I'm moving my accounts, but that's because of you. Real friends stick together."

Over the next few years I had many opportunities to remember that statement. When the financial markets tumbled after 9/11, when my marriage collapsed and I went through a painful divorce, when the markets rebounded, I could always count on an encouraging word from Ron.

Then one day he had tough news of his own: He had pancreatic cancer. I visited him frequently those last few months. I hated to watch his illness take its toll, but he had lifted me up so often I wanted to try to do the same for him.

The last time I saw Ron, he raised his head from the hospital pillow and said, "What are you doing hanging around this place, Brock?"

I swallowed the lump in my throat and told him, "Just what you taught me. Good friends stick together."

Father, thank You for the friends who lift us up and for the chance You give us to return the favor. —BROCK KIDD

LET US TAKE OUR JOURNEY, AND LET US GO. . . .
—*Genesis 33:12*

Will gets into the driver's seat and I sit in the passenger seat, a change I'm not sure I can get used to.

"Okay, just pull away from curb. Don't forget to look behind you. Check the rearview mirror. Yes, that's right. You're doing fine."

I want to be encouraging but, frankly, I'm scared out of my wits. He's taken driver's ed classes, but this is the first time we've done this together. He bites his lip. He's a little worried too.

"Do you see that stop sign ahead?"

"I see it, Dad."

"Good. Just let your passengers know you see it." I'm trying to put it in a way that won't sound alarmist. "You want to slow down, so they know you're going to stop in time." I feel my body jerk against the shoulder harness. Okay, it's a stop, just not a very smooth one.

"Which way should I go?"

"Let's turn right. There's a divided highway up there. It'll be good for practice." My mind thinks of all the challenges ahead. Highway driving, freeway driving, night driving. All the bad drivers on the road. The perils of the unexpected. I can find good reasons to be scared. But I look over at Will. He's always been very responsible. I trust him. Does he see the red light? Yes, and he's letting me know.

"How was that?"

"Nice stop." There must be a prayer for the parent of a driving teen. But then it's probably not much different from the prayers of a parent at any time.

Be with my child, Lord, on this journey. —RICK HAMLIN

GIVE INSTRUCTION TO A WISE MAN, AND HE WILL BE YET WISER: TEACH A JUST MAN, AND HE WILL INCREASE IN LEARNING. —Proverbs 9:9

A cup of tea. A stretch. A pat for the kitty. A yawn. Even washing a few dishes sounds like fun right now. I'm taking a break from grading research papers: Eight done and thirty-two more to go. Grading each paper takes at least fifteen to twenty minutes, so the "done" stack rises slowly. I still face hours of intense work.

Over the past month, my community college students have invested twenty to thirty hours of their lives in this project. They brainstormed topics, evaluated references, drafted, revised, complained—endlessly—and documented sources. I coaxed them through obstacles like jobs, cranky computers, balky vehicles, fussy children, colds and flu to meet their deadlines.

But now I wonder, *Who's encouraging me?* I sink down with a small stack and my purple pen, ready to read. But first I read the students' evaluations of their own papers.

"This turned out to be fascinating," writes one. "I didn't know so much had happened in my hometown."

"The more I read about this, the more I wanted to do something to change it," says another.

"One-on-one with the instructor helped me the most," admits the one who nearly dropped the course. "I didn't know I could write." *Wow,* I think, *I reached him after all.*

I sit up straighter, energized by these writers and their newfound confidence. By the end of the week I'll know a lot more about topics as diverse as kidney stones and Contoocook, New Hampshire. I urged them on for the first fourteen weeks of the semester, and they're supercharging me for the final two.

Now, back to the stack.

Lord, give me the wisdom, love—and energy—to instruct well.
—GAIL THORELL SCHILLING

BLESSED IS THE MAN WHOSE STRENGTH IS IN YOU, WHOSE HEART IS SET ON PILGRIMAGE. —*Psalm 84:5* (NKJV)

This has not been a good week. Things did not work out as I had hoped, and the last few days have brought disappointment and discouragement. No matter how mature and experienced I become, these "days in the valley" do not become easier.

I went for a long walk this morning. Stepping out into a clear, crisp autumn day, I slipped a small Bible into my coat pocket. As I walked, I flipped open my Bible to Psalm 84:5-6 (NKJV): "Blessed is the man whose strength is in You, Whose heart is set on pilgrimage. As they pass through the Valley of Baca, They make it a spring; The rain also covers it with pools."

The Valley of Baca is associated with weeping. Indeed, the word *Baca* is derived from the verb *bakah*, "to weep." Reading these verses reminded me that to follow God is to be on a long journey—a pilgrimage—that traverses all kinds of terrain. We wind our way up mountains and down steep valleys. There are deserts and ocean vistas. We experience moments of laughter and weeping, excitement and boredom, comfort and pain, birth and death.

I began my walk this morning in the depths of the Valley of Baca. But the Bible reminds me that I do not walk alone. God can change my tears of disappointment into refreshing springs and the dismal rain into pools of pleasure.

Dear Lord, help me to remember that wherever I go, I'm on a pilgrimage with You. Amen. —SCOTT WALKER

The Lord God has given Me the tongue of disciples,
That I may know how to sustain the weary one with
a word. . . . —Isaiah 50:4 (NAS)

One of the associate pastors of our church asked me to give my
testimony in front of the congregation. *Anything but that!*
Please, Lord, no! I thought. Public speaking has always been
the number-one fear in my life. But I didn't want to turn down
my pastor, so I said I would. A week of dread and sleepless
nights followed.

The next Sunday I was playing the piano in the praise band
and looking at the stage in front of me, knowing that the following Sunday, I'd have to be there, microphone in hand, speaking to all those people. God would have to do a minimiracle to
get me calm enough to be of any use to Him.

When our praise songs were over, I had to get off the
stage and find a seat in the congregation. Stage right seemed
like a good choice, so I took a few steps in that direction
until my shoe got caught in a cable. I didn't fall, but it took a
series of modern-dancelike movements to keep me standing.
My face turned beet red, and my ears began to sizzle with
embarrassment.

The next Sunday I walked up onstage to give my testimony
with a lot more confidence than I'd ever had before. Compared
to last week's mishap, speaking seemed like a breeze. And after
church a man came up to me to tell me that what I'd said had
touched him deeply.

If I hadn't tripped the week before, I don't think I'd have
been as effective a speaker that Sunday. I guess God will do a
minimiracle to get His message out, even if it's sometimes a little hard on the messenger.

Lord, help me always to speak Your Word boldly.
                                            —Dave Franco

To BE SPIRITUALLY MINDED IS LIFE AND PEACE.
                                                    —Romans 8:6

Have you ever had one of those days when everything goes wrong? That's how this particular Monday started out. I cut myself shaving and, reaching for the styptic pencil, knocked a glass tumbler to the floor. After sweeping up the pieces, I went downstairs for breakfast and burned my hand on the frying pan. Later I drove my younger son to school and dropped him off without his book bag. And so it went. Nothing terrible, just enough minor mishaps to call it a "bad day."

The only thing is, I had labeled the day a bit too soon. When I left my office to buy lunch, the air was warm, my spirits rose and I whistled as I walked. I found a quarter on the sidewalk and lifted my hat to some ladies. Arriving at the deli, I discovered that my favorite sandwich, a curried turkey stroller, was on sale. On the way back to the office, I ran into a friend whom I hadn't seen in months. And so it went.

Was it a good day or a bad day? I asked my family over dinner. "You know," my wife said, "if you look hard enough, every day has its share of good and bad. That's the way it's meant to be. God keeps us off balance—and that's how we learn to find a balance of our own."

Now, no matter how my day goes, I make an effort to take both good and bad with equanimity—and keep an even keel.

Teach me, Lord, to see everything that happens today in the light of Your abiding love. —PHILIP ZALESKI

*BLESSED ARE THE PEACEMAKERS: FOR THEY SHALL BE
CALLED THE CHILDREN OF GOD.* —*Matthew 5:9*

I often substitute-teach English as a Second Language classes
for adults from a dozen different countries. In these classes,
Salim from Iran may practice dialogue with Miguel from
Venezuela. A sixty-year-old Egyptian grandfather, Wahib, works
with young, pregnant Sanju from India to solve a crossword
puzzle. Svetlana from Russia translates a newspaper article with
Matzuko from Japan.

Lively debates occur over countable or noncountable nouns:
Do we have *much* chairs and *many* furniture in our classroom?
We construct a model town, then ask and give directions.
Sung-he from Korea and Tao from China determine if the post
office is "across" the street or "next door to" the library? Is the
gas station "behind" or "between" the grocery store and the
Laundromat?

At the school's annual international fair, students delight in
sharing their cultures with visitors. Fourth-grade American girls
try on a beautiful *hanbo*, the Korean festival dress. Lupe from
Mexico samples Japanese *yakitori*, proclaiming it *deliciosa!*
Each student takes pride in sharing his or her own country's
delicacies and traditions. The Brazilians demonstrate the samba
and then bravely attempt a lively dance from Africa.

As I watch my students work together, I yearn for our world
to become like their classroom. Instead of our differences leading to violence and war, couldn't each nation help each other
solve problems together, and share and appreciate our unique
cultures?

*Dear God, please guide the leaders of every nation and put in
each one's heart a desire for peace that burns stronger than
any other.* —MARY BROWN

THE LORD MY GOD WILL ENLIGHTEN MY DARKNESS.
                                                    —Psalm 18:28

It's a blustery, rainy, end-of-October afternoon. I could easily
match my mood with the weather. Gray . . . chilly . . . mournful.
This past year has been exhausting. Pieces of my life I once
thought secure have come apart. They lie at my feet like tat-
tered autumn leaves.

Today I am helped by Jesus' "Be of good cheer" words. Just
before His Crucifixion, Jesus said, "In the world ye shall have
tribulation: but be of good cheer; I have overcome the world"
(John 16:33). When He healed a paralytic man, He reassured
him: "Son, be of good cheer; thy sins be forgiven thee"
(Matthew 9:2). Jesus calmed His terrified disciples by saying,
"Be of good cheer: it is I; be not afraid" (Mark 6:50). And the
risen Jesus stood beside Paul in prison and encouraged, "Be of
good cheer, Paul: for as thou hast testified of me in Jerusalem,
so must thou bear witness also at Rome" (Acts 23:11).

These accounts give me four reasons to "be of good cheer."
First, Jesus has power that transcends every heart-wrenching
situation. Second, nothing is beyond His forgiveness when I
put my trust in Him. Third, because He is near, I do not have to
succumb to fear in any crisis. Fourth, even when I feel most
cornered, I can dare to hope, knowing that He has redeemed
my future.

My personal storm continues to buffet me. But like those
few straggler leaves still clinging to the branch, I hang on in
faith to the "good cheer" promises of Jesus. I know that, ultimately, they will not let me fall.

*"Be of good cheer"—four small words reverberating with hope
because You, Lord, have spoken them.* —CAROL KNAPP

LET THE BEAUTY OF THE LORD OUR GOD BE UPON US. . . .
                                    —Psalm 90:17 (NKJV)

I was chatting with my college students before class. "I've got a bad case of dysmorphophobia," I admitted.

"What's that?" they wanted to know.

"It's the fear of getting old and ugly."

"Hey," one boy fired back, "you don't need to worry about getting ugly, Mr. Schantz. You've been ugly for years."

"Very funny, Jason. And when grades come out, you'll see what ugly is."

In my job as a college teacher I deal every day with students who think they are without redeeming value. Burdened by impossible standards, many students are down on themselves for being ordinary.

A young man came into my office to talk. He's handsome and muscular, with thick hair and bold blue eyes. A 4.0 scholar, he's also witty and charming. When he suddenly began to cry, I feared that he had done something terribly wrong, something of which he was ashamed.

His problem? "I'm short. I hate being short."

I wanted to laugh out loud, but I knew better. "That's odd," I replied. "I've never once thought of you as short. When I look at you, I see someone strong, handsome and smart as a whip."

"Really?"

He left in a good frame of mind. Each of us needs somebody who thinks we're okay. You could be that person to someone today, by holding up a mirror to his or her unnoticed beauty.

Help me to see Your beauty, God, in the people I meet each day. —DANIEL SCHANTZ

WHEN I CONSIDER THY HEAVENS, THE WORK OF THY FINGERS, THE MOON AND THE STARS, WHICH THOU HAST ORDAINED; WHAT IS MAN, THAT THOU ART MINDFUL OF HIM? . . . —Psalm 8:3-4

I had gone to bed early, exhausted from the sheer frustration of my workday. I was almost asleep when the phone rang. I heard my husband's voice downstairs, talking briefly, and then his footsteps in the hallway. "Honey, you asleep?" he asked as he opened the door.

"How could I be?" I asked, just wanting the day to end.

"Want to come outside and look at the moon? We're having a total lunar eclipse."

I was wide awake now. "Really?"

A few minutes later, Gary and I stood on the front lawn, the sky an amazing arc of black velvet studded with stars. And center stage was the pale, marvelous moon. I broke the silence and asked, "How did you know about this?"

Gary put his arm around me. "That phone call. It was some lady, all excited, telling me to go out and look at the moon. She was pretty embarrassed when I told her she had a wrong number."

I stood there looking at the sky, my frustration and exhaustion giving way to wonder and awe. God really was in control —of the universe and my own life too. "You know," I said, snuggling closer to Gary, "I don't think she got the wrong number at all."

How marvelous are Your works, God! —MARY LOU CARNEY

ENCOURAGE THE TIMID, HELP THE WEAK, BE PATIENT WITH EVERYONE. —I Thessalonians 5:14 (NIV)

The day of the Special Olympics began with a slight drizzle. It was 6:30 A.M. Since I'd been at college, I'd hardly seen 9:00 A.M., much less a sunrise, but here I was, up and at 'em with the birds.

I trudged down to the parking lot, clearing my throat. I'd been sick for the past week, and the car was parked nearly half a mile away. I grumbled the whole way down about the miserable day and wished I could excuse myself. But as the student coordinator for the Mercer County Special Olympics, I had to organize the volunteers from school and provide lunch for them and the athletes. I had to show up.

When I got to the track, I tried to give the volunteers a pep talk. "I know you're cold and wet," I said to the volunteers. My voice trailed off. I looked around and noticed what was going on just outside our circle. Athletes circled the track, warming up and stretching. Two hundred kids with developmental and mental disabilities were here to compete today.

My tone changed, "Remember that today, you're not just helping out by giving your time, you're making someone else's day. Enjoy it."

I got down off my makeshift podium and made my way over to where the athletes were stretching. "Y'all ready to race?" I asked.

"We were born for this!" one girl replied, grinning despite the raindrops that were now dripping from her soaked bangs. I forgot all about the rain, the cold and my throat.

After the meet I shared snacks with the athletes and listened to their game plans for next year.

Next year. Maybe it'll rain, maybe it won't. Either way, those kids will make my day.

Lord, thank You for opportunities to share in the joy of others.
— ASHLEY JOHNSON

THEN JOB REPLIED TO THE LORD: "I KNOW THAT YOU CAN DO ALL THINGS; NO PLAN OF YOURS CAN BE THWARTED."
                                                   —*Job 42:1-2 (NIV)*

I had just finished putting the dinner dishes into the dishwasher and was wiping off the kitchen counter when I heard the refrigerator door open. Turning around, I saw three-year-old Maggie peering into the fridge. "Are you looking for something, honey?" I asked her.

Maggie turned around and glared at me. "You ruined my plan!" she shouted. "I was going to sneak some food!"

I offered her some fruit. "No," she scowled and stomped off to the living room.

I wasn't sorry to have ruined Maggie's plan—I have enough firsthand experience with bad eating habits to want to keep her from forming them—but I was impressed by her anger. And I think I understood it. There have been plenty of times in my life when I failed to get something I very much wanted, and it made me angry too. Whether it was a promotion or a relationship, sometimes my most cherished plans have come to nothing, and the immediate aftertaste was bitter.

But as I look back at my life, all those frustrations along the way seem, literally, providential. If I'd gotten what I thought I wanted so much then, I wouldn't be working at Guideposts, and I wouldn't be the husband of Julia and the father of Maggie and Stephen and John and Elizabeth and Mary.

Maggie has a hard time seeing that sometimes it's best for her that she doesn't get what she wants. I'm old enough to know better.

Lord, Your plans for me are better than anything I can imagine. Help me to remember that when You tell me "No."
                                                   —ANDREW ATTAWAY

BE STRONG AND OF A GOOD COURAGE. . . .
—*Deuteronomy 31:6*

It seems odd that I should have traveled to remarkable Machu
Picchu, "The Lost City of the Incas," and afterward the first
thing I think of is a ten-year-old Indian boy. I roamed for hours
in that city that Hiram Bingham came upon in 1911, hidden
away on a high, impregnable mountain peak. It was awesome
wandering among the vast stone structures, more than four
centuries old, and yet I felt an eeriness there too.

It came time to get on the bus for the downward trip. It
would be the same as coming up but in reverse: numerous
horseshoe turns, one after the next. As we left, I noticed a boy
who ran alongside the bus, then disappeared into the brush.
When the bus rounded the turn, there he was, smiling. Then he
raced into the tangled brush again and was waiting for us once
more. By the time he dashed down again through the rocks
and thicket, the people on the bus, including me, were urging
him on.

"Hey, kid! Go get 'em." And he did, time and again, until we
reached the bottom. The driver opened the door, and Fluvio
(I found out his name) came aboard to much applause and,
not to be forgotten, an offering of tips.

Fluvio helped to dispel the eeriness that had bothered me
earlier. Machu Picchu was an ancient wonder, but it holds a
sad mystery: the absence of its people. Fluvio made me feel
that I was back among the living. The tip I gave him was well
and cleverly earned.

I think of Fluvio, Father, and ask You to watch over him.
—VAN VARNER

BE ON THE ALERT. YOUR ADVERSARY . . . PROWLS ABOUT . . .
SEEKING SOMEONE TO DEVOUR. —*I Peter 5:8* (NAS)

The Halloween tradition of trick or treating is just a little
spookier and a whole lot scarier for children in Churchill,
Manitoba, a town several hundred miles north of us. The rules
are a little different too.

Rule one: No polar bear costumes.

Rule two: No white costumes such as ghosts, nurses or
brides. And definitely no seal costumes.

The reason? Polar bears. Churchill lies in proximity to the
world's largest denning area for polar bears. After spending the
summer on land, in late fall the bears head back to the waters
of Hudson Bay to hunt seals. By the end of October most of the
twenty holding pens in the town's "bear jail" are already filled
with occupants awaiting release.

To protect children going door to door on Halloween night,
conservation officers and game wardens are out on patrol
armed with dart guns to tranquilize any bears wandering into
town. A helicopter does surveillance over the area. Local volunteers with two-way radios patrol in cars. Police constables
carry shotguns to frighten away any furry white marauders.
And while noise may help, authorities agree that the most effective deterrent against prowling bears is light. Each year more
than a dozen fire trucks, ambulances and police cruisers are
positioned around the perimeter of Churchill, their bright lights
flashing into the night.

I don't know about you, but sometimes when I read the
morning newspaper, I feel very small and vulnerable. Should
anxiety threaten my peace of mind, however, I find the best
protection is to "walk in the light" (I John 1:7). It's advice that's
equally effective whether dealing with polar bears or the pow-
ers of darkness.

Thank You, Lord, that You are the Light of the world.

—ALMA BARKMAN

*THE PEOPLE THAT WALKED IN DARKNESS HAVE SEEN A
GREAT LIGHT. . . .* —Isaiah 9:2

A gallery of saints in glowing stained glass filled the windows
of the little church: Mary holding the Child, St. Peter with his
keys, St. John on Patmos. Watching the figures transform ordinary daylight into radiance and glory, I remembered a definition
I heard once: "Saints are people who let the light shine
through." And I thought, *The words apply not just to revered
individuals like the ones in the windows but to the unsung
saints we honor today.*

I've known a lot of them, as different from one another as
an English teacher and a Paris street sweeper. Yet, through each
one, God's light shone on those around them.

I think of a book report that came back to me in my sixth-
grade English class with a line at the top in Miss Cathcart's
green-ink script: "You're capable of seeing more in this story."
And because she saw something better in me, I reread the book
and I did see more.

When I was a student in Paris a few years later, my worn,
much-mended jacket was in shabby contrast to the elegant outfits of Parisian women. A man was sweeping a gutter with his
straw broom as the daily rush of water carried debris into the
sewers. As I started to cross the street, he held up his hand
and halted traffic so my frayed old coat wouldn't be sprayed by
passing cars. The gesture said, *You're valued just as you are.*

And there was the friend who paid a visit after our second
child was born, when all I could see ahead was dirty diapers
and a sink full of dishes. Margaret pointed out the sacredness of
daily chores, and when she left, my untidy apartment looked
like a shrine.

Through all these people and scores more, light shone.

*Faithful Lord, send me a saint today to shine Your light on my
path. And let me be a saint where another needs it.*

—ELIZABETH SHERRILL

"AS FOR ME, I WOULD SEEK GOD . . . WHO DOES GREAT
THINGS AND UNSEARCHABLE, MARVELOUS THINGS WITHOUT
NUMBER." —Job 5:8-9 (RSV)

On my street, the chestnut trees by the creek all let go at once,
and there is a steady rain of hard fruit the size of tennis balls.
On windy days, my children and I hear the nuts falling from our
house, and we amble down the street and watch from a safe
distance as the heavy green nuts leap from the trees. We take
home handfuls and burnish the lovely brown nuts, and my
young sons throw them at each other and at their sister until
I insist they desist and put the boys to bed, but not the sister,
who is a teenager and so never sleeps.

I work the nuts through my fingers like fat oily coins and
consider the parallels between chestnuts and children. Both
are wrapped in soft pebbly skins. Both have stubborn centers.
Both gleam when polished. Crows are fascinated by both.

I watch the gangs of crows in the street flare and hammer
and bicker and chortle among the shards and scraps of nuts
and then go kiss my sons and nod to my daughter, who deigns,
for once, to nod back. Her nod this evening seems like a blessing beyond price to me, for she has been sharp and sassy and
supercilious, and I grow weary of being the tree from which
she must carve her independence. But tonight she nods to me:
a subtle message, a silent prayer, a fleeting gift. And we know all
gifts are fleeting; yet they come to us all day and night, an
ocean of generosity from the One Who made and makes everything that is.

Dear Lord, I ask this one crucial, necessary, nutritious pri-
mary gift: Will You help me just see and smell and hear and
taste and touch Your unimaginable sea of miracles every
moment? Please? —BRIAN DOYLE

"SURELY GOD IS MY SALVATION; I WILL TRUST AND NOT BE AFRAID. . . ." —Isaiah 12:2 (NIV)

Recently, I've had to choose between taking a job with a steady income that would limit my freedom to minister and pursuing a business that had great potential but no security. The new venture had almost run out of cash, and my fear of an uncertain future had just about made up my mind to take the safer course, when I took a ministry trip to Madagascar, the island nation off the southeast coast of Africa noted for its magnificent forests and exotic wildlife.

While I was in Madagascar, I visited a national park that is home to a variety of lemurs, adorable creatures that look like a cross between raccoons and monkeys. To see them, I took a canoe across a narrow creek to a small island. "Why not just build a bridge?" I asked.

"Lemurs are afraid of water," our guide replied. "The ones on the island won't cross the creek, so it's easier to protect and study them."

The lemurs leaped from treetop to treetop, often covering twice the distance it took to cross the creek. Yet none of them jumped over the water. Even though they had the opportunity and ability to leave, their fears had turned the island into a prison. I watched as a group of lemurs sitting in a tree branch looked longingly at the mainland.

Those lemurs made my decision for me. When I got home, I would face my fear and do whatever it took to keep the new venture alive.

Lord, show me the places where my fears have me trapped and help me trust You to face them with faith.

—ERIC FELLMAN

*"ALL MY WORDS THAT I SHALL SPEAK TO YOU RECEIVE IN
YOUR HEART, AND HEAR WITH YOUR EARS."*
                                        —Ezekiel 3:10 (RSV)

Saturday afternoon I joined about eighty mourners gathered
for the two o'clock funeral of Grasty, one of our older church
members. At the end of the service we processed to the outdoor altar and columbarium, committing Grasty's ashes to the
earth and his soul to eternal rest.

Midway through the short liturgy, I heard a chainsaw in the
distance. I imagined its blade disfiguring a tree's grand form.
The buzz seemed to add an exclamation point to the pastor's
somber message: To dust we will return. I soberly filed back
indoors for the reception. "Wasn't the timing amazing?" someone remarked. "The church carillon playing right at the pastor's last amen? Bells of blessing—what a fitting farewell."

"I didn't hear bells. Only that chainsaw. Did you notice?"

I asked around. Hardly anyone had heard both the buzz and
the bells. On the way to my car, I listened to the neighborhood
noises, determined this time to hear the full range of God's
message.

Lord, open my ears to Your promises. —EVELYN BENCE

"THE LORD HAS KEPT THE PROMISE HE MADE. . . ."
—*I Kings 8:20 (NIV)*

Awhile ago I told you about my challenge of teaching Sunday school to a Spanish-speaking class of two-, three- and four-year-olds at a mission church begun by our congregation. For me, it was a test of whether I truly believed that God wouldn't ask me to do something I wasn't capable of doing. God said, "Trust Me," and I'm glad I did.

First, the children were adorable, freshly scrubbed in their best Sunday clothes, as anxious to teach me some Spanish words as they were to learn about the colorful children's Bible in my hands. Then, the first day's lesson was perfect for a beginner. We showed the children a small cross woven in a rainbow of colors. *I remember colors from high school Spanish,* I thought, pointing at *rojo* (red), *azul* (blue), *negro* (black), *blanco* (white), *verde* (green) and *amarillo* (yellow).

Fortunately, a friendly teenage girl from the church visited our class and stayed to translate as I explained how the colors remind us of our sin and Jesus' sacrifice, the cleansing of baptism and God's promises. But at those times when we still didn't understand each other, I just smiled and the children always smiled back.

As I handed each child a cross to take home, I carefully said the words Pastor Jose had taught the teachers before class: *"La cruz de Cristo, tu Salvador"* (the Cross of Christ, your Savior). Even if the children didn't exactly understand, I hoped they felt the love and trust that had brought us together.

Gracias, Señor—thank You, Lord—for helping me to speak in the familiar language of Your love. —GINA BRIDGEMAN

BE CAREFUL TO MAINTAIN GOOD WORKS. . . . —Titus 3:8

After undergoing angioplasty and stent replacement surgery, I felt pretty good. But I was told I needed therapy, so I enrolled in a cardiac rehabilitation class at our local hospital. I joined four others in a compact, air-conditioned room where exercise machines lined the wall like tanks. "Welcome," said the physical therapist. "The exercise you get here will improve the function of your heart and lungs."

The cardiac rehabilitation nurse added to that, "The exercise will also increase your confidence and feeling of well-being."

It was clear, though, that we would have to do the work.

At each hour-long session, we had to exercise on three different machines. The physical therapist pushed us. The treadmill moved faster, the hand crank became more tiring and the exercise bicycle more resistant. All the while we patients also got to know one another better.

Charlie was worried about his Florida home, battered by two hurricanes in the space of three weeks. Steven felt guilty being away from his desk three mornings a week. Helen hoped she would not collapse under the stress of all this exercise. I wondered if I would ever attain the endurance of the others.

Music played and the cardiac rehab team kept urging us on: "Lift that arm a bit higher. Keep those elbows even. Watch your breath."

The secret of recovery seemed to combine our personal efforts with the monitoring of the cardiac rehab team. But I was most grateful for the support and encouragement of my fellow patients. What we could never have done on our own we could do in a group. Getting better was a collaborative process.

Embracing Father, thank You for the people in my life who help me reach my goals. —OSCAR GREENE

IN THE FOURTH YEAR WAS THE FOUNDATION OF THE HOUSE OF THE LORD LAID. . . . —*I Kings 6:37*

I'd never considered working at the polls on Election Day, but a co-worker had signed up and asked me if I wanted to do my civic duty too. Too embarrassed to refuse, I agreed and dragged myself out of bed before sunrise so we could set up at the polling place before people trooped in to vote. The place was mobbed. A few—students voting for the first time, bleary-eyed waitresses coming off the night shift, hardhats starting their day—had been waiting at 7:00 A.M. when we opened for business. I'd always heard so much about those people who don't vote; I was pleased to see up close how many do.

"Come into the booth with me, honey," a young mother told her kindergartner as she stepped behind the curtain. After a few minutes, the twosome came out and the youngster dropped her mother's paper ballot in the box.

"Did you vote?" I asked the child jokingly.

"Yes," she answered, "but don't ask me who I voted for. It's a secret who we vote for in America!"

"This is how we teach the next generation," her mom said to me, smiling.

I immediately flashed back to the first time I'd gone to the polls. It was in the 1950s, and the presidential race had been between Dwight D. Eisenhower and Adlai Stevenson. I remember seeing two red, white and blue buttons: Mom told me that one read, I LIKE IKE, and the other, I'LL GLADLY VOTE ADLAI. I toddled along, holding on to my mother's plaid skirt as she took me into the booth with her and showed me how to pull the lever and cast her ballot for . . . well, I won't tell you, of course. It's a secret whom we vote for in America!

Lord, though I may not say for whom I voted, let me be proud to say I voted today. —LINDA NEUKRUG

*PREACH THE WORD! BE READY IN SEASON AND OUT OF
SEASON. CONVINCE, REBUKE, EXHORT, WITH ALL
LONGSUFFERING AND TEACHING. —II Timothy 4:2 (NKJV)*

"You're quite a salesman!" the man said, pumping my hand. I
had just given a talk to the group he was a part of. "Boy, you
really know how to sell Guideposts."

I was a tad taken aback. I'd come down to this conference
in Florida to talk about Guideposts and all the good things it
does. Still, I'd never thought of myself as a salesman.

My father was a salesman but not by choice. He had to drop
out of college during the Depression to help support his family, abandoning his dreams of a medical career for a job selling
cash registers. He wasn't a natural salesguy, but he was a good
one and he had plenty of awards to prove it, along with high
blood pressure and bleeding ulcers.

My friend Jim, a consummate sales professional, says you
can't sell something unless you truly believe in it. My father
was a good salesman because he believed in working hard at
an honest job to support his family. I work for an organization
I believe in. It's a blessing that I sometimes overlook because
I'm too busy. But that man in Florida was right: I'm absolutely
convinced that everyone in the world should be reading our
publications. If that makes me a salesman, then so be it.

Dad would have been proud.

*Dear Lord, in word and deed today, let me make a sale for
You.* —EDWARD GRINNAN

*THEY HELPED EVERY ONE HIS NEIGHBOUR; AND EVERY ONE
SAID TO HIS BROTHER, BE OF GOOD COURAGE.* —*Isaiah 41:6*

When my son Greg was in kindergarten, he had a classmate
named Wayne. Wayne's mother Anna didn't have a car. She
walked him to and from school every day, passing our house
around 7:45 each morning. After a few days of watching them,
I decided I could pick up Wayne for school in the morning
and take him home in the afternoon.

Anna didn't have a telephone, so there was no easy way for
her to contact me if Wayne wasn't going to school. That meant
I'd sometimes drive to her house, bang loudly on the downstairs door so that she could hear me in her upstairs apartment, only to discover that Wayne wasn't going to school that
day. Sometimes Anna would wait for me on the days Greg
couldn't attend, and I'd feel a terrible pang of guilt as she and
Wayne hurried past our house late for school, wondering, I was
quite sure, why I hadn't come to pick up Wayne.

Pretty soon, I began to wish I'd never gotten myself into
such a predicament. I complained long and often to my husband Larry about the situation, and one night he said rather
gruffly, "Would you rather be Anna and have to depend on
someone else all the time?" That was all it took. I suddenly realized how difficult it was to be a care-receiver.

Jesus said, "It is more blessed to give than to receive"
(Acts 20:35). Being a gracious giver was the least I could do to
pass on that blessing.

*Lord, please keep me from losing sight of how hard it some-
times is to be on the receiving end of my time and patience.*

—LIBBIE ADAMS

*"THE SPIRIT OF THE LORD IS UPON ME. . . . HE HAS SENT
ME TO PROCLAIM RELEASE TO THE CAPTIVES . . . TO SET
FREE THOSE WHO ARE DOWNTRODDEN. . . ."*

—*Luke 4:18 (NAS)*

Eddie Dwyer has been a special friend for a dozen years. We
first met when I became his pastor. For nearly four decades,
Eddie served as a professor of New Testament at Baylor
University. His students loved him for the care and support he
gave them. Eddie died last week at age ninety-two. Yesterday
I stood by his grave and read the Scriptures he had taught for
a lifetime.

When Eddie was in the eighth grade, his teacher assigned
her class a term paper, warning them that she wouldn't accept
late papers. Several days later, Eddie came down with the flu.
He missed three weeks of class and couldn't finish his term
paper on time. His teacher refused to give him a second
chance. Angry and frustrated, Eddie emptied his desk, packed
his books and dropped out of school. For the next three years,
he picked cotton and worked odd jobs in the midst of the
Great Depression.

One day a businessman approached Eddie on the street and
said, "Eddie, I've been watching you. You're a hard worker and
you've got a lot of promise. If you'll go back to school, I'll buy
your books for you."

Eddie was seventeen and was embarrassed to go back in
the eighth grade. But late that night, he decided to accept the
man's offer. He graduated from high school when he was
twenty-one.

All Eddie needed was a second chance. And his life was
changed forever when someone saw his potential and gave
him that chance.

*Dear Father, help me to lift up the downtrodden and set the
prisoners free with a second chance.* —SCOTT WALKER

THE LORD WILL GIVE STRENGTH UNTO HIS PEOPLE; THE
LORD WILL BLESS HIS PEOPLE WITH PEACE. —*Psalm 29:11*

My Bible is stuffed with prayers and notes and clippings that
encourage me. One clipping quotes a letter from a Civil War
officer to his beloved wife. He desperately hoped that he would
return to her and their sons unharmed. But, "If I do not, my
dear Sarah, when my last breath escapes me it will whisper
your name. I shall always be near you, in the gladdest days and
in the darkest nights. And if there be a soft breeze upon your
cheek, it shall be my breath. Do not mourn me dead; think I am
gone and wait for thee, for we shall meet again." The soldier,
Major Sullivan Ballou, was killed in the Battle of Bull Run seven
days after writing the letter.

   We have a veterans' memorial in our city park, directly
behind a rock sculpture named the Weeping Wall. Water flows
constantly over it, bringing out the beauty of the stone as only
water can. Let us go through this day with reverence as we
remember the price so many paid, generation through generation, to preserve our freedom.

Around the world, night and day, those in the armed forces
stand watch for us. Oh, blessed Lord, be their strength, their
courage, their protector and their shield. For those who have
endured, who still serve in hospitals and on the battlefield of
their own daily lives, be their peace, their comfort and their
hope. —FAY ANGUS

"BRING THE FULL TITHES INTO THE STOREHOUSE . . . AND THEREBY PUT ME TO THE TEST, SAYS THE LORD OF HOSTS. . . ."
—*Malachi 3:10 (RSV)*

It was a bad year. I was reeling from my divorce. Not only did I feel spiritually beaten, but my personal finances were suffering from legal fees, counseling, mediation and a large settlement. To top it off, my business wasn't going well. I was worried about my clients and worried about my son Harrison. I was worried about everything.

And there I was sitting in church listening to my dad preach a sermon on tithing. *Surely God must realize the challenges I'm facing,* I thought. *I've been tithing ever since I was a kid. This year I can skip it.*

"Whatever you give or don't give won't make God love you less," Dad said. "But tithing is an adventure in trusting God. Give God a chance at your life. Try something big. Unfold your soul's wings. Put God in charge." And his closer: "The law of the tithe holds: You can't outgive God."

Those words clinched the deal. Without further hesitation, I pulled a pledge card from the pew in front of me and filled it out. This would be the most difficult tithe I had ever made, and the most exciting. I dropped the card in the plate with a sense of total freedom.

Three days later I found an unexpected envelope on my desk. A commission check had been forwarded to me from my former company. Even before I read the amount, I smiled, remembering my dad's words: "You can't outgive God."

Thank You, God, for Your overflowing blessings—whether I deserve them or not. —BROCK KIDD

"Cease striving and know that I am God. . . ."
—*Psalm 46:10* (NAS)

I hadn't yet turned sixteen when I learned to drive. I'd sat through driver's ed in school, but now I was getting some hands-on experience. My mother sat in the passenger's seat of our station wagon, and I eased it out of our driveway and into the street.

"What on earth are you doing?" my mother said.

"I'm driving, Mom." My eyes were hawklike, focused straight ahead. My neck and shoulder muscles were knotted. My sweaty hands gripped the wheel tightly at the two and ten o'clock positions, just the way I'd learned in driver's ed. *A good driver keeps her hands on the wheel at two and ten at all times and keeps her eyes on the road.* I'd memorized the rules for safe driving and gotten an A.

"Julie, what are you looking at?"

"The nose of the car. I'm steering the car between the two lines. It's hard!"

"Nobody drives like that! Look way out down the road."

"How will I stay between the lines if I quit focusing on the car?"

"Trust me, you drive by looking ahead. Focus as far down the road as you can see."

I shifted my glance to the horizon. Until recently, I approached life the same way: I wanted to be in control with my hard-steering technique. But now I'm learning to let go, focus far down the road and look only toward God.

Father, for today, I'm trusting You. —Julie Garmon

IN HIS HAND IS THE LIFE OF EVERY CREATURE AND THE BREATH OF ALL MANKIND. —Job 12:10 (NIV)

I was driving home from grocery shopping on a mid-November afternoon; it was drizzling and foggy, and traffic was heavy on the four-lane interstate. *The older I get,* I thought, *the scarier it is to drive in this kind of weather and traffic. Are You there, Lord?*

About a mile from my exit, an eighteen-wheeler cut right in front of me, forcing me into the left lane. By the time my heartbeat returned to seminormal, I'd crossed a small bridge and caught a split-second glimpse of a black kitten peering into traffic, her mouth open in a cry for help.

I maneuvered back into the right lane. Soon I'd be home—unless I went back for the kitten. *But that would be crazy. How would I find her? What were the chances of her still being there?* Then two bold words flashed into my mind: *Trust God.*

I got off at my exit and back on the interstate, going the other way. I drove to the side of the bridge and pulled onto the right shoulder, putting on my hazard lights. The kitten was right where I'd seen it, perched on the median strip on the edge of traffic. My heart pounded as I crossed the highway. *Trust God.*

I stood on the side of the median strip and called, "Here, kitty, kitty." She turned her head. Holding my breath, I called again. This time she whipped around and came running to me, wet and bedraggled. I scooped her up and she snuggled into my arms as if she'd been waiting for me.

Today, five years later, as I pet her sleek, black fur, I still see her on that foggy day, by the side of the highway, tiny mouth open in a cry that couldn't possibly be heard, yet was.

Almighty God, how much more do You hear the cries of Your children, no matter how weak or small. —SHARI SMYTH

SO THE LAST SHALL BE FIRST, AND THE FIRST LAST. . . .
—Matthew 20:16

Powder-puff football was a popular fall event at my high school. Every year the junior and senior girls put on uniforms, pads and helmets, and played each other on the school field.

I had a difficult time making it through gym class—unless it was folk dancing season—yet my heart was set on making the powder-puff team. My father offered me as many pointers as he could before he dropped me off at tryouts, but when he came back to pick me up, I threw myself into the car and burst out into tears. "It's not fair! It's not fair! I didn't make the team!" I wailed.

The next morning I had to force myself to go to school. No sooner had I walked in the front door than I was being called to the office. "Pam, one of the faculty sponsors said, 'Since you didn't make the team, we want you to be the manager.' All you have to do is round up the guys on the football team and get them dressed up to be cheerleaders at the game." Standing in the middle of the entire male football team, enjoying twice as much attention as the mud-caked girls out on the field, I was mighty glad that life wasn't fair.

Powder-puff football may seem a little silly, but I always think of that game when I read Jesus' parable about the vineyard owner who pays all his workers the same, whether they came to work early or at the end of the day. God's gifts don't depend on our output but on His heart. Sometimes we get a double dose of what we don't deserve.

Father, Your grace is for everyone: the first, the last, even me. Now that's something to cheer about! —PAM KIDD

THOU DIDST CLEAVE THE EARTH WITH RIVERS.
—*Habakkuk 3:9*

I'm a fan of the TV show *Jeopardy*, from way back when Guideposts' friend Art Fleming was the host. On a recent show, the contestants were given the answer "China's Yangtze River." The question they were being asked to provide was "What is the third longest river in the world?" I'd have thought the Mississippi was the answer, but at 2,348 miles it's only the longest river in the United States.

It's the Nile that is the longest river in the world, measuring 4,160 miles; the Amazon second longest at almost 4,000 miles. I've boated on all three and find it hard to believe there's anything bigger than the Amazon; more water flows through it than the Nile, Mississippi and Yangtze combined, it's that humongous. My memory of the Amazon is of fishing for piranhas that would bite on anything that moved. "Don't put your finger in the water," our guide joked.

There are important rivers in the lands of the Bible, too, like the River Jordan, which flows through the Sea of Galilee into the Dead Sea. And two rivers now in the news, the Tigris and Euphrates, are important in biblical history for Babylon and Nebuchadnezzar, Nineveh, possibly the Garden of Eden, and the land of Ur, the birthplace of Abraham, the common patriarch who defines the faith for half the world— Jews, Christians and Muslims.

For me, Abraham personifies obedience to God. When the Lord told him to leave his home and go "unto a land that I will shew thee" (Genesis 12:1), Abraham didn't say, "But I'm seventy-five years old," or "How about next year?" No, Abraham and Sarah obeyed, taking all their possessions out of Haran, in today's Turkey, and headed south, no doubt along the Euphrates and Jordan rivers. They and the sheep and goats they probably took with them needed water to survive, and God provided. He always does to those who are faithful.

Teach us, God, both to listen and lace up our shoes,
To obey all Your orders, not pick and choose.

—FRED BAUER

THEREFORE, BRETHREN, STAND FAST, AND HOLD THE
TRADITIONS WHICH YE HAVE BEEN TAUGHT. . . .
—*II Thessalonians 2:15*

It started the night the electricity went out. I was seven, and my father, sisters, brother and I sat around the kitchen table with a stack of board games as my mother put together a platter with cheese and crackers, pretzels, and celery sticks. The room was lit by candles, and the sound of the storm outside gathered us close together around the table.

A transistor radio played big band music in the background as we exhausted our supply of board games. Then we went around the table playing the "name game." My mother called out a category and we took turns naming things that fit. "Birds!" Mom said.

"Cardinals," my sister said.

"Woodpeckers," my brother followed, and so it went. My father whispered hints and clues to me, the youngest, as the rain pelted the window. When one of us was stumped, a new round was started. Flowers followed birds and then countries, trees and vegetables. The lightning flashed, the platter of snacks dwindled, and the candles dripped wax.

When the name game lost its magic, my father told stories from when he was a boy. "We didn't have television," he said. "Our neighbor had one, but we didn't."

We looked at him in amazement. "What did you do?" we asked.

"We did this," my father said.

The light above the sink came on, and my mother quickly got up and turned it off. Listening to our father's voice, his face lit by the candlelight, we pretended not to notice the electricity had returned.

And so "no electricity night" was born. One night a month, we turned off the lights and gathered around the kitchen table. They were among my childhood's brightest nights.

Lord, thank You for the traditions that bind our family together. —SABRA CIANCANELLI

TRUTH LASTS. . . . *—Proverbs 12:19* (MSG)

I sat on the edge of a circle of friends at a baby shower recently, watching Sara, a young mother-to-be, open her gifts. My friends and I exchanged wistful sighs as we passed around the gifts. So much had changed since we became mothers a generation ago.

Sara already knew she'd be having a girl, so there were many frilly, gender-appropriate gifts. She also received a baby monitor that lets you hear and see what the baby is doing in another part of the house, a bouncy seat that gently vibrates the baby, a wet-wipe-warmer to toast up the diaper changes, and a pillow designed to help prop up the baby while nursing.

The hostess asked us to go around and offer advice to this first-time mom. From moms of all ages came these tidbits:

- Trust your instincts.
- Write down the cute things the baby says and does. You think you'll never forget, but guess what? You do.
- Disappear for several hours at least a once a week and leave the baby with Daddy. Try to do this during the baby's cranky time, so Dad "gets it."
- When people offer to help, let them.
- It's never too early to start reading to the baby.
- Ask for help.
- Cultivate patience.
- Go easy on yourself. Mothering is the hardest job you'll ever have.
- And finally, enjoy these years, they pass so quickly! (*Aha!* Some things never change.)

Father, Your timeless truth endures forever.

—CAROL KUYKENDALL

GREAT PEACE HAVE THOSE WHO LOVE YOUR LAW. . . .
                                        —*Psalm 119:165 (NKJV)*

My lifelong love affair with the Bible and its Author was kind-
led by some great examples in my youth, such as George
Stansberry, an itinerant preacher from Kentucky, who held
meetings all over the Midwest.

George was every inch a gentleman, a young Peter O'Toole
in navy blue suits and crisp white shirts and classic ties. His
voice was so rich that when he read from the Bible, we were
sure it was the voice of God Himself. Like the Music Man,
George floated across the platform, his dark eyes flashing and
his warm smile charming us. He told lots of Bible stories, acting
them out with a skill he had picked up in drama school.

Most of all, I remember the way George handled his Bible.
He held it with the care you would give a newborn baby. When
he turned its pages, he was like a professor examining a priceless manuscript.

When George gave me a Bible of my own, I treasured it. I
set about memorizing key passages that I thought I might need
in the future.

National Bible Sunday would be a good time to give a modern version of the Bible to some young person you love: a high
school or college graduate, or a young couple with stars in
their eyes. It might be the very thing that will start them out
right in life. It certainly did that for me.

*I'm grateful, God, for the instruction manual of Your Word,
so that I didn't have to learn everything the hard way.*
                                        —DANIEL SCHANTZ

GIVE THANKS TO HIM AND PRAISE HIS NAME.
> *—Psalm 100:4 (NIV)*

After I had surgery to remove a large tumor behind my eye a couple of years ago, I telephoned the churches who had prayed for me to thank them and give a praise report. Because of a new medical procedure, I'd had very little bleeding and my surgeons were able to remove most of the tumor with no nerve damage.

"That's wonderful, Roberta," Barbara at Judson Baptist Church in Eleanor, West Virginia, said. "We'll be sure to put it in the bulletin. We have two columns: 'Prayer Requests' and 'Answered Prayers.' Of course, the request column is always a lot longer."

I couldn't get Barbara's comment out of my mind. *How often am I like that in my personal prayer life? My "Please Help Me" column is always much longer than my "I'm Grateful" column.*

But with God's help, I vowed to change that. I started a prayer journal to record my requests and the ways God moves in my life to answer them. Doing so also reminded me to give feedback to the people I've asked to pray for me about a particular situation.

I'm continually amazed at the many answers to prayer that I long took for granted. Being grateful is such a wonderful place to be, I'm making it a lifelong habit.

Great is Your faithfulness, Lord, when I make my requests known to You. Thank You. —ROBERTA MESSNER

*BECAUSE HE IS AT MY RIGHT HAND, I WILL NOT BE
SHAKEN.* —*Psalm 16:8 (NIV)*

I'm extremely nearsighted and so dependent on my glasses
that I only remove them to sleep.

One afternoon I felt very tired and decided to take a short
nap. The sound of someone knocking at the door woke me
up, but when I reached for my glasses, they had vanished.

The knocking grew louder and the phone started to ring.
I felt panicky as I realized I was alone in the house and virtually
blind. "Lord," I said as I groped, "would You please help me out
here?"

I couldn't find my glasses, so I gave up searching and followed the sound of the phone. On the way I tripped over
something. The phone stopped ringing before I reached it, but
someone was still at the door. I retraced my steps and tripped
over the same thing again.

"What *is* this?" I said as I picked it up. It was my purse; the
same purse in which I kept a pair of prescription sunglasses!
Grinning, I put them on and answered the door. I had to laugh
at the very odd look the deliveryman gave me.

Later I found my glasses under the bed. One of our cats had
knocked them down there, but I definitely know Who made
me trip over my purse.

*Dear Lord, knowing that You are the light means that I never
have to be afraid.* —REBECCA KELLY

MY FLESH AND MY HEART MAY FAIL, BUT GOD IS THE
STRENGTH OF MY HEART AND MY PORTION FOREVER.
—*Psalm 73:26 (NIV)*

Our sons were all born with a rare blood disorder. Ryan and
Joel barely survived it, but by the time of our third son's birth,
a machine was available that would cleanse Kathy's blood of
antibodies so that it could be given to the baby and prevent the
severe reactions Ryan and Joel had suffered. The doctor set a
definite date for the procedure—the baby would be delivered
by C-section—and assembled an expert medical team.

But Kathy's labor pains began on a holiday weekend. She
called the doctor, and he was dismayed: Except for the technician who operated the blood-cleansing machine, the members
of the team were all away for the holiday. The hospital staff
was tense, and so were we.

Everything seemed to be going well until it was time to
begin the blood-cleansing. The technician couldn't get the
machine started. She tried a few times, with no success. At that
point even Kathy, the most positive thinker I know, began to
look frightened and her blood pressure began to rise.

"Aren't you a pastor?" asked the technician. "Let's pray for
God's help."

I prayed. And after our prayer, the machine began its work
and soon a healthy Kyle Vincent Nace was in his mother's arms.

Father God, I know my weakness. I depend on Your strength
to make my life a joy. —TED NACE

IT IS A GOOD THING TO GIVE THANKS UNTO THE LORD. . . .
                                                  —*Psalm 92:1*

It seems to take hours for everybody to get seated on Thanksgiving. The steaming mashed potatoes fog up people's glasses, the stuffing spills off the serving platter, the dish of cranberry sauce gets passed around, there's a request for salt and pepper from one end of the table—sometimes two tables in our cramped dining room. And then, something that's a tradition in our house: There's a clink of a spoon against a glass for silence. "Pam, do you want to start?" I ask. Pam, an old friend, is good at setting the mood.

"I'd like to say how grateful I am for my mother and what she gave me when I was growing up," she begins. The opportunity is passed around the table, just like that dish of cranberry sauce. From five-year-olds to ninety-five-year-olds, everyone gets to express what they're thankful for. The litany is wide-ranging, from a winning soccer season and the life of a pet rabbit to good health. Tears well up behind the fogged glasses. The teenagers roll their eyes at first, then rise in eloquence to the occasion. I start worrying that the succotash is growing cold and the pie will burn in the oven. But blessings must be said. We are a group of many faiths, and one or two with no declared faith at all. But thanksgiving runs deep.

Lord, I'm thankful for this day when thankfulness is on everyone's lips. —RICK HAMLIN

ESAU RAN TO MEET JACOB AND EMBRACED HIM. . . . AND THEY WEPT. —*Genesis 33:4 (NIV)*

My older brother and I were close when we were children—Dave's fist was often close to my nose, and I was often close to tears during those rare occasions when we were together. We don't talk about our former animosity—it's grace enough to know that we love each other today.

Last year my wife and I spent Thanksgiving with Dave and his family. Dave's grandsons Grant and Nathaniel wanted us to play kickball with them. Nathaniel offered to referee. He wanted his grandpa to referee too. Grant angrily pointed out that we couldn't have teams if half the players were refs.

"But I can't be the referee for two teams," Nathaniel whined. He set up two chairs, one for each ref. He tried to sit in both chairs at the same time, straddling the edge of each. "It's not working!" he wailed. Nathaniel was behaving exactly as I had as a child. Grant was behaving just like Dave.

Dave may have been like Esau to my Jacob as a child, but he now had to become Solomon for his grandchildren. He declared Grant the captain of one team, me the captain of the other and himself the other referee. He and Nathaniel kept track of Grant's numerous ghost runners, calling them out or safe depending on the skills of my imaginary outfielders. I don't remember the score or the rules of the game, but I'll always remember the love and patience my brother had for his grandchildren—for the child like him and for the child like me.

Dear God, thank You for the love and wisdom You give me when I need them both. —TIM WILLIAMS

THEN GOD SAW EVERYTHING THAT HE HAD MADE, AND INDEED IT WAS VERY GOOD. . . . —Genesis 1:31 (NKJV)

Many times (usually Saturday mornings) I've deceived myself into thinking that a day doing nothing would be the most wonderful day imaginable. *Nothing* doesn't literally mean nothing, of course. It means doing only the things that I want to do, like kicking back with a good book in my cushy recliner or catching up on three months' worth of magazines or watching political talk shows for a few uninterrupted hours.

To do that I have to ignore not only the clutter, the house that wants cleaning, the projects that need completing and the finances that need attention, but also the sick sense of dread at tackling it all. That's tough to ignore, but too often I manage. And you know what? A day like that has never been all that wonderful. In fact, I almost always regret it.

On the other hand I've never regretted a productive Saturday. I love relaxing after a hard day's work, when everything's in its place, vacuum marks are still on the carpet and the scent of furniture polish lingers in the air.

I recently heard a speaker suggest that after all God's creating, He designed a day of rest just so He could sit back and savor the joy in work well done. That's exactly how I feel when I've resisted the urge to do nothing and have a Saturday full of finished chores behind me.

Father, would You remind me every Saturday morning how good hard work feels? —LUCILE ALLEN

NOVEMBER 26

IT IS THE LORD YOUR GOD YOU MUST FOLLOW, AND HIM
YOU MUST REVERE. KEEP HIS COMMANDS AND OBEY HIM;
SERVE HIM AND HOLD FAST TO HIM.
—*Deuteronomy 13:4* (NIV)

Our refrigerator's icemaker and water dispenser had stopped
working; not even a dribble was coming through. Hesitating
to pay for a repairman, I mentioned the problem to a friend at
church.

"It's probably the solenoid," he said. "I had that happen
twice, and both times I replaced the solenoid. That's all there
is to it."

I checked my home handyman manual, which explained
how to test the solenoid, an electrical coil that opened and
closed the water valve. So I pulled the refrigerator away from
the wall, removed the solenoid-valve assembly, which is a single
piece, and tested it with a meter. Surprisingly, the reading
showed there was nothing wrong with it. Confused, I gave up
and called a repairman.

"You can't go by the reading," the repairman said. "There
can be current flowing through the solenoid, but the valve can
still be stuck." He replaced the assembly with a new one, and
the refrigerator has been dispensing ice and water ever since.
If only I'd known what the repairman knew, I thought, *I could
have saved the cost of his bill.*

But I'd learned a valuable lesson. Reading a handyman's
guide didn't make me a repairman. Some things need to be
learned by experience.

That's true with my spiritual life. I pray and read the Bible,
but those practices alone aren't enough. It's when I do what
God tells me to do that I really see results. Prayer and Bible
reading provide the current, but my obedience is required for
God's blessings to flow.

*Father, show me what You want me to do today. I want to
hear and obey.* —HAROLD HOSTETLER

"IF YOU HAVE FAITH AS SMALL AS A MUSTARD SEED. . . .
NOTHING WILL BE IMPOSSIBLE FOR YOU."
—*Matthew 17:20-21 (NIV)*

I grew up in the church, but my friend Stacey didn't. Now, as a young woman, she was awakening to the whole spiritual side of life. It was exciting for me, but a bit frightening too. Her faith was so young and tender—I was afraid that one great trial would send her reeling.

Then her dog Arkus got sick—very sick. Stacey was devastated. She took Arkus to the vet, and when they hooked up Arkus to IVs and other machines, Stacey spent whole afternoons lying beside her, praying.

Late one evening Stacey stopped by my house in tears. "I don't want Arkus to die! She's my best friend!" Silently, I considered the facts. Arkus was twelve years old. She had a severe digestive problem. The vet had not been encouraging. So I talked to Stacey about how there is a time for everything, about how much joy Arkus had given her over the years, about how God was a god of love and could give us peace no matter what happened. Then Stacey went her way—and kept praying that Arkus would be well again.

Two weeks later, my back door opened and in romped Arkus, complete with shaved areas where the IVs had been. Stacey glowed as she said, "See, God healed her! I knew He would!"

Mature faith is wonderful, but maybe it takes a new believer to remind us that all things are possible—for herself, for me and for a much-loved pooch.

Thank You, Father, for the exuberance of newfound trust—and for Your love for all Your creatures! —MARY LOU CARNEY

*AND THIS IS LIFE ETERNAL, THAT THEY MIGHT KNOW THEE
THE ONLY TRUE GOD, AND JESUS CHRIST, WHOM THOU
HAST SENT. —John 17:3*

We had been sailing for a week in the waters and ice of
Antarctica, stopping at peopleless islands, taking rubber rafts
from the *Explorer II*. We saw firsthand a world forbidding to
humans yet teeming with wildlife—chinstrap penguins, leopard
seals, storm petrels, humpback whales and orcas. What can I
say? I can only begin to list what was there.

Twice a day there were lectures on everything from wildlife
to paleontology. One day my nephew Gordy and I were listening to a talk on Sir Ernest Shackleton's heroic escape from
Antarctica's subzero conditions. The speaker stood across a
bare dance floor in front of an oak lectern—heavy, solid oak.
Suddenly, a mighty rogue wave hit the ship abeam.

"Look out!"

I heard the cry as the ship rolled and the podium plunged
straight at me. I moved a fraction. The podium struck my leg.

"Are you all right?" There was a crowd around me.

"Yes," I mumbled, "I'm okay." My right leg was a little sore.

"I thought you were a goner," a man said. "It was lucky that
you moved that little bit."

That night, I couldn't sleep. About 3:00 A.M., I went out on
deck. It was already dawn. The mystery of Antarctica surrounded me, the desolate icescape filled with a pristine wonder.

It was there that I communed with God.

*Thank You, Father, for the continued privilege of being alive
in Your beautiful world.* —VAN VARNER

THE WISDOM FROM ABOVE IS FIRST PURE, THEN
PEACEABLE, GENTLE, REASONABLE, FULL OF MERCY AND
GOOD FRUITS. . . . *—James 3:17 (NAS)*

More than fifteen years ago, I went through an emotionally draining period. I spent a good deal of time alone in my basement office, struggling to come to grips with things. Then one day the postman rang the doorbell to deliver a small parcel. I recognized our daughter's handwriting on the label and wondered what had prompted her to send me a gift. Inside, nestled in some crumpled tissue paper, was a pewter pear.

As I lifted the pear's lid, a gentle breeze blew through the open window, scattering the contents of the pear across the kitchen floor. Scrambling to retrieve the snippets of colored paper, I noticed our daughter had printed out a different Bible promise on each one. There must have been several dozen all told. I could just imagine her in her pajamas, sitting cross-legged on her bed with her Bible in her lap, painstakingly printing out each promise she found. I phoned her that evening to thank her.

"That's your prayer pear, Mom. I found it in a secondhand shop and decided to fill it with some encouraging verses. And you know what? I think I benefited just as much as you will."

Thank You, Lord, that the fruit of Your Spirit blesses the one who manifests it just as much as the one who is refreshed by it. —ALMA BARKMAN

*"AND WHO KNOWS WHETHER YOU HAVE NOT COME TO THE
KINGDOM FOR JUST SUCH A TIME AS THIS?"*
—*Esther 4:14 (RSV)*

Long before the wildly successful show *CSI* introduced all
America to the language of crime scene investigations, it was a
language I knew. That's because the police-detective father of
a childhood friend of mine often talked to us about his work.
His message was the same as the hit TV show: "You never
know where you might find the one essential fact that solves
the case. So pay attention."

Recently I had to decide whether to leave my current job
for a new opportunity. The choice was neither easy nor clear-
cut. There were good reasons to stay and good reasons to go,
and no one reason seemed to rise above any of the others.
Frankly, I was stymied.

In the end, I didn't take the new job. But not because my
long list of pros and cons finally swayed me in a particular
direction, and not because of salary or opportunity for advance-
ment or power. Rather, it was because of a small clue I found in
a book I was reading about a group of Belgians who helped
Jews during World War II—one brief phrase that resounded
within me for days: "We chose to stay with those who needed
us most."

Like Moses stumbling upon the burning bush or Peter hearing the call of a stranger, I've learned to pay attention to what's
around me. You never know where you might find an essential
word from God.

*Your guidance is still real today, God. Open my eyes and heart
to those unexpected places of Your leading.* —JEFF JAPINGA

FOR GOD SO LOVED THE WORLD, THAT HE GAVE HIS ONLY BEGOTTEN SON. . . . —John 3:16

It was December 1, and I hadn't even started on Christmas preparations. I hadn't picked our cards, bought a single gift, gotten ready for the houseguests arriving in two days. I'd come back the night before from a Thanksgiving trip to our son's home in Miami—an anxious time following his recent surgery.

As I waited for my computer to come to life, I thumbed through a stack of unanswered letters. My desktop appeared on the monitor; every icon seemed to scream *overdue assignment!* I was staring at a bottomless scroll of e-mails when the phone rang, then the doorbell.

And so it went for two increasingly frantic hours as each thing I turned to meant not doing something else equally pressing. I was near tears when the printer suddenly gave a cough and a whir and flung a piece of blank paper onto the tray. I snatched the unasked-for sheet from the tray and slapped it back on the paper stack.

And as I did, something caught my eye. Way up in the far left corner was a tiny black mark. I picked it up and looked closer.

It was a heart.

Now the tears that had been building really did come. Anxiety, weariness, pressure—all of it poured out, released and relieved, at the sight of that small symbol appearing in a totally unexpected place. As unexpected as a stable for the birthplace of a king, as small as a baby born to save the world.

It's love, that little heart said. *Love was the reason for the trip to Miami. Love is the reason for the cards and the gifts and the guests and the letters to answer and the work God has given you to do. The loving chores you've taken on are simply your response to the Love that came down at Christmas.*

Faithful Lord, keep my focus this busy month on the reason for the season. —ELIZABETH SHERRILL

THEN THE LORD SAID TO MOSES, "I WILL RAIN DOWN
BREAD FROM HEAVEN FOR YOU. THE PEOPLE ARE TO GO
OUT EACH DAY AND GATHER ENOUGH FOR THAT DAY. . . ."
—*Exodus 16:4 (NIV)*

Humming a Christmas tune, I rinsed the fresh cranberries in my stainless steel colander. Time to start baking my first batch of cranberry nut bread. Although I'd never had much interest in cooking, baking bread was a fun and economical way for me to give to others at Christmastime.

My husband Roy walked into the kitchen, his brow wrinkled with concern. "We really need to replace the tires on the car," he said. "I know the budget is tight for the holidays, but we'll just have to figure something out."

My thoughts raced ahead. *We could use my expense check next month, but what if it isn't enough? What if we have to use some of our Christmas budget?* I didn't feel so festive anymore.

But then as I sifted the flour and the baking powder together, I recalled a conversation I'd had years ago with a close friend. I was a single mother and a full-time student at the time, and worried about paying my tuition for my next two semesters. We spent some time in prayer. After we'd recited the Lord's Prayer, she said, "God promises us our *daily* bread—not flour for tomorrow. We need to have the faith that He will provide for our future as well as our present." One week later an unexpected scholarship more than covered my school expenses.

That day I'd learned an important lesson. Today I would share that lesson with others. So when the cranberry nut bread cooled off, I wrapped the loaves in the usual green cellophane with a red ribbon and a handmade message that said, *Merry Christmas!* But this year I added the following prayer to the label:

Master Provider, may we always remember that the bread we eat in the here and now becomes the promise of bread forevermore. —MELODY BONNETTE

SING UNTO THE LORD A NEW SONG. . . . —*Psalm 149:1*

Although I sang and played guitar with the children at our church before religious education classes every Sunday, I hadn't reckoned on being the music director for a full-blown Christmas pageant. Didn't I have enough stress in my life already? *We'll do a few familiar tunes and get through it,* I told myself.

Then Julie, my friend and accompanist, turned up with a new song. "You'll just love it!" she exclaimed, launching into a bouncy rhythm on the piano. "Come on, ring those bells . . ." Well, it *was* catchy, but how were we going to teach it to ninety kids?

Over the next month we worked on our song once a week. I loved it just as Julie had predicted, and the kids seemed to catch my enthusiasm. "Come on, ring those bells," we sang. "Everybody say 'Jesus we remember this, Your birthday.'" But how were they going to learn all those words? We printed the lyrics on poster board to cue the readers. We dreamed up gestures to remind the prereaders: *Jesus is our King* (finger crown overhead).

Christmas Eve arrived. Our once-squirmy crew, now outfitted in white, glittery ponchos and crowned with tinsel halos, looked angelic indeed. The service progressed serenely. At last we were ready for the recessional, our new song. The children belted it out, exuberantly ringing the huge jingle bells hidden all evening under their ponchos. So much jingling! So much joy! The congregation caught the spirit with wide smiles and a few tears.

For the next ten years the youngsters at our church continued to sing our "new" song at the close of the Christmas Eve service. Several former students, now parents themselves, recall it as one of their best Christmas memories.

I'm glad Julie pushed me to learn a new song.

Lord, thank You for those who nudge me out of the status quo to keep my praises fresh. —GAIL THORELL SCHILLING

*"STORE UP FOR YOURSELVES TREASURES IN HEAVEN, WHERE
MOTH AND RUST DO NOT DESTROY, AND WHERE THIEVES DO
NOT BREAK IN AND STEAL."* —*Matthew 6:20 (NIV)*

When I was little, my dad drove an old car that was painted a
dull shade of gold so that you wouldn't notice the rust unless
you looked closely. Each day he drove the car home for lunch,
and as soon as we heard the front door swing open, we
sprinted toward him. "Daddy!" we yelled.

Except for the hottest months of summer, he always wore a
knee-length leather coat. When we reached him at the door,
we jumped and tried to grab hold of his coat as high up as we
could and then ascend it like rock climbers on the side of a
cliff. The leather was smooth and cool, and I can still remember
its sweet fragrance.

After lunch he climbed back into his little gold car, and
we waved good-bye with our noses pressed so close against
the window that our breath fogged the glass. After he drove
away, we wrote our names with our fingers in the condensation
on the window.

One night when he came home for dinner, he walked by
the windows and scowled. "I don't want you boys to get too
close to the windows anymore," he said. "And please don't rub
your hands on them. They look smeared."

We obeyed and stood several feet away from the glass. We
did this for several days. Then one day Dad said, "I've changed
my mind. The glass might look a little messy, but soon you guys
are going to be grown up, and I'll wish you could come back
and write your names on the window again."

Looking back, I see evidence of a man who had his priori-
ties straight. He was storing up his treasures in heaven, a place
where the streets are made of real gold and rust doesn't even
exist.

Thank You, Lord, for the saints You give us here on earth.
                                              —JOSHUA SUNDQUIST

*ON HIM WE HAVE SET OUR HOPE THAT HE WILL CONTINUE
TO DELIVER US, AS YOU HELP US BY YOUR PRAYERS. . . .*
— *II Corinthians 1:10-11 (NIV)*

Nine years ago, I had to have back surgery for a very painful cyst in one of the tiny joints that connect the spinal column with the sacrum. I was told that the operation was a delicate one that could damage the nerves of the spinal column, but I was in such severe pain that I chose to have it anyway. Many people were praying for the success of my surgery. Thanks be to God, I came through the operation well and the pain gradually subsided.

Now that unwanted visitor is back! A few weeks ago, I began to have pain in the identical place on the other side of my body. An MRI confirmed the diagnosis.

As I write this, piercing pain is shooting from my lower back down my left leg, ankle and foot. The date for my spinal surgery is two months away. How can I bear it?

I looked through my journals from my previous back surgery and discovered that pain has been a strong teacher for me. The following words are from 1995:

> 4/14/95. Looking back on my last few entries, I see I've been using the words *my pain* over and over again. But I also realize I'm certainly not the only one hurting today! So I'll pray for all of us who are in pain, whoever and wherever we are. As I write these words in my journal, I seem to see candles glowing in hearts all over the world. Pain is the great connector, linking us with all others who are, at this very moment, in great pain too. We truly are one body, and maybe if I could focus on opening my heart during episodes of pain, I could embrace all others in their suffering and pain, praying that all of us may be comforted.

O Comforter, may we pray for each other now in our shared pain. How brightly our candles shine with Your healing love!
— MARILYN MORGAN KING

*"AND MANY OF THOSE WHO SLEEP IN THE DUST OF THE
EARTH SHALL AWAKE. . . ." —Daniel 12:2 (RSV)*

Los Angeles is the largest city in the world built in a desert. So
when it rains several inches a day, and continues to do so on
and off for a couple of weeks, the ground becomes saturated
pretty fast. Runoff achieves mythic proportions as flash floods
sweep down the control channels.

Yet, during all the drama of recent rainstorms, a small wonder in our front yard evoked more awe in my husband Keith
and me than the forces of nature on a rampage: The dirt in
which our roses grow became carpeted with moss. Looking at
it, we felt a wonder born of nature's surprising lesson—that
spores of the moss could hibernate in the desert ground for
years without ever sprouting, and yet the potential to sprout
was always there, under the surface.

God gives every growing thing all the potential to sprout.
We may lie dormant for a long time, but when conditions are
right, we, like the humble, velvety green moss, can still appear,
thrive and grow.

I'm ready to answer Your call, God. What is Your will today?
                                                    —RHODA BLECKER

"Thou liftest me up on the wind, thou makest me ride on it, and thou tossest me about in the roar of the storm." —Job 30:22 (RSV)

"This is the captain speaking. There's a lot of weather around the Denver airport, so you might want to buckle up early as we try to land."

Whoa! What was that? Try to land? I dutifully fastened my seatbelt and attempted another article in the in-flight magazine, but no chance. We were beginning the roughest reentry since Orville at Kitty Hawk, bouncing around like a Chihuahua on caffeine. Finally the runway came into sight. We were still all a-jolt, but at least we were on the ground.

Wrong! The pilot aborted the landing at the last second and we went screaming skyward. After a few minutes of top-notch roller-coaster action, the pilot informed us that we were going to Colorado Springs. Some people applauded. No one complained about the abrupt delay; phone calls were made, plans changed, meetings rescheduled. Once we were on terra firma, I was tempted to kiss the ground.

I cannot tell how many times my life has met with rough weather and bumpy rides, and usually without the warning to buckle up. Birth, death, joy, sorrow—they pop up like a sudden thunderstorm. Sometimes you land. Sometimes you try to land, then take off again. Sometimes you end up in a completely different place, and there's nothing to do but call on the Almighty and ride it out.

Lord, when the storms of life are tossing me about, help me to remember that only You can say, "Peace, be still" (Mark 4:39).
—Mark Collins

THE LORD HATH APPEARED OF OLD UNTO ME, SAYING, YEA,
I HAVE LOVED THEE WITH AN EVERLASTING LOVE. . . .
                                                    —*Jeremiah 31:3*

I'd been cleaning up for about fifteen minutes when I saw then-seven-year-old Elizabeth in the kitchen doorway. "I can't get to sleep," she said.

I took my daughter back to the kids' room and tucked her into her top-bunk bed. "Will you snuggle with me a little?" she asked.

"Of course, honey," I said. I leaned against the bunk and put my arms around her. "Is everything okay?"

"I feel bad about something," Elizabeth said.

I straightened up and looked at her as I stroked her hair. Elizabeth is a bright, inquisitive, articulate girl where most things are concerned, but her emotions are an exception. Most of the time, if she seems troubled and I ask her how she's feeling, her answer is "I don't know" or "I won't tell you." But this time was different.

"I don't want to grow up," Elizabeth said.

"Why?" I asked.

"I'm afraid I'll be too big to snuggle." At seven, Elizabeth no longer fit over a shoulder or in the crook of an arm the way five-year-old John and three-year-old Mary did.

"You'll never be too big for a hug, honey," I said. "Mommy and I won't stop loving you just because you're getting bigger."

"But I want to be little, so you can carry me."

"I know you do. But God made us so that we grow from children into adults, and although that might seem scary right now, it has its rewards—like an Elizabeth to snuggle and to watch grow up."

"I know that," Elizabeth said. "But it still makes me sad not to be little."

My arms ached as I leaned over her bunk. I hugged her for a long while before I went back to cleaning up.

Father, no matter how grown-up I get, I'll never be too big for Your arms. —ANDREW ATTAWAY

I WILL SING OF THE LORD'S GREAT LOVE FOREVER. . . .
—*Psalm 89:1 (NIV)*

Not long ago I heard our son Ryan talking on the phone in his room. He'd gone through a lot over the course of the year—a wonderful trip to Germany, a week at a Young Life camp in Georgia, the loss of his older brother Reggie in a car accident and his seventeenth birthday in July. He was a young man now, and I wondered how much longer his mother and I would be the defining influences in his life.

I walked past Ryan's room and saw him on his knees, the phone in one hand, a Bible in the other. Later I asked him about it.

"Dad, I was talking to one of my friends," he said. "She was having some difficulties, and I was encouraging her with Scripture."

Wow! Ryan had been practicing what we had been teaching him all his life. I wanted to praise God.

Now, whenever I start to wonder if my children—or anyone else—is really listening to me, I remind myself that if I'm faithful and share the truth as best I can, our heavenly Father will accomplish all that He wants to accomplish through me.

Father, help me to do my best to be faithful and entrust the rest to You. —DOLPHUS WEARY

I ALSO WILL REQUITE YOU THIS KINDNESS, BECAUSE YE HAVE DONE THIS THING. —II Samuel 2:6

What would Christmas be without a tree? From the lodge-pole pine that resembled a coat rack our first year in Wyoming to the firs we wired to the ceiling to withstand energetic cats and toddlers, each year's tree had a story. When the children were small and the budget tight, we'd buy a five-dollar permit and cut our own tree in the Shoshone National Forest. Squabbles over who dragged the tree and who rode the sled were part of the adventure. In later years I bought trees from a World War II veteran in town who never rushed me, even at night in a snow-fall. But none of those were the tree that I remember best.

That year our family friend Larry offered to buy us a tree. He liked doing nice things for us and wanted to support a church youth group selling trees twenty-five miles away. We thought the fifty-mile drive generous, indeed, and thanked him. He said he'd deliver our tree that afternoon.

Larry turned up on our doorstep on time but empty-handed. "They were closed," he said simply. "I'll go back tomorrow." We protested, but he would have none of it.

The next evening when I returned home from work, I found a lovely spruce on my front porch. Larry had driven one hundred miles to keep his promise—and make sure we had a Christmas tree.

Maybe my imagination played tricks on me, but I think the Christmas tree lights twinkled more brightly that year.

Lord, thank You for the gifts that can never be boxed and wrapped—my precious friends. —GAIL THORELL SCHILLING

I RISE BEFORE DAWN AND CRY FOR HELP; I HOPE IN THY WORDS. —*Psalm 119:147* (RSV)

My eyes were barely open when I looked at the alarm clock. Who could be calling at 4:00 A.M.? My wife Elba reached over and picked up the phone. "Christine, are you all right?" she asked. It was our daughter calling from her college dorm in Miami.

"Why are you crying?" Elba asked. "What happened?"

There was a long pause, then Elba said, "Christine, it's four in the morning. You ought to go to bed. Talk to your professor tomorrow."

Elba paused to tell me what had happened: Christine had a mental block and couldn't finish the term paper that was due that morning.

At first I was happy because it wasn't a life-threatening situation, but then I became upset. *How could Christine be calling us at this time of the morning? Didn't she know that we needed our rest?*

I lay back and tried to let go of my irritation, focusing on Elba's voice instead. "You're going to be fine," she told Christine. "If you explain what happened to your professor, she'll understand."

How patient she is, I thought. *It's as if there's nothing she'd rather be doing than listening to her child and helping her with her problem.*

I turned over, and as I drifted back to sleep, I whispered a prayer for Christine, confident that God was listening. Even at 4:00 A.M.

Dear God, there's never a wrong to time to call out to You.

—PABLO DIAZ

*HE HEALETH THE BROKEN IN HEART, AND BINDETH UP
THEIR WOUNDS.* —*Psalm 147:3*

I really love the Christmas season, and I do my utmost to share
that love with family and friends. But with all the hustle and
bustle, I need to be reminded that Jesus is the reason for it all.
So I've made the nativity scene under our Christmas tree the
centerpiece of my decorations. Mary and Joseph are two feet
tall, and Jesus lies in the manger with His arms outstretched as
if to embrace the whole world.

Last year, it was particularly hard for me to feel the Christmas
spirit. It would be the first one without my father, and his
absence had never seemed more profound. Also, a good friend
had recently been diagnosed with breast cancer, and my heart
ached each time I prayed for her.

During an especially hectic day I paused in the doorway
of the den to admire the crèche and right away noticed that
something was wrong: One of the wise men had toppled over
onto Baby Jesus. One of His arms had broken off and rested
on the carpet next to the manger. *Oh no,* I thought, *my perfect
Christmas scene is ruined!*

I bent down to pick up the broken figure, then got out the
glue and repaired the little arm. As I worked, I thought about
the love that brought this Child to birth in Bethlehem. That
love would hold our family together now, even though Dad
was gone, and keep my ailing friend whole in spirit.

I put the baby back in the manger. I still had lots to do to
get ready for Christmas.

*Lord, You came among us to heal our brokenness. May Your
love hold us all together now and always.* —DEBBIE MACOMBER

Do not neglect to do good and to share what you have, for such sacrifices are pleasing to God.
        —Hebrews 13:16 (RSV)

"Mom, I did the *spwinkles*."

I looked up from cutting out sugar cookies and inspected Maggie's work. "Those are great colors, honey. But if you were a hungry three-year-old, would those cookies look like they had enough sprinkles?"

Maggie looked doubtful. "No. But I want to save the rest for us!"

"Don't worry. We have plenty of sprinkles. Right now let's think about the hungry people who will get these cookies."

The cookies were slated for the neighborhood food pantry. Along with two dozen families in our neighborhood, we were making home-baked goodies for the bags of food given out the week before Christmas. For the older kids the project was a hands-on way to help the poor. For Maggie, baking for others held a more basic lesson.

Maggie put a few more sprinkles on the cookies. "There, Mom."

"That looks better, sweetie. I think a hungry three-year-old would like those cookies. Unless you think she'd be happier with even more sprinkles."

Maggie's eyes lit up and she sprinkled the bottle of non-pareils madly. I almost regretted urging her to put herself in someone else's shoes. But some of the tiny candies did actually land on cookies. As hundreds more scattered across the floor, I picked my way across the multicolored sea to retrieve the vacuum. A little bit of texture in the rug is a small price to pay for broadening the heart of a preschooler.

Lord, remind me that the reason You gave me sprinkles is so that I can share them. —JULIA ATTAWAY

*A DREAM COMETH THROUGH THE MULTITUDE OF
BUSINESS. . . .* —*Ecclesiastes 5:3*

Since I can remember, I've had dreams in which I'm flying.
That's far from unusual, of course. Any psychology student will
tell you that dreams of flight are universal. Iowa corn farmers,
Alaskan Eskimos, Australian investment bankers—everyone in
the world, it seems, dreams at one point or another that they
can leave the earth and gravity behind.

What's interesting to me about my flying dreams, however,
is that they're of two distinct kinds. The ones I remember most
vividly the next morning aren't those in which I'm swooping
around far above the ground. Those are fine, but the ones that
carry real magic are of a more low-key variety. I'll be walking
along someplace, on a beach perhaps or maybe just on the
street where I live, when suddenly I'll find myself lifting up
and floating a few inches off the ground. The difference is so
slight and subtle that the people around me—if there happen
to be any—don't even notice it.

Why do these modest dreams of flight mean so much to
me? I think it's precisely because they are modest. In dreams,
anything can happen. But these dreams where I'm lifted and
carried just a few inches off the ground remind me that in
dreams, just as in waking life, the most wonderful changes of
perspective often come with the smallest change in viewpoint.
Sometimes just a few inches will do it.

*Lord, keep me awake to the little changes in perspective that
can make all the difference in how I see the world.*

                                        —PTOLEMY TOMPKINS

PUT YOUR HOPE IN GOD. . . . —*Psalm 42:5 (NIV)*

An out-of-town friend was stopping in my area on business and we'd arranged to meet for coffee before she headed back home. I looked forward to seeing her, yet dreaded it at the same time.

Helen had lost her job several years back and now was losing her home. A brand-new Christian, she was facing her first real crisis of faith. "Every sermon I hear and every book I pick up says God is going to take care of me," she had challenged me the last time we spoke. "But where is He now, Roberta?" Every response that came to my mind seemed feeble in light of Helen's losses.

Fix her the nicest present you can think of. The idea came totally unbidden and seemed pointless. But I filled a gift bag shaped like an old-fashioned purse with a butter rum candle and a package of pansy-printed tissues, then tied a miniature teacup on the handle of the gift bag. When I presented the gift to Helen, she didn't even make eye contact.

It was several days later that I heard from her. "That candle," she gushed, "is absolutely wonderful. I burn it a little each day, so it will last. And the tissues—at least now I cry pretty." I heard a smile in her voice. "Can you help me find some more of those itty-bitty cups? Wherever I end up living, I want to have a little Christmas tree filled with them. God's going to take care of me, Roberta, just like He says."

May I always listen, Lord, for Your urgings, like the ones that turn despair into Christmas hope. —ROBERTA MESSNER

*EACH OF YOU SHOULD LOOK NOT ONLY TO YOUR OWN
INTERESTS, BUT ALSO TO THE INTERESTS OF OTHERS.*
                                        —*Philippians 2:4 (NIV)*

I'd seen them all my life. I'd even dropped coins and the occasional bill into their bright red buckets. But today I was going
to be one: a Salvation Army bell-ringer. And, frankly, I was feeling pretty pleased with myself. Here it was—just a couple of
Saturdays before Christmas, and despite a long to-do list, I had
volunteered to ring the bell that afternoon in front of a busy
drugstore.

I headed out early, determined to check at least a few
things off my list. When I encountered a Salvation Army
bucket outside my first stop, I couldn't resist saying "I'm going
to be doing that later" to the man behind the bell. He smiled
and kept ringing.

Later, when I came out of the store, he was ready with
advice for me. "Dress warmly," he said, "and make sure you wear
comfortable shoes." I think I saw a slight grimace as he said
that.

"How long are you here for?"

"Until nine P.M."

"But that's twelve hours!" I was scheduled to man my
bucket for exactly thirty minutes.

He smiled, shrugged his shoulders and went back to ringing
his bell.

At 3:30 that afternoon, I reported for duty. I wore a red
Santa hat and jingle bells on my wrists. I rang my bell with
enthusiasm and with gratitude too. Gratitude for all those people who sacrifice, in large and small ways, so others can have a
happier Christmas.

*At this holy season, Lord, make my heart tender and my
hands eager to bring joy to others. One coin, one half-hour,
one kindness at a time.* —MARY LOU CARNEY

THERE WAS NO ROOM FOR THEM IN THE INN. —*Luke 2:7*

For fifteen years while we lived in Wyoming, our friends Dick and Julie Lefevre always invited us to their *posada*. This Mexican Christmas celebration combines caroling with a reenactment of Mary and Joseph seeking shelter that holy night in Bethlehem. Although few of us were Mexican, all of us enjoyed the tradition, which kept us close to the heart of Christmas.

Carolers, bundled in parkas and carrying lanterns, would trek to friends' homes and sing a plea to be let in so that Mary could rest. The "innkeeper," usually someone from our choir, would step outside and sing an unaccompanied refusal from his or her porch. When temperatures plunged below zero, the singer's breath hung in the air like smoke.

While the carolers sang traditional carols, the innkeeper would quickly pack up his or her family and Mexican food to share, then join the procession to the next inn. After three or four stops, the carolers, now stamping feet to keep warm, wound up at the Lefevres. These gracious innkeepers sang, "Yes! Come in!" to the chilled singers, who duly trooped past flickering candles into their home. The fiesta had begun.

For the next several hours we savored a groaning board of Mexican fare, including huge pans of enchiladas and a Christmas salad with beets. When the older kids left to ice skate, the younger ones whacked the *piñata*. Then someone would start strumming a guitar. We'd sit on the floor and sing Christmas songs until, with a start, we realized that the ice rink had closed and we dashed to fetch our youngsters.

While I lived in Wyoming, we rarely celebrated Christmas with our relatives from the East Coast. But my *posada* family always made me feel at home in this ritual of food and song.

There was always room in the inn.

Divine Comforter, help us to remember that when we welcome others, we welcome You. —GAIL THORELL SCHILLING

APPLY THINE HEART UNTO INSTRUCTION, AND THINE EARS TO THE WORDS OF KNOWLEDGE. —*Proverbs 23:12*

My routine exam had shown no signs of the melanoma I'd had in the past. I'd just signed an eighteen-month lease on a beautiful home by the water. My children's book was being illustrated by an award-winning artist. Christmas was coming, and I was actually ready! So why was I so upset?

I sat by my glowing Christmas tree, tears running down my face, wondering what was wrong with me. I resisted sharing my silly troubles, knowing full well how ridiculous they seemed. But there was one person I could confide in: Kathy and I had grown up together, and there must have been something in the air in our neighborhood, because she, too, was an inveterate worrier. Like me, she worried about accidents, losing people she loved, money, dangerous weather and aging . . . among other things!

Knowing that she, at least, wouldn't think I should be committed, I called Kathy and listed my worries to her. Bless her, she deemed every one of them justified! Then she told me her worry bell clanged whenever her husband was late. She'd imagine an accident in every terrifying detail. Early in their marriage, she had told him how distressing this was for her, so they established a system. He would call if he had to be more than thirty minutes late. If he was less than thirty minutes late, she would wrestle her fears.

"Marse," Kathy concluded, "some things you change, and some things you manage." I hung up, thinking management was easier with a little help from my friends.

Father, everyone worries. Grant me the courage to share mine more often. —MARCI ALBORGHETTI

THEREFORE LET US STOP PASSING JUDGMENT ON ONE ANOTHER. INSTEAD, MAKE UP YOUR MIND NOT TO PUT ANY STUMBLING BLOCK OR OBSTACLE IN YOUR BROTHER'S WAY.
                        —Romans 14:13 (NIV)

Today I have some questions:

Why don't people walk faster in the cold, so they can get someplace warm sooner?

Do folks really need to be gabbing on their cell phones at the same time they're attempting to pay for purchases, thus slowing down the line? And while I'm on the subject, if you're going to take my money, can't you at least look at me when you do?

Don't people realize that yelling "Hold the elevator!" holds up the rest of us?

To the person who lingers over the paper in a crowded coffee shop: Can't you see there are other hungry customers waiting for your table?

And what's up with those people who don't bother filling out a deposit slip until they actually get up to the ATM?

Do fellow motorists really think that blowing the horn is going to make traffic move faster?

Finally, in a world full of God's beauty and blessings, where we see His glory and goodness at every turn, why do I allow myself to become so bogged down by life's small and unimportant irritations?

Lord, keep me from judging others. Grant me patience and understanding and the wisdom to love every moment of every day that You've given me. —EDWARD GRINNAN

MINE EYES ARE EVER TOWARD THE LORD. . . .
> —*Psalm 25:15*

The December my husband Terry and I cut our first Minnesota balsam, everything about the experience seemed strangely different from what we had done during our fourteen years in Alaska. There was barely a sprinkling of snow, and we had to go to a tree farm instead of tromping through the woods. When the farm turned out to be adjacent to the interstate, I rebelled. We headed away from the highway and found a more peaceful place situated among isolated farm fields.

Finally, we spotted a tree that looked about the right size and shape. Among its branches, tucked snugly in the boughs, was a bird's nest! Nearly twenty-five years before, while tree-hunting in a thick forest with our young children, we had unwittingly cut down a tree with a nest in it. When we decorated the tree, we left the nest exactly where we'd found it, figuring it was "God's ornament." Ever since then we had always placed a real bird's nest in our Christmas tree.

The nest decided us: This was our tree for the year. While we were cutting it, a second surprise startled us. From a barnyard somewhere close by, a rooster crowed! Our last Christmas Eve in Alaska had been spent with friends on their alpaca farm. Their independent-minded rooster had roused from his bed of straw and followed me about when I stepped outdoors alone, echoing my late-night praises to God with his own vigorous crowing—exactly as if he knew what he was saying. It had been unforgettably hilarious.

Now, here we stood, preparing for our first stay-at-home Christmas in our new home in a new state. Yet some things hadn't changed. I leaned into our fragrant tree and gave glory to God for His reminders that He can use any means—however unorthodox—to make me feel welcomed and cared for wherever Christmas finds me.

Lord, in this season of Your birth, keep me watchful for Your joyous presence. —CAROL KNAPP

*AND THOU SHALT HAVE JOY AND GLADNESS; AND MANY
SHALL REJOICE AT HIS BIRTH.* —*Luke 1:14*

I just received a 1977 clipping from a friend that brought my
brother Ham vividly to mind. Ham was a vice president of the
Quaker Oats Company and a member of numerous corporate
boards. When it came to himself, he was—let's just be frank
about it—a tightwad. That's why the clipping surprised me. It
concerned the fiftieth anniversary of Pan American Airways
and a different kind of round-the-world flight, this one over
both the North and South Poles. Some 117 passengers who
"like to fly" (no, not Ham) and who "wanted to be a part of a
historical aviation adventure" (hardly Ham, especially when I
thought about what the fare for such a flight must have cost).
Then, alongside the article, there was a picture of a man with
flowing white whiskers and a red cap bestowing gifts and
laughter to an enchanted group. *That* was Ham.

During the fifteen-minute countdown as the 747 Clipper
New Horizons approached the North Pole, Ham appeared from
the restroom with jingle bells and "Ho, ho, ho" to delight the
young and the old. Frugality was forgotten. It was so like him
after all. It made me think of my mother's saying that "Hamill
loves Christmas more than anyone." And he did. I saw it
Christmas after Christmas, when we went to the Winnetka
Congregational Church (where he was on the church's council), and we sang the hymns and celebrated the birth of the
Christ Child. No one sang louder, or with more tenderness,
than Ham.

*I have no doubt that he has found a way to amuse You, too,
Father.* —VAN VARNER

IN THIS WAS MANIFESTED THE LOVE OF GOD TOWARD US,
BECAUSE THAT GOD SENT HIS ONLY BEGOTTEN SON INTO
THE WORLD. . . . —I John 4:9

Every year on her birthday, my daughter Maria asks me to tell her the story of her birth. I tell her how I loved her from the moment I first saw her tiny heart beating on the ultrasound exam; how she surprised us, arriving five weeks early; and how we were nearly afraid of her, so small at four pounds, thirteen ounces. "Tell me again how Daddy sang 'Maria' from *West Side Story* the first time he brought me into your hospital room," she says. She wants to hear every detail again and again.

I imagine it's both powerful and mysterious for Maria to realize that, by some miracle and God's grace, she entered the world. But at its heart, it's a love story. Each time Maria hears it, she knows how very much we love her.

Perhaps that's why I never grow tired of hearing the story of Jesus' birth. Like a child, I savor every detail. *What did the angels say that night?* I think as I listen. "Glory to God in the highest!" And I wait to hear again how the astounded shepherds ran from their flocks to Bethlehem to see the wonderful mystery unfold.

This familiar story tells of more than a baby's birth. It reminds me that on one unforgettable night long ago, the great love of God came down to earth to save us from our sin. I've heard the story many times, but this season I'm listening even more closely, knowing that in all its familiar detail, it's simply telling me how very much God loves me.

Dear Father, show me again the way to the manger, the birth-place of Your love. —GINA BRIDGEMAN

FOR UNTO YOU IS BORN THIS DAY IN THE CITY OF DAVID A
SAVIOUR, WHICH IS CHRIST THE LORD. —*Luke 2:11*

It's 6:00 P.M. Christmas Eve 2003. My favorite service of the
entire year is about to begin. The sanctuary of our rural church
is richly dressed. Dark, fragrant greens drape the doors, blood-
red poinsettias adorn the altar, and candles flicker in each
window. The tree glistens with silver and white ornaments,
symbolizing our faith. Each star, dove, rose and cross was
crafted with love by a woman in the congregation.

The service follows a familiar pattern. The four purple candles of the Advent wreath are lighted, and members and guests
are welcomed. The Christmas story is read, interspersed with
familiar carols: "O Little Town of Bethlehem," "Hark, the Herald
Angels Sing" and "Joy to the World." After Holy Communion, we
take small white candles and make a circle around the dark
sanctuary, waiting in total silence for the pastor to light her
candle and send the flame around the room.

Then a cry breaks the silence. Our youngest grandson, four-
month-old Caden, begins to wail. His mother tries to hush him,
but he whimpers until we sing, "Silent night, holy night, all is
calm, all is bright."

"A baby cries out in the darkness," Pastor Sheryl says when
the song fades. "How appropriate! How wonderful. Go in
peace, and remember the baby born in Bethlehem, the Savior
of the World."

"There's a song in the air! There's a star in the sky! There's a
mother's deep prayer and a baby's low cry!" Amen.
                                                        —PENNEY SCHWAB

THE LORD IS GOOD UNTO THEM THAT WAIT. . . .
                                    —*Lamentations 3:25*

Christmas Eve 1983, Wyoming. My daughter Tess, four, sleeps in her peppermint-striped pajamas. On the sofa eleven-month-old Greg snoozes on his daddy's chest. I'm rocking six-week-old Tom, singing lullabies by firelight. My living room is rich in miracles this holy night.

After years of infertility, I now had two baby boys this Christmas Eve: Greg, adopted in January when he was three days old, and Tom, born to us in November. Last Christmas Eve my heart ached with longing. When I asked Tess what she wanted for Christmas, she said, "A baby brudder"—the one present we could not promise. Despite years of prayer, it appeared that we would never give birth to a child. *God must have something else planned*, I told myself.

Then a mere three weeks after Christmas 1982, our case-worker phoned, "You have a son in Rock Springs!" Our family felt complete—we had a daughter *and* a son. Who could want more? I stopped feeling sorry for myself and plunged into joyous, full-time mothering.

Now here I was with a toddler and *two* babies, one asleep in my arms. As I rocked him, I wondered what Mary sang to Baby Jesus in that stable long ago. I wondered how many mothers and fathers would sing lullabies to their babies on this holy night. I wondered how many would sing songs about the special baby who will guard their children forever.

Only embers glowed in the fireplace as I finished singing "What Child Is This?" Tom didn't understand the song yet, of course, but he would. I thought, *I'll keep singing to my children at home, at church and in the car, not just on Christmas, but every day.* God has blessed me beyond my wildest imaginings; I have only begun to sing my praise.

Infant Jesus, in the tumult of Christmas, hear the lullabies of love from the stillness of my heart. —GAIL THORELL SCHILLING

AND YET I AM NOT ALONE. . . . —John 16:32

Our family opens gifts on Christmas morning—quietly, with coffee and quiche before the children were born; with bewildered toddlers, who preferred the boxes to the gifts; amid preschooler pandemonium. Then, as the children grew older, we could take turns and savor the experience. A lighted Christmas tree, soft carols and a special coffee cake add to the festivities.

But in 1996 my daughter Tess, seventeen, was in Spokane, Washington, about one thousand miles away. She couldn't come home. Then a few days before Christmas, she injured her knee. Overwhelmed with pain, loneliness and memories of happier holidays, she called crying on Christmas morning.

"Oh, honey, I wish you could be here too. Did you like your presents?"

"No. I'm too depressed to open them."

"Well . . ." How to comfort long-distance? "You aren't alone now! We're here. Kids, get on the bedroom phone. Tess is going to open her gifts!"

Tess stopped sniffling and dug into the box. First she opened the red fleece cloche hat and mittens. "So soft. They fit great, Mom."

Then the surfboard-shaped pillow her brother had sewed in home economics class. "You really did this? Way to go, Tom!" Now there was energy in her voice.

Next, slippers. The harp tape. "I love them!"

Sounds of paper tearing. "What are you opening now, honey?"

"A book—must be from Mom!"

A squeal. "Now what?"

"Peppermint patties, pinwheel cookies and fudge!"

Finally a soft "wow" as she found her Christmas card and check to buy the coat she had admired. By the time we hung up, her dismal mood had vanished.

God bless the phone circuit that keeps our family circle from unraveling!

Lord, on this Christmas Day, bless with comfort those separated from their loved ones. —GAIL THORELL SCHILLING

PRAISE YE THE LORD. PRAISE GOD IN HIS SANCTUARY. . . .
                                        —*Psalm 150:1*

God certainly could've created a palace for the newborn Jesus
to lie in. So why did He choose a barn for the birthplace of His
Son?

I think of the barn on my family's farm during my growing-
up years. It was a sort of sanctuary. I loved the dim interior's
safeness, the softness of hay underfoot, the odor of seasoned
wood, the musty tang and feel of aged leather harnesses. The
loft's peaceful silence was broken only by the *chitter-chitter*
of nesting sparrows, the *whoo-hoohoo* of gray doves seeking refuge in the rafters, and the shouts of small boys and
girls transforming themselves into whoever or whatever they
wished they could be.

But I've seen other barns that weren't so enchanting.
Recently I spotted one in the countryside. Rampant ivy clung
to its clapboard siding; huddling weeds fringed alongside;
loose shingles flapped, letting in sunshine and rain to soak its
interior. Mice had gnawed its walls and colonies of fat termites
had pitted them.

Yet, despite its exterior appearance, as soon as I stepped
inside that decaying barn, the same, age-old sense of security
and warmth engulfed me. And at that moment, it dawned on
me maybe just why God chose a barn instead of a castle for the
baby's beginnings. He didn't need a glittering TV setting for
His Son. He was showing us that we can create something
memorable and magical in the roughest surroundings. We can
find safety wherever He is near.

*Father God, I'm sure You love old barns too. Otherwise You'd
not have chosen one to be Your Son's birthplace.*
                                        —ISABEL WOLSELEY

"HAVE YOU COMPREHENDED THE VAST EXPANSES OF THE EARTH? TELL ME, IF YOU KNOW ALL THIS." —*Job 38:18 (NIV)*

Near Tucson, Arizona, stands an expensive experiment that didn't work as planned. The Biosphere 2, a multistory bubble with sixty-five hundred windows, cost millions of dollars. It was painstakingly designed with rainforest, ocean, tropic and desert environments to support life. One day, its builders hoped, it might be reconstructed on Mars as a base for manned exploration. But their hope was disappointed. Scientists struggled to fix the Biosphere's oxygen-carbon dioxide imbalances, belatedly discovered that insects were essential, battled the premature dying of plants and animals and finally gave up.

One small thing they found, however, struck me as profound: The cottonwood trees they planted began falling over as they grew tall; they had to be propped up. Why? Because the scientists had not included wind in their world, and wind was necessary if the cottonwoods were to develop strong root structures.

Perhaps we'll always be trying to create a perfect world. In my own life, I hope for blue skies, good health and few trials. Yet confusion, disappointment and death enter my life no matter how hard I try to avoid them. As the cottonwoods in Biosphere 2 proved, the ill winds that invariably blow through my life can make good things happen: They can help me develop strong roots and a deeper faith.

Prop me up, Lord, until my roots run deep. —MARJORIE PARKER

*MAY YOU BE BLESSED BY THE LORD, THE MAKER OF
HEAVEN AND EARTH. —Psalm 115:15 (NIV)*

"I need to go to the bank to cash some traveler's checks," I told
my daughter. I was visiting Esther in Senegal, where she lives.

Esther phoned ahead to make sure the bank was open. But
when we arrived just after noon, a teller told us, "We don't
cash checks in the afternoon. You must come back in the morning and stand in line."

Esther hesitated for a split second. Then she forged ahead,
"My mother cannot come back tomorrow and stand in line.
She's too old, you see."

The clerk peered at me through the grate and must have
agreed with her. "Why don't you see the manager. He may
make an exception."

We joined the men sitting in the waiting room. When a
buzzer sounded, my daughter walked into the manager's office
and explained our problem.

"I would like to help you," the manager said. "Unfortunately,
my computer is down. But if you don't mind waiting, I'll buzz
you when I'm ready for you."

About an hour later, the manager greeted us and cashed my
traveler's checks. When the transaction was complete, my
daughter spoke earnestly to the man in his native Wolof. The
smile on his face grew wider and wider.

"What was all that about?" I questioned Esther once we
were back out on the street.

"Oh, I just gave him a Senegalese blessing," she said with
a smile. "I said, 'May God give you long life and good health.
May He bless your coming and your going. May He prosper
your work and your rest. May He bless your wife and your
children.' Senegalese people are quick to bless me when I buy
something at the market or when I do someone a favor."

On our way home, I reflected on this delightful custom.
Wouldn't it be good if everyone I met today received a personal blessing from me?

*Father, I pray that my walk and talk will gladden someone's
heart today.* —HELEN GRACE LESCHEID

Teach me, O Lord, the way of thy statutes; and I shall keep it unto the end. —*Psalm 119:33*

I'm always glad when a favorite author quotes the Bible to clarify an idea or shore up an argument. But I have to admit that until recently I was sometimes unfamiliar with the passages being cited. I knew the Good Book in bits and pieces, but I longed to explore all its nooks and crannies and at the same time gain a better sense of it as a whole.

Why not, I thought, *read the Bible from cover to cover?* A friend assured me that the project would never fly; I would grow weary halfway through and bail out. I didn't like being told that something was impossible, especially something so valuable. So I decided to follow Jesus' advice to "take therefore no thought for the morrow" (Matthew 6:34); I'd read a portion of Scripture each day and not worry about how much further I had to go.

I thought I could handle four pages a day under just about any circumstances. So that night I opened our family Bible and read from the beginning of Genesis to the list of generations from Adam to Noah. In the months that followed, I never missed a day. I read whether healthy or sick, alert or sleepy, energized or exhausted. And as the teachings and stories came and went, I discovered a vast store of wisdom, truth and revelation that shed light on every aspect of my daily life. Above all, I came to see the Bible as a whole, as the magnificent, coherent unfolding of the Word of God. And along with these spiritual rewards, I enjoyed a sense of real accomplishment: I'd met the challenge, and the rewards outweighed all my expectations.

Lord, make me eager to do the things that will bring me closer to Your kingdom. —Philip Zaleski

*O THE DEPTH OF THE RICHES BOTH OF THE WISDOM AND
KNOWLEDGE OF GOD! . . . —Romans 11:33*

Years ago, a small town in Europe decided it needed a clock in
the town square that would chime the hour for the whole
countryside. So the villagers hired a renowned clockmaker
from a distant city. He made them a majestic clock that played
a beautiful tune on the hour, complete with dancing figures
that kept time to the music.

But as the years passed, things began to go wrong with
the clock, until finally it quit running. No one knew how to
repair it, and a great depression descended on the village. Then
the mayor had an idea: Maybe they could find the original
clockmaker.

And they did. The man, now white-haired and stooped, had
been retired for nearly twenty years, but he agreed to come
back to their village and try to repair his creation. The villagers
helped the frail man into the clock's innards and waited outside, hoping he would be successful. An hour passed, then two.
Suddenly, the clock began ticking, the chimes rang out over
the valley, the dancers danced and everyone cheered.

That story has implications for all of us as we embark on a
new year. When we have problems in the days and months
ahead, and we surely will, it will behoove us to go to the One
most qualified to help us deal with them. As our Maker, He
knows us inside and out, and He knows what we need to make
us tick.

> *Lord, we don't know what the future holds
>   for us,
> But we know You do, and that emboldens us.*
> —FRED BAUER

I WAS GLAD WHEN THEY SAID TO ME, "LET US GO INTO THE HOUSE OF THE LORD." —*Psalm 122:1* (NKJV)

As my daughter Lanea and I stand in line, I wave to people I know, popping in and out of the line to hug those I haven't seen in a while. We are blessed; we've made it inside the main building, but we're still outside the seating area, and we're praying that we will be able to get one of the few remaining seats. I have flown in from Chicago, Lanea from North Carolina, and we're hoping we won't be turned away.

We can hear the music beginning inside. In the line, people begin to fidget and look about anxiously.

Lanea and I are at church—New Psalmist Baptist Church in Baltimore. It's New Year's Eve. We've been in line for almost an hour. We will not give up hope of getting into the sanctuary. Over the loudspeakers, we hear a voice praying inside and we bow our heads.

New Psalmist has more than eight thousand members; the sanctuary seats just over two thousand and there are three services each Sunday, but there is always a press for seats. The atmosphere is always alive—it sizzles, buzzes and pops. It's high-powered praise and worship, and an anointed message from a pastor who is at once scholarly, compassionate, entertaining, inspiring and down-home.

Beyond the main sanctuary, the three-hundred-seat chapel is full and the overflow room is beginning to fill. I've been away awhile, and I'm hit with the reality that church isn't like this for everyone. In most places tonight, people aren't running to get inside.

Finally, Lanea and I inch our way around, up the choir loft steps and inside the door to our seats, and we join in the worship. Hallelujah! And happy New Year!

Thank You, God, for giving us the privilege, power and excitement of worship, praise and prayer this and every year.

—SHARON FOSTER

"In May 2004, my husband Larry and I bought a house in Berne, Indiana, and moved from Richlands, North Carolina," writes *LIBBIE ADAMS*. "I accepted the position of news editor at the city newspaper. My passion has always been feature writing, and searching out stories on a regular basis has brought me into close contact with the residents of Berne. Larry closed the door of his doghouse and storage building business, and found work in an Amish cabinet shop. We are most richly blessed."

MARCI ALBORGHETTI of New London, Connecticut, writes, "When I think about it, I see His faithfulness in my life in so many ways. My fifth book, *When Lightning Strikes Twice* (based on my *Daily Guideposts, 2005* series), was published by 23rd Publications/Bayard last year, and I'm working on a sort of New Testament sequel to *Twelve Strong Women*. Through all this, I can only pray that my own faithfulness will continue to grow."

"My life in Van, Texas, has been all about our little country church where I served on the women's ministry leadership team, coordinated the ladies' book club and volunteered to put together a new pictorial directory. What *was* I thinking?" says *LUCILE ALLEN*. "Camping in Yellowstone and our annual family reunion in Grand Junction, Colorado, was the perfect prescription for my husband Curtis. Deanna, 11, is a bright student, a loyal friend, a fun-loving, affectionate daughter and a budding pianist."

"Aunt Min is 90," writes *FAY ANGUS* of Sierra Madre, California. "The highlight of my year was flying to Vancouver, British Columbia, to help her celebrate. The floral displays in the botanical gardens restaurant were breathtaking, the food gourmet and the party such fun that even the servers were laughing themselves silly. This year we praise the Lord for His great faithfulness. As my heart is filled with gratitude, I'd like to extend it also to the faithfulness of those who have shared in and loved us through all the sunlight and shadows in the unwinding of our years."

"We've had so many reminders of God's faithfulness this year," writes *ANDREW ATTAWAY* of New York City, "most especially in our children's growth in mind, body and faith. John, 9, and Mary, 7, have joined sister Elizabeth, 11, onstage at our neighborhood children's theater. Chess has joined math on the list of Elizabeth's passions, while Maggie, 4, is enjoying gymnastics and delighting us all with her wry sense of humor, and 2-year-old Stephen's enthusiastic explorations keep us on our toes."

"This year was eventful in ways both big and small," writes *JULIA ATTAWAY* of New York City. During the summer the Attaways' son John was diagnosed with a serious anxiety disorder. "That was good news, since it finally put a name to John's struggles and allowed us to develop a strategy for addressing them. As he's grown more stable, the family has flourished."

"To see God's faithfulness, I simply open up my journal and look in the column where I've numbered my latest answer to prayer," writes *KAREN BARBER* of Alpharetta, Georgia. "This year I've recorded my father's adjustment to living in a nursing care facility, our son Chris's safe return from Afghanistan, our son John's transition to high school, and the move by our son Jeff and his wife Leah to North Carolina. Although these are all big events, I see that each was made up of smaller answers that I numbered day by day."

"Leo and I were thrilled when our daughter Gae and husband Blair announced we were to be grandparents again," says *ALMA BARKMAN* of Winnipeg, Canada. "Max Isaac arrived safely in August. *Isaac* means laughter, and he is certainly living up to his name. We now have eight grandchildren ranging in age from a newborn to a young man in his twenties."

"As a child, one of my favorite hymns was 'Great Is Thy Faithfulness,'" writes *FRED BAUER* of State College, Pennsylvania, and Englewood Beach, Florida. "I've always sung the lyrics with great enthusiasm because they so revealingly describe God's steadfastness. Now as the shadows of my life lengthen and I look back on the manifold blessings God has sent my way, I see even more clearly how great His faithfulness has been unto me."

"In July, with the help of my sisters, I organized and hosted a reunion for the descendants of my maternal grandparents," says *EVELYN BENCE*. "Sixty people, ages 2 to 86, gathered under a picnic pavilion at a church campground in western New York. When my one surviving uncle told us that he prayed regularly for his extended family, I remembered being a child and hearing how my housebound grandmother spent hours praying for her children and grandchildren. God has faithfully answered those petitions."

"My husband and I are both in life-changing circumstances," *RHODA BLECKER* of Los Angeles says. "Keith is finally retiring, and he and I are moving to the Pacific Northwest. We've been in our present home for twenty-three years, and we love it very much. But we want to be nearer to the monastery, in the fresh air, and we're looking forward to having a new community and new friends. As for the community and friends we'll be leaving, we say, 'Thank God for e-mail!'"

"I'm turning 50 this year," writes *MELODY BONNETTE* of Mandeville, Louisiana. "It's caused me to reflect on the milestones in my life, one being when I realized I wanted to become a writer. We had to practice our letter writing in third grade by sending a note to someone. I wrote a five-page letter to my grandmother and ended it with *Love with all hope*. The next time Grandma came to visit, she knelt down to hug me and said, 'I loved your letter, but I especially loved the way you ended it. *Love with all hope* is a sign of your faith in the future. It reminded me of my faith too.'"

"We're blessed with friends, health and love, and our life together is overflowing with one of God's greatest gifts—music," writes *GINA BRIDGEMAN* of Scottsdale, Arizona. Ross, a high school junior, plays in several bands, from jazz and rock to church concert band. Maria, a fifth-grader, makes music in voice and chime choirs, and sang and danced in the church musical. Husband Paul continues to teach musical theater, and Gina returned to her church choir after a few years off.

A highlight last year for *MARY BROWN* of East Lansing, Michigan, was a twentieth-wedding anniversary trip with Alex, which included a few days in New York City. "I enjoyed visiting Guideposts and praying with the Monday morning prayer group." The family also headed for South Africa where Alex conducted nuclear physics research. Through contacts arranged by a hospice chaplain who ministered to Mary's mom last year, the Browns brought supplies to children suffering from the HIV/AIDS crisis and visited several orphanages and hospices.

MARY LOU CARNEY's year was filled with the *whoosh-bam!* of power nail guns as the family built a new house for daughter Amy Jo, her husband Kirk and 2-year-old Drake. The family will now live just one mile from Mary Lou and Gary in Chesterton, Indiana. Son Brett was the general contractor for the project, taking time out from his hectic schedule of remodel and rental work. Mary Lou continues to edit Guideposts *Sweet 16* magazine, as well as manage www.gp4children.com and www.sweet16.com.

SABRA CIANCANELLI of Pawling, New York, writes, "Restoring an old farmhouse keeps my husband and me busy! As we tear away the siding, sills and footings that need replacing, it's as if we're uncovering the strength and history not only in the structure of the house but also within ourselves. Chasing after our 3-year-old son Solomon helps us to remember the fun to be had building snowmen, stomping in puddles, catching fireflies and watching birds at the feeder." Sabra is Web editor of Guideposts Online.

"Our dek-hockey team plays in the 'old-guy' league—26 and over," explains *MARK COLLINS* of Pittsburgh. "Meanwhile, most of our players haven't seen 26 since Jimmy Carter was president. When we're losing, we'll tell each other, 'We're better than this, we're better than this.' I've had that feeling a lot recently, that I could be better." Luckily Mark has a solid team at home: his wife Sandee and their daughters Faith, 14, Hope, 13, and Grace, 9.

"Elba and I have reached a significant milestone in our marriage," writes *PABLO DIAZ* of Carmel, New York, "our twenty-fifth wedding anniversary. Our marriage has been filled with many joys and sorrows, but mostly joy. We are having a wonderful time as empty nesters and are especially blessed to see our children living out their dreams. Paul is enjoying his college experience, and Christine is busy in her career."

BRIAN DOYLE lives in Portland, Oregon, with a wee, tiny, extraordinary woman and a passel of small children who move so quickly that their father is never quite absolutely sure if they have eaten, are clothed properly, have done their homework and/or are responsible for the latest misdemeanor committed in the hallway. Doyle wishes to be a man of great faithfulness, being convinced, he says, that running away from things is easy and sticking at them is hard.

"Our family saw God's faithfulness in several new beginnings this year," writes *ERIC FELLMAN* of Falls Church, Virginia. "Jonathan graduated from college and promptly moved to Los Angeles to seek out a career in the music business. Nathan got engaged to Jesse, who becomes the first daughter Joy and I have been expecting. We hope grandkids will be along in the next decade. Jason settled into a challenging career at a trade association near us in Alexandria. Then, probably most importantly, Joy finished her master's degree as a nurse practitioner."

"My daughter Lanea and my son Chase continue to do wonderful things," says *SHARON FOSTER* of Chicago. "Chase earned a scholarship at the school where he studies opera, sang at the governor's inauguration, is getting great grades and still lights up the church choir. Lanea is completing her master's degree and continues working in youth advocacy programs while she teaches Spanish at a charter school. My sixth novel, *Ain't No Valley*, was published last year, and I'm working on the next one. I keep smiling and thanking God for each day. God is faithful."

"This year a most amazing thing happened," says *DAVE FRANCO* of Solana Beach, California. "My wife came home from a meeting at the church office one day and said, 'Guess what? I've been asked to head up the drama ministry . . . and you're going to write the scripts!' It never occurred to me to write dramatic scenes before, but I was intrigued. 'Okay,' I said. And so far, my wife has been in four productions, and my daughter, 6, in one but is pining to do more. My son, 9, is far too shy or too cool to be seen onstage."

"My husband didn't sleep much last year," says *JULIE GARMON* of Monroe, Georgia. "Rick built our log house. After his real job, he'd drive out to the property and work during the night. He laid the floors and the tile. He perched on twenty-foot high beams to line the den ceiling with tongue and groove boards. He caulked between each log. We moved in right before Valentine's Day last year."

After seven years of entertaining guests at local restaurants, circumstances took *OSCAR GREENE* of West Medford, Massachusetts, and his wife Ruby back to entertaining at home. Once again, the dining room table was the gathering place where delicious meals were filling, but not as filling as fellowship, conversation and laughter. When Oscar stepped away from teaching at writers' conferences, writing for his church newsletter and speaking engagements, he felt much was lost. But God has handed him a new ministry right in his own home.

EDWARD GRINNAN of New York City writes, "I know many of the *Daily Guideposts* writers personally, yet I discover something new about them through their devotionals. I learned that Van Varner's long-ago houseboat was named *Ashland*. Van is one of my closest friends. I've heard many stories about life on the boat. All of them, I thought. How come I never knew how the vessel got its name? It is a gift to learn something new about an old friend." Edward is editor-in-chief and vice president of Guideposts publications. His newest project is the launch of a magazine called *Positive Thinking*. For more information, check out www.PositiveThinkingmag.com.

"I always imagined the day when our family would be able to cover all four parts in the hymnal," says *RICK HAMLIN* of New York City. "I guess I hadn't figured out how brief that moment might be. Sure, Carol and I have carried the soprano and tenor lines for years (that's what we do in our church choir). And William, 18, when his voice changed, turned out to have a nice baritone. For a while Timothy could carry the alto line, then at 15 he turned into a true tenor, and the moment passed. But we are grateful for two boys who seem to enjoy our company even as they spend less time at home."

MADGE HARRAH of Albuquerque, New Mexico, writes, "My husband is heading up the personnel committee for our church and building an observatory behind our summer cabin in the high country of Colorado. We feel very close to God under that star-spangled canopy. I'm busy, too, writing children's books, giving seminars at writers' conferences and teaching a Sunday school class. One thing that helps Larry and me deal with these challenges is God's faithfulness. He's always there when we need Him."

"Over the past year we've traveled to the East Coast twice to visit our younger daughter Kristal and her family," writes *HAROLD HOSTETLER*. "In between, Kristal and Derrick moved from Massachusetts to New York. Now they are urging us to move back East. Our older daughter Laurel and granddaughter Kaila, who live just two miles from us in Vista, California, feel the pull of family togetherness too. In forty-three years of marriage, we have lived in the West almost as long as in the East. As you might expect, this is going to be one very difficult decision."

"Welcome back! It's been awhile" might be an appropriate greeting for *JEFF JAPINGA*, who last appeared in *Daily Guideposts* almost twenty years ago. Jeff and his wife Lynn live in Holland, Michigan. Jeff coordinates ministry work for the Reformed Church in America. Lynn teaches religion at Hope College, runs triathlons and has a huge oral history project going. Their son Mark is now a college freshman; Annie, their seventh-grader, is likely busy with her sport du jour—she'll tell you basketball is her favorite—squeezing in studies on the side.

ASHLEY JOHNSON joined the Guideposts family through the American Society of Magazine Editors summer internship and, while in the New York City offices, got bitten by the devotional writing bug. A native of Florence, Alabama, she graduated in May 2005 from Princeton University with a degree in literature and a renewed love of writing. "This year has been a whirlwind! My sister Kristi got married, my brother Lloyd and his wife Holly welcomed the first grandchild into the family, and I finished writing my senior thesis."

"I have never needed my faith more than this past year," writes *REBECCA KELLY* from her new home in Mount Dora, Florida. "Less than a month after we moved, we were struck by Hurricanes Charley, Frances and Jeanne. Just as we recovered from the storms, my husband had to undergo cancer surgery and our son broke his arm playing basketball. Yet throughout our troubles, I never doubted for a moment that God was with us. His presence in our lives gave us the love and strength to endure everything as a family should: together."

BROCK KIDD of Nashville, Tennessee, writes, "My son Harrison is thriving in school and loving his time out of it. This past year marked his first season as a soccer player, and I was fortunate enough to be his assistant coach. My career is going quite well, and I take much happiness from helping my clients along with their financial goals. I'm slowly learning that while life is a series of unexpected storms, it's worth weathering them for the calming sunsets that follow."

"When I found myself standing on a desolate street in Harare, Zimbabwe, in 1999, wanting to shout my anger to the heavens, it's almost impossible to comprehend what has happened since," writes *PAM KIDD* of Nashville, Tennessee. "Why had God sent David and me to such a place? We were surrounded by hungry street children orphaned by AIDS, and there seemed no plausible way we could make a difference. Now, because of the generosity of many caring people, the lady who brought tea and bread to the children that morning has a compound of buildings to work from, and there is a lovely farm where an amazing man and his wife have made a home for more than twenty orphans."

For *MARILYN MORGAN KING* and her husband Robert of Green Mountain Falls, Colorado, the past year has brought some serious pain and loss. Death claimed Cheryl, the wife of Marilyn's oldest son Paul, leaving four young children still at home. The blessing is that they also have four grown children who, along with their Aunt Karen, have generously given of their time and talents to help care for the little ones. Marilyn has suffered from a back problem that may require a second surgery in the coming year. Is she discouraged? "How could I not trust in the faithfulness of our loving God, Who continues to show us such abundant love and care?"

CAROL KNAPP of Lakeville, Minnesota, writes, "It took five airplanes, but I got to an Arctic Ocean island to help our daughter Tamara welcome a new son, Joshua. In April I celebrated spring in north Idaho with a visit to my mother, 82. In June, we had our first-ever family reunion on our daughter Brenda's farm in Alaska. Terry and I had laps overflowing with seven grandchildren, the newest being Clay, born to our daughter Kelly in March. Thanksgiving found us back on the Alaskan farm dining on homegrown turkey. We are about to head to my brother's for a Colorado Christmas."

"We've seen many evidences of God's great faithfulness in our lives this year," writes *CAROL KUYKENDALL*. "At the top of my list is my husband Lynn's miraculous recovery from his brain hemorrhage last year. Another is our grandchildren. I held the video camera at the birth of my daughter Lindsay and husband Jeff's first child, Karis Noel, born just before Christmas. They live in Solana Beach, California. Our 2-year-old granddaughter Gabriella lives in Denver, a half-hour from our home in Boulder, Colorado. She is expecting a little brother or sister this spring."

"Now that I'm a senior, it's easy for me to trace God's faithfulness throughout the years," writes *HELEN GRACE LESCHEID* of Abbotsford, British Columbia. "As a child I experienced the horrors of World War II and later, as a married woman, the devastation of mental illness. Although my husband did not recover, I've been aware of God's gentle, abiding presence. I will be visiting my three grandchildren, Miriam, Nathan and Philip, in Senegal, where their parents work. I feel truly blessed."

"After my father died last February," *DEBBIE MACOMBER* says, "I moved my mother into an assisted living complex close to our family here in Port Orchard, Washington. Our Florida condo took a direct hit from not one, but two hurricanes. But through it all, God's loving arms have held us close." Debbie's four grown children make it a point to visit often. "Best of all, they bring the grandchildren." Wayne, her husband of thirty-eight years, is retired and enjoys traveling with Debbie when possible.

ROBERTA MESSNER of Huntington, West Virginia, met a woman this past year who told her that she reads the devotional in *Daily Guideposts* each day to her mother, who is in a coma in a nursing home. "It showed me just how far our *Daily Guideposts* family extends," says Roberta.

Ever since *TED NACE* of Poughquag, New York, was a little boy, he remembers singing "Great Is Thy Faithfulness!" Ted and Kathy's three sons, now grown, have multiplied the examples of God's faithfulness. One of life's greatest joys is when Kyle (who graduates from Mansfield University this May), Joel and his wife Alyssa join them to travel to Ryan's church in Red Hook, New York (where he is pastor), to worship with his wife Jennifer and their children Mandy, Jim and their new baby. Great is thy faithfulness indeed!

LINDA NEUKRUG of Walnut Creek, California, still likes her job at the bookstore and, since she's surrounded by books, is trying to learn a few new things this upcoming year. She's starting with Gregg shorthand, which seems to be a lost art. She also hopes to overcome a few fears with God's help. "I've read that every day you should do one small thing that you fear, just to show yourself that you can. I've always been too afraid to commit to that, but this will be the year I do it."

As *MARJORIE PARKER* and husband Joe of Byers, Texas, have helped care for their octogenarian mothers, she has felt God stretching her time, increasing her faith, giving her energy and making things happen when she couldn't. Marjorie experienced His faithful generosity in a glorious trip to Italy to meet daughter Sarah, who was studying there. She observed it in the lives of newlywed daughter Joanna and her husband Vince. But, most of all, she's seen God's faithfulness in and through the thirteen people she has helped train for lay ministry in their church.

RUTH STAFFORD PEALE of Pawling, New York writes, "At 99, I hold the title of chairman emeritus of the Guideposts board. I have a lot to be grateful for through the many ways God reveals Himself to me. What an exciting blessing! It is His great faithfulness that has brought me to the celebration of my 100th birthday on September 10, 2006. I rejoice to see my family actively involved with Guideposts: my daughter Elizabeth as chairman of the board, and my son John and eldest daughter Margaret as board members. Along with a brilliant and dedicated staff, I know that our work of prayer and publications started by my husband Norman Vincent Peale and me will go on to help a great many more people in the years to come."

"God's utter faithfulness has been real to us this past year," writes *ROBERTA ROGERS* of New Market, Virginia. "In joy, as we awaited the birth of our first grandchild to Susan and Tom; as Peter got the 'stay behind' slot just before his reserve unit deployed to Iraq; as Bill went past his 500th volunteer EMT call and became a squad officer; as John began publishing an online golf column; as Dave and Matti moved to Fort Knox, Tennessee, and bought their first home. And in sorrow, as my mother died at 95 and Bill's mother at 98. Through it all, the Lord has sustained us in His faithful love."

DANIEL SCHANTZ and his redheaded wife Sharon have moved to a new home just outside the city limits of Moberly, Missouri. "As I sorted through thirty-five years of accumulated stuff, I could see the faithful hand of God at work in my life." Dan is in his thirty-ninth year of teaching at Central Christian College. "I enjoy young people more than ever," he admits. "They are like family to me."

After twenty-six years of parenting, *GAIL THORELL SCHILLING* found her empty nest unsettling at first. "I always thought I'd move back to Wyoming once Trina graduated from high school, as she did this year. Yet here I am, still in New Durham, New Hampshire, still loving my teaching, writing and choir singing.

Nor is the nest always empty. Trina, Tess and her daughter Hannah, 5, often spend weekends for giggly "girl time." Tom, a junior at MIT, sometimes zips up from Boston. Only Greg, a carpenter in Los Angeles, can't come home often. Like the others, however, he phones a lot and always says, 'I love ya!'"

"We experienced anew God's faithful love and care," writes *PENNEY SCHWAB* of Copeland, Kansas. "My husband Don remains cancer-free three years after his surgery. I am in my twentieth year as director of United Methodist Mexican-American Ministries. Son Patrick, wife Patricia and family moved to Friona, Texas, where he manages a feedlot. Son Michael and wife Jerie remain in Fort Collins, Colorado. Daughter Rebecca and husband Frank moved into an old 1920s house while she was finishing up her master of science from Fort Hays State University. Our grandchildren Ryan, David, Mark, Caleb, Olivia and Caden add mystery, delight and lots of travel to our lives."

The highlight of the year for *ELIZABETH SHERRILL* of Chappaqua, New York, was watching granddaughter Lindsay receive her bachelor of science in nursing from the University of Florida. "When Lindsay addressed the auditorium as president of her class, I saw not only an erect and lovely young woman, but the faithfulness of God. Growing up, Lindsay endured many hospitalizations to correct severe scoliosis. In my distress and daily prayers for her, God kept telling me, *I will use this pain not only to heal Lindsay but, through her, many others.* Because of the healing she herself received, Lindsay has dedicated her life to the healing arts."

"I'm constantly learning from the kids," says *JOHN SHERRILL* of Chappaqua, New York. "By high school, our grandson Daniel already knew he wanted to be a chef. Last year, all by himself, he mounted Thanksgiving dinner for eight, including a twenty-pound turkey, all the trimmings and two pecan pies made from scratch. Just as we were about to sit down, his sister's new puppy swallowed a fishhook! Daniel, who took sister and dog to the vet, came back an hour later with a good report, then at last brought his slightly overcooked turkey to table. Daniel taught me the art of doing my best with what I can control, then relaxing into events I can't control."

"This year Whitney and I got the pot of gold at the end of the rainbow," says *SHARI SMYTH* of Nashville, Tennessee. "We've become grandparents. Frank Whitney Dean was born February 5 to our youngest daughter Sanna and her husband Glen. Wendy, our oldest, is in Hawaii. Laura is in Pawling, New York, managing a horse barn and continuing her painting. Jon is in Nashville and works as a chef. Whitney is active on the worship team at church. I continue my work with children in church and at an inner-city community center."

JOSHUA SUNDQUIST attends the College of William and Mary in Williamsburg, Virginia, where he is a business marketing major and a member of the Fellowship of Christian Athletes. He divides his time between college and ski racing in Colorado. As of now Josh has reached near-competent levels in several areas: guitar playing, writing, soccer, reading and eating. Last year he edited a book that features personal experiences written by young people from around the world.

"I love looking for books in junk shops and library sales," says *PTOLEMY TOMPKINS* of New York City. "Sometimes I'll stumble on an old volume of *Daily Guideposts*. When I do, I always turn to the back pages and look around for familiar faces in the contributors' bios. It's a little like looking at an old high school yearbook, except that most of the faces I recognize in those back pages are still a part of my world at Guideposts. Life is full of changes—the biggest one for me this year being my stepdaughter Mara's departure for college. It's wonderful to be part of a community that stays so consistent year in and year out."

"An extraordinary thing happened to me," writes *VAN VARNER* of New York City, "when, in going through papers in my safe deposit box, I opened an envelope marked 'Letters of Importance from Joe W. Varner.' Joe was my dad. I had always bypassed the envelope because I thought it dealt with my parents' divorce, the one thing that had anguished me since I was five. Inside the envelope was a telegram and a score of love letters from Dad.

The telegram had arrived too late and Mom, whose love for Dad I discovered later was infinite, had married another man. I am left with a bittersweet feeling, but I believe that at last they are together. Sometimes, in one way or another, prayers are answered, even though it can take a lifetime."

SCOTT WALKER writes, "Drew graduated from Furman University; Luke graduated from high school and is attending Samford University; Jodi is finishing her junior year in high school and is considering where she will attend college. I have completed twelve years as pastor of the First Baptist Church of Waco, Texas, and Beth continues her work with international students at Baylor University. With each passing year, I am more deeply impressed with God's grace and love, in both the good times and the difficult moments. God is using all things to teach me that He truly is a very good Shepherd."

DOLPHUS WEARY of Richland, Mississippi, writes, "Our son Reggie went home to be with the Lord in June 2004, and the pain of missing him continues for Rosie, Danita, Ryan and me." Since Reggie's death, REAL Christian Foundation started the Reginald Weary Memorial Scholarship Fund, which provides partial scholarships to aid young people from rural Mississippi as they go to college. "Rosie and I are experiencing the empty nest phase as Ryan is now in college. Danita practices medicine in Natchez, Mississippi, Rosie continues to serve as executive director of the foundation, and I still work with Mission Mississippi, encouraging unity in the body of Christ across racial and denominational lines."

"This has been a growth year for my family," writes *BRIGITTE WEEKS*. "My first grandchild, Benjamin, made his appearance. He will have a cousin in a few months, so I am knitting another shawl. I also made a memorable trip to Cuba with Samaritan's Heart to repair a few houses and meet some wonderful people. My next stop with my trowel and screwdriver will be in Mexico in the summer."

MARION BOND WEST of Watkinsville, Georgia, says, "*Pray for Your Life*, based on Habakkuk 3:17-19, evolved because of my passion for the Scripture, but I doubted that God had actually wanted me to write the book and maybe it wasn't good enough to be published. The day of its completion, my prodigal son Jon happened by. 'Hey, Mom, look what I found. I know it belonged to a believer. See how it's all marked up?' I thumbed through the Bible to the very back. There, written in magnificent handwriting, I read 'Habakkuk 3:17-19 (NAS). Though the fig tree should not blossom, And there be no fruit on the vine. . . .' It was all there! The Scripture I so loved, hand-delivered by my son whom I so loved."

"I see God's great faithfulness in the most ordinary circumstances," writes *TIM WILLIAMS* of Durango, Colorado. "I am grateful when my sons Ted, in Seattle, and Patrick, in La Playas, Mexico, call me. I am grateful every time my wife Dianne arrives home safely from the school where she teaches. I still volunteer as an EMT and firefighter, and work for Mothers Against Drunk Driving."

"When Lawrence Torrey and I married six years ago," says *ISABEL WOLSELEY* of Syracuse, New York, "he never suspected I would want chickens as pets! But he's grown to enjoy them as much as I, even building the five bantam hens a small bedroom inside the garage, complete with a kitty-door-opening for them to go to the fenced-in yard." Isabel is in her thirty-fifth year as a newspaper columnist and authored the book *Don't Holler 'til You're Hurt*. Lawrence, a semiretired pharmacist, fills in for colleagues at his company's outlets. Both continue their support of Wycliffe Bible Translators.

"It's been another year of growth for everyone in the family," says *PHILIP ZALESKI* of Northampton, Massachusetts. "John, our high school senior, has been trying his hand at writing a novel, in addition to being on the varsity baseball and ski teams, while young Andy has been tackling piano, geography and chess. Carol and I have finished our book on prayer and are mulling other projects."